...TWO SIDES TO EVERY STORY

MOON OF THE SNOW-BLIND

SPIRIT LAKE

▲▲▲▲▲▲▲▲▲▲▲▲▲▲▲▲▲

TEXT AND PICTURES BY GARY KELLEY

Ice Cube Press, LLC
North Liberty, Iowa, USA

Moon of the Snowblind: Spirit Lake

Copyright ©2021 Gary Kelley

First Edition

Isʙɴ 9781948509213

Library of Congress Control Number: 2020950999

Ice Cube Press, LLC (Est. 1991)
1180 Hauer Drive
North Liberty, Iowa 52317 USA
www.icecubepress.com | steve@icecubepress.com

The paper used in this publication meets
the minimum requirements of the American
National Standard for Information
Sciences—Permanence of Paper for Printed
Library Materials, ANSI Z39.48-1992.

Manufactured in Canada

IN MEMORY
OF MY LATE UNCLE
EUGENE KELLEY

A WWII veteran,
Minneapolis Institute
of Arts student,
newspaper man;
he taught me to draw
as a preschooler,
shared with me his
amazing library of
art books and history
books, including
Abigail Gardner Sharp's
autobiography;
HISTORY of the
SPIRIT LAKE MASSACRE

THE WAR DID NOT
SPRING UP HERE
ON OUR LAND...

THE WAR WAS BROUGHT
UPON US BY FOLLOWERS
OF THE GREAT WHITE FATHER

...WHO CAME TO TAKE
OUR LAND.

— *SPOTTED TAIL*

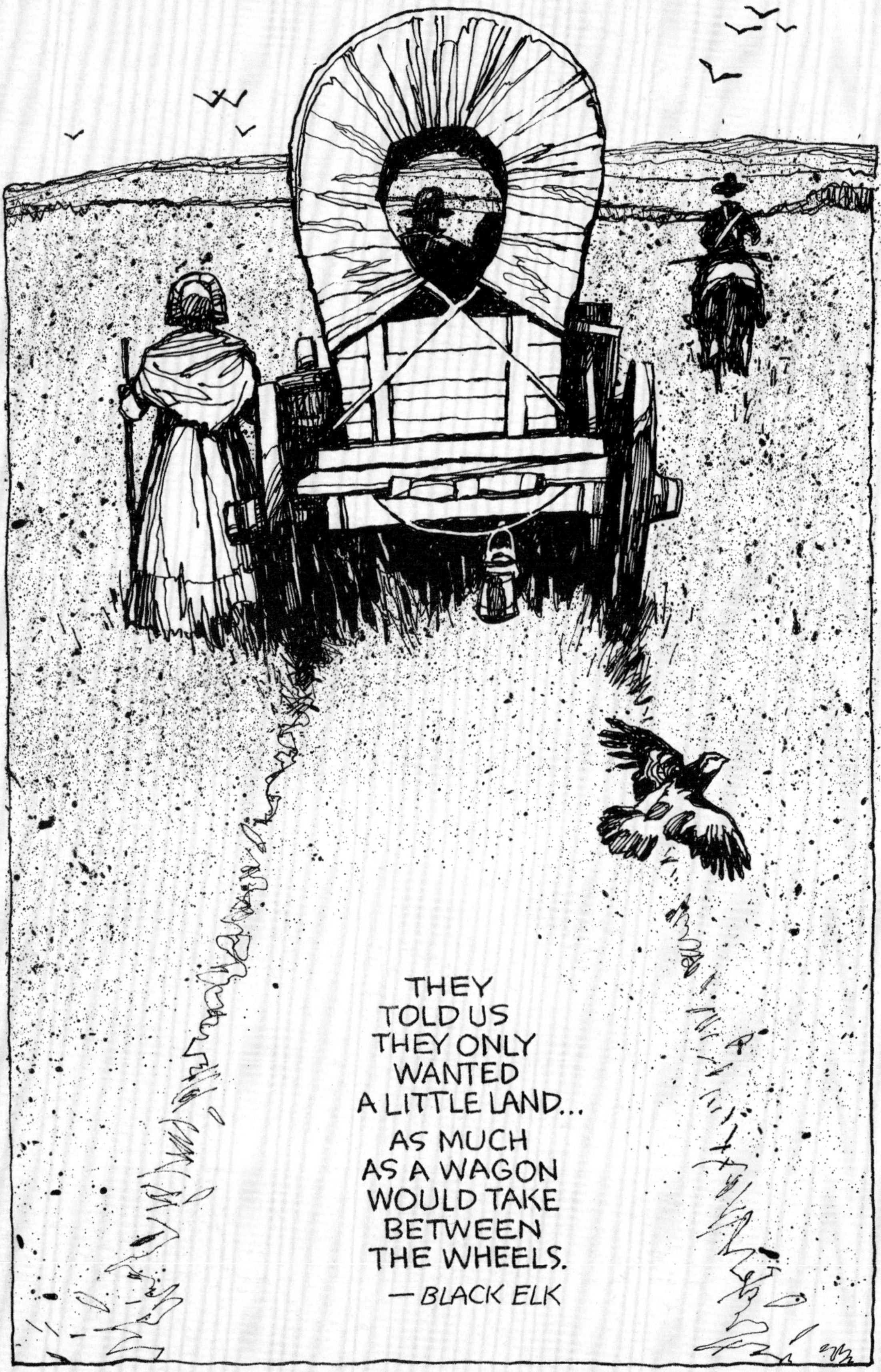
THEY TOLD US THEY ONLY WANTED A LITTLE LAND...
AS MUCH AS A WAGON WOULD TAKE BETWEEN THE WHEELS.
— BLACK ELK

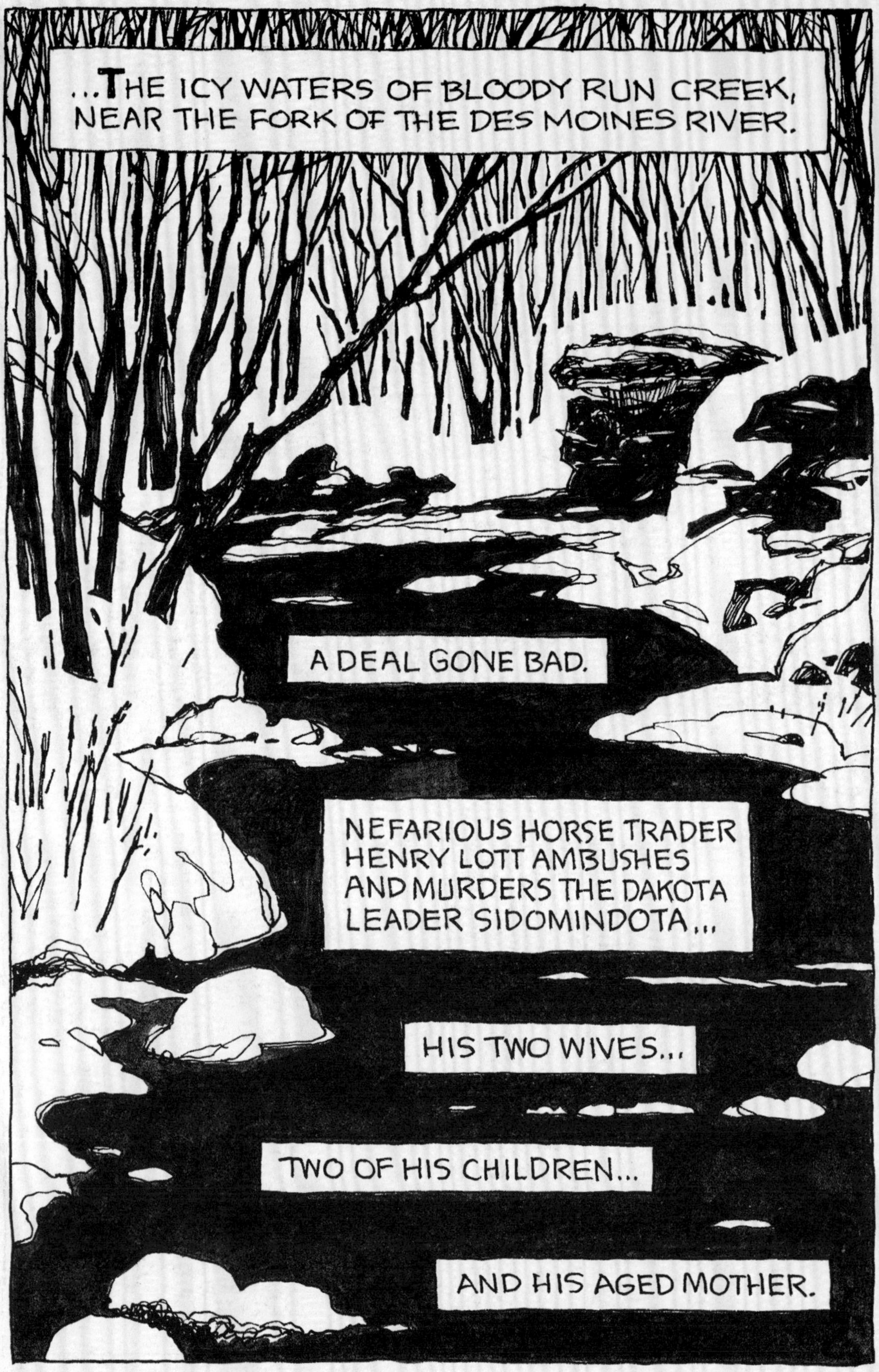
...THE ICY WATERS OF BLOODY RUN CREEK, NEAR THE FORK OF THE DES MOINES RIVER.
A DEAL GONE BAD.
NEFARIOUS HORSE TRADER HENRY LOTT AMBUSHES AND MURDERS THE DAKOTA LEADER SIDOMINDOTA...
HIS TWO WIVES...
TWO OF HIS CHILDREN...
AND HIS AGED MOTHER.

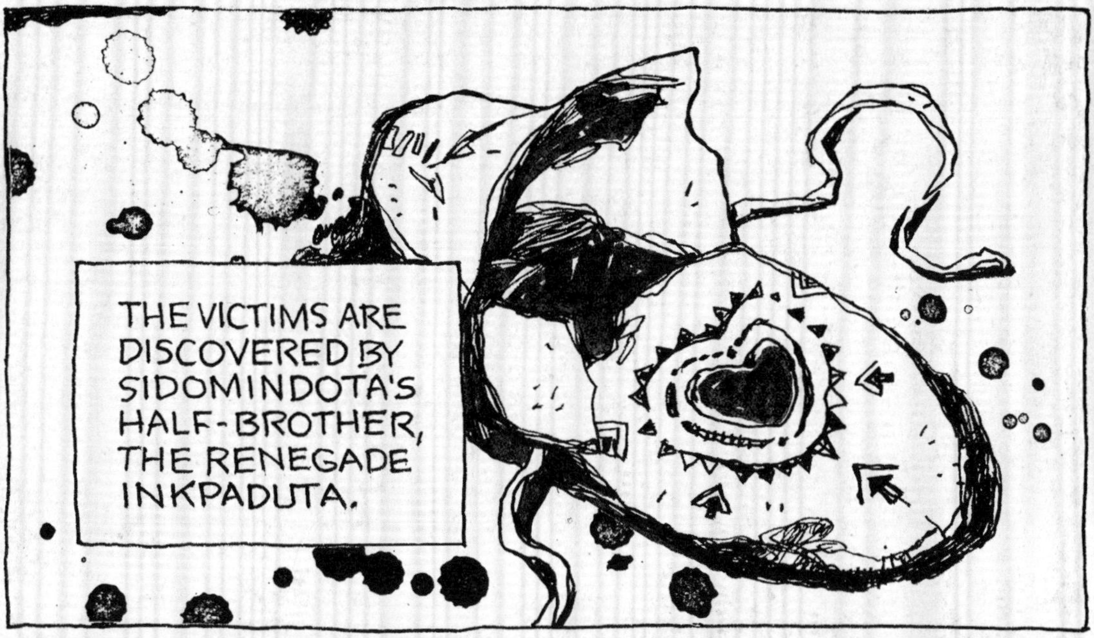
THE VICTIMS ARE DISCOVERED BY SIDOMINDOTA'S HALF-BROTHER, THE RENEGADE INKPADUTA.

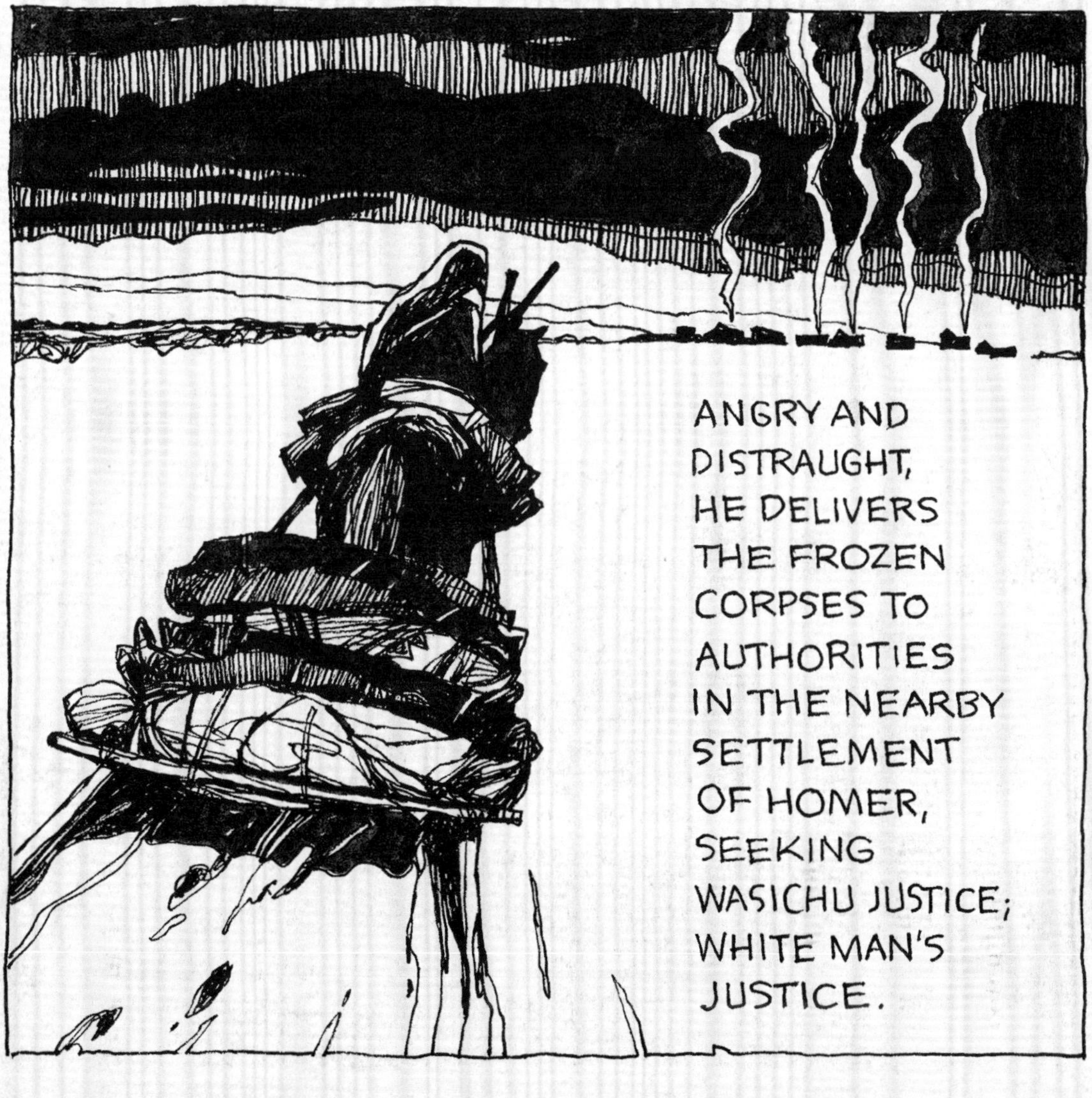
ANGRY AND DISTRAUGHT, HE DELIVERS THE FROZEN CORPSES TO AUTHORITIES IN THE NEARBY SETTLEMENT OF HOMER, SEEKING WASICHU JUSTICE; WHITE MAN'S JUSTICE.

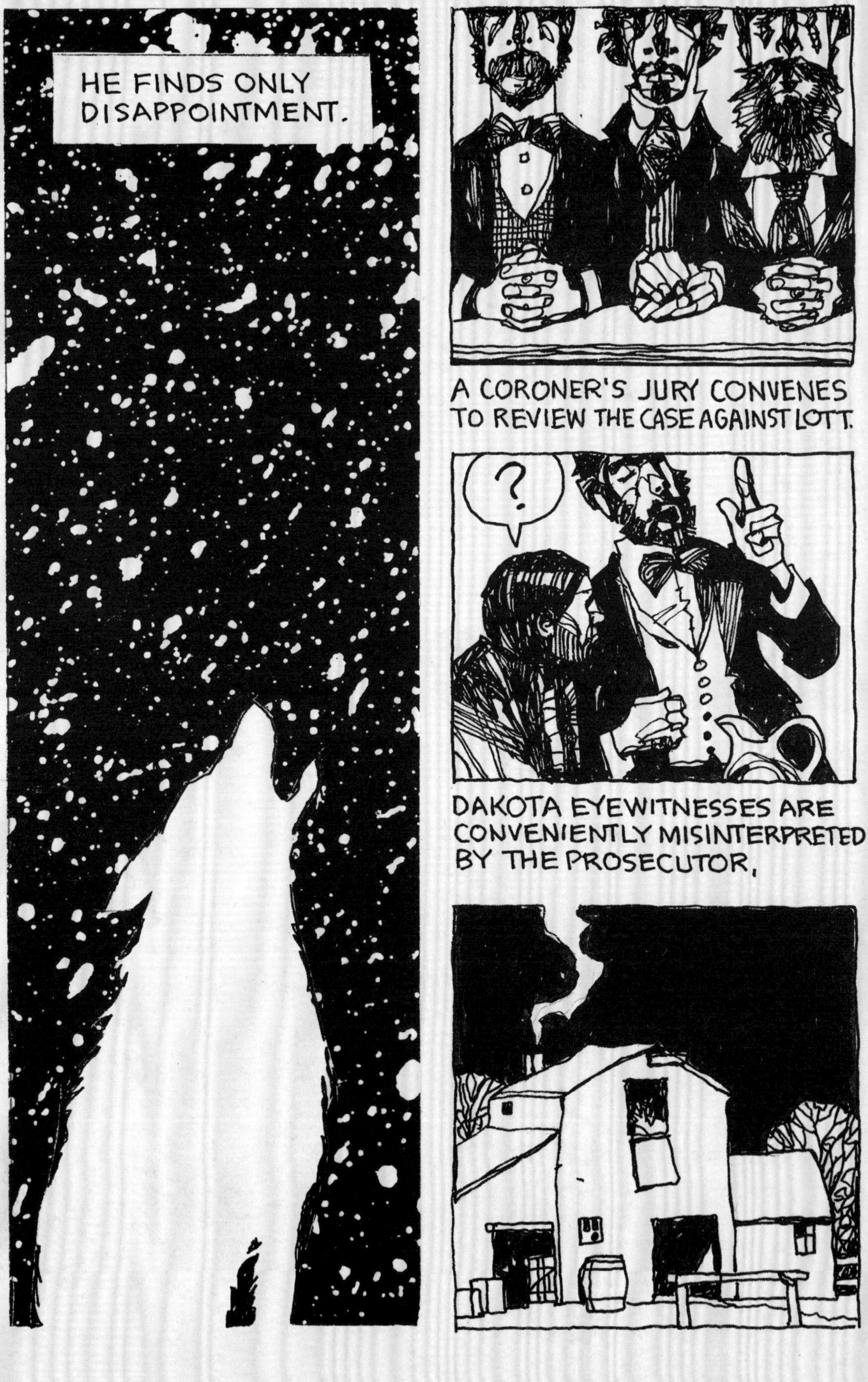
HE FINDS ONLY DISAPPOINTMENT.
A CORONER'S JURY CONVENES TO REVIEW THE CASE AGAINST LOTT.
?
DAKOTA EYEWITNESSES ARE CONVENIENTLY MISINTERPRETED BY THE PROSECUTOR,

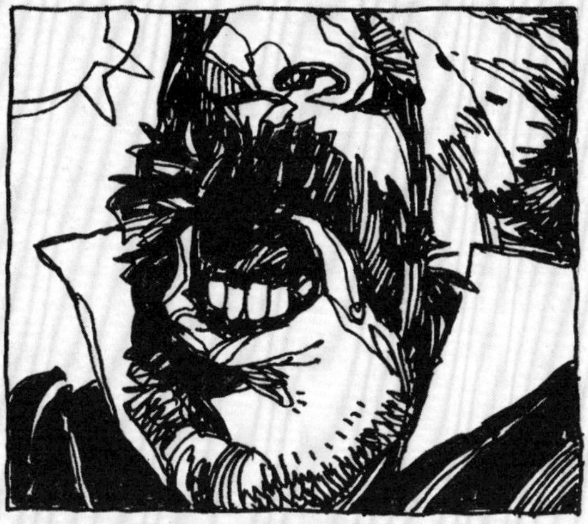

THE HEARING RAPIDLY
DEGENERATES INTO A FARCE.

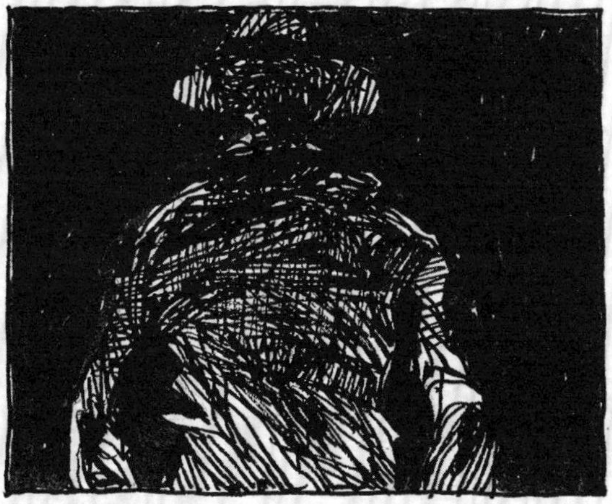

WHEREUPON HENRY LOTT
HAS LONG GONE, VANISHED
INTO THE FAR WEST...

CASE CLOSED.

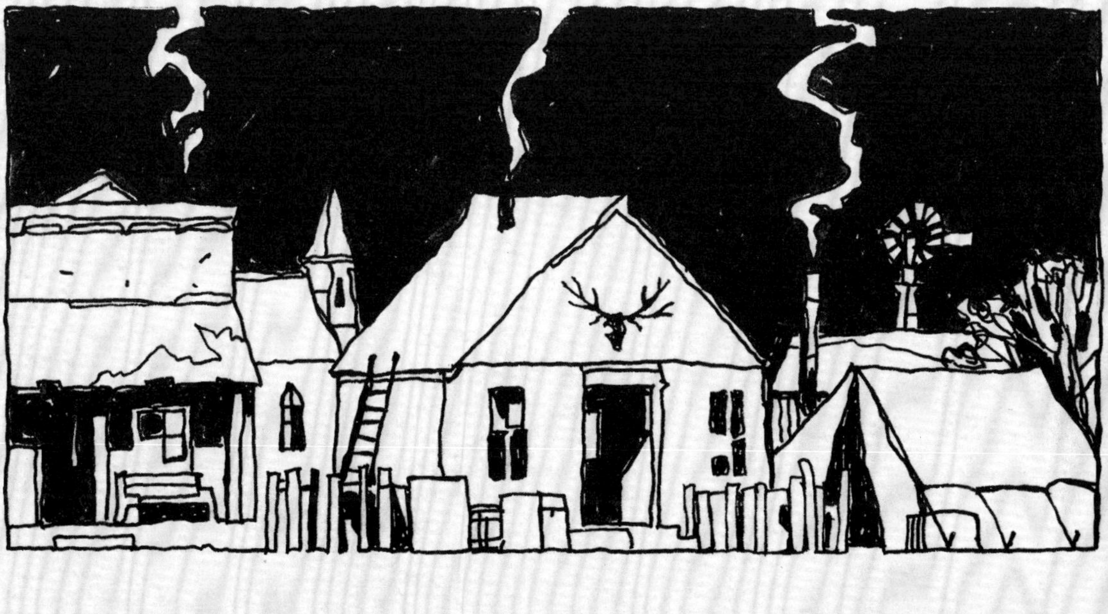

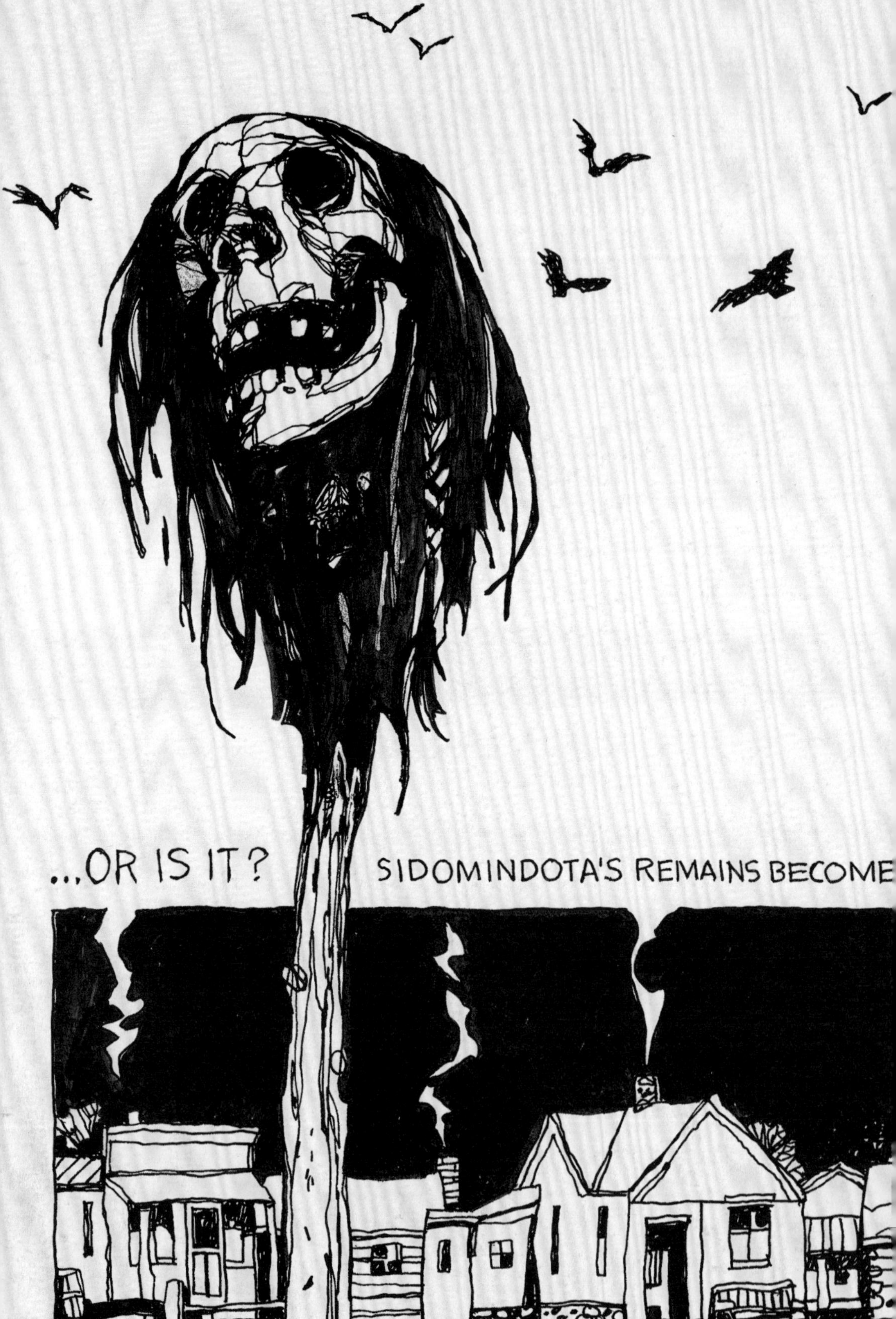
...OR IS IT?
SIDOMINDOTA'S REMAINS BECOME

AN UNFORGETTABLE SIDESHOW FOR ALL TO SEE.

MEANWHILE...
1OOO MILES EAST

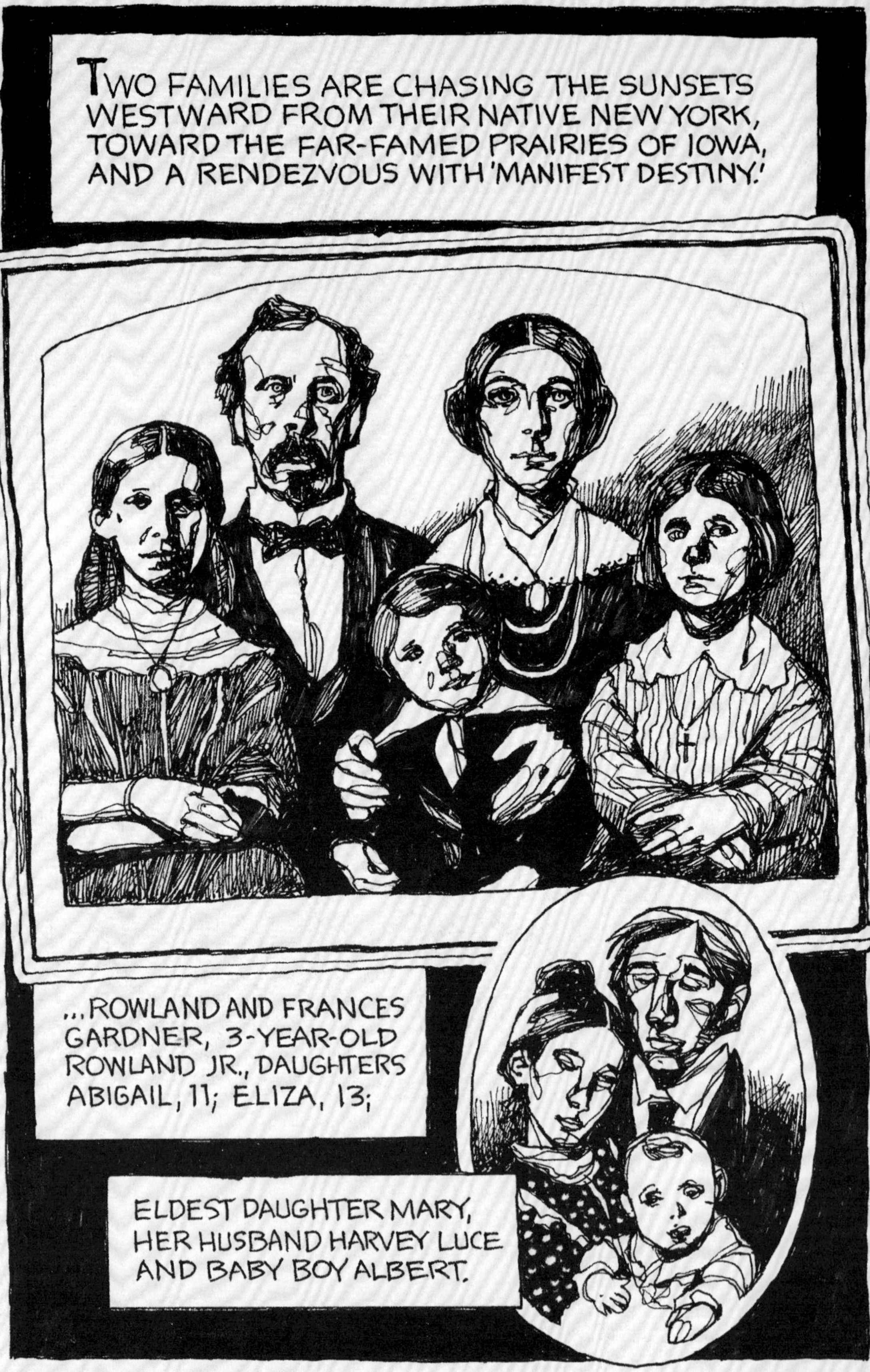
TWO FAMILIES ARE CHASING THE SUNSETS WESTWARD FROM THEIR NATIVE NEW YORK, TOWARD THE FAR-FAMED PRAIRIES OF IOWA, AND A RENDEZVOUS WITH 'MANIFEST DESTINY.'
...ROWLAND AND FRANCES GARDNER, 3-YEAR-OLD ROWLAND JR., DAUGHTERS ABIGAIL, 11; ELIZA, 13;
ELDEST DAUGHTER MARY, HER HUSBAND HARVEY LUCE AND BABY BOY ALBERT.

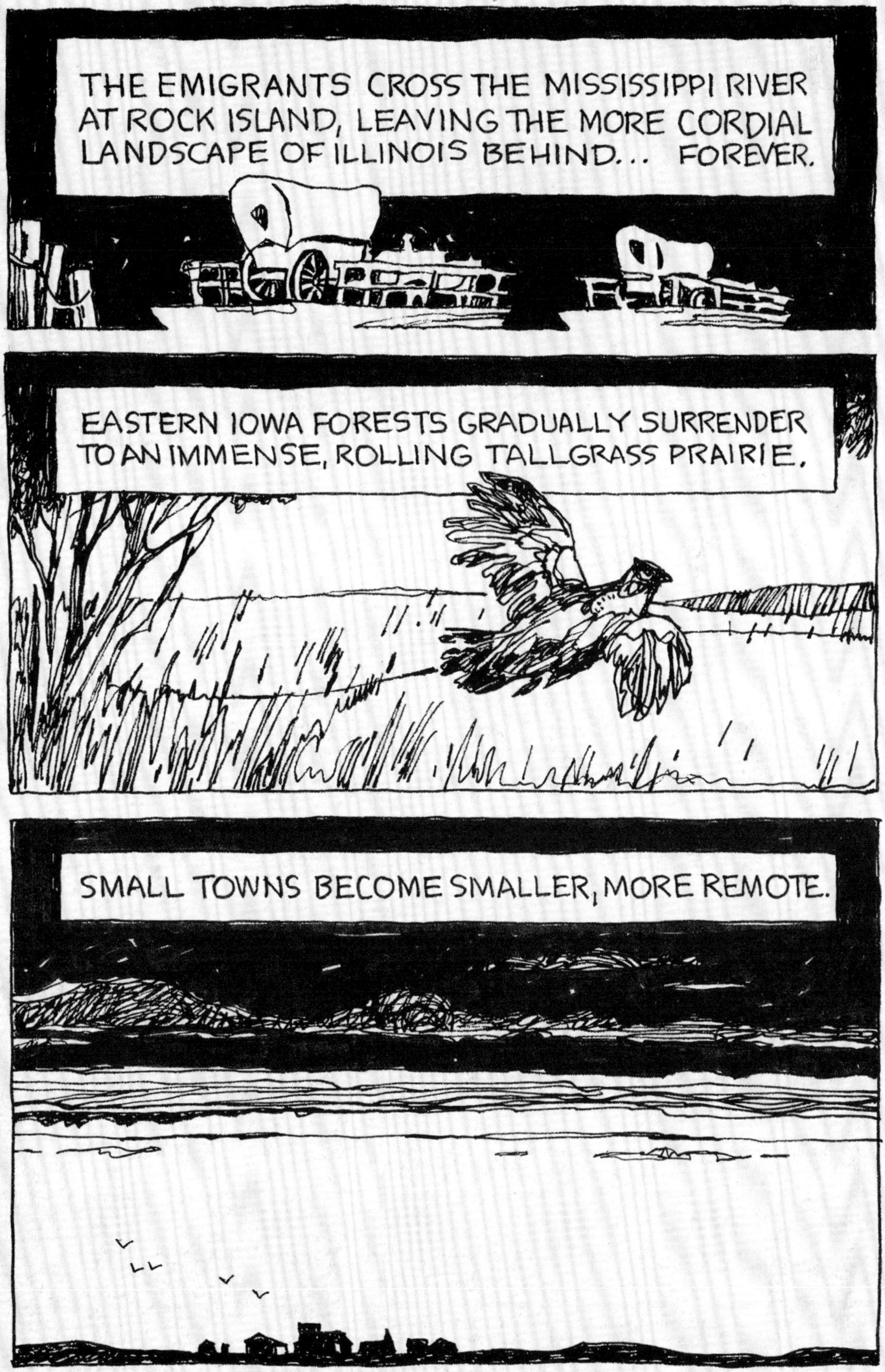
THE EMIGRANTS CROSS THE MISSISSIPPI RIVER AT ROCK ISLAND, LEAVING THE MORE CORDIAL LANDSCAPE OF ILLINOIS BEHIND... FOREVER.
EASTERN IOWA FORESTS GRADUALLY SURRENDER TO AN IMMENSE, ROLLING TALLGRASS PRAIRIE.
SMALL TOWNS BECOME SMALLER, MORE REMOTE.

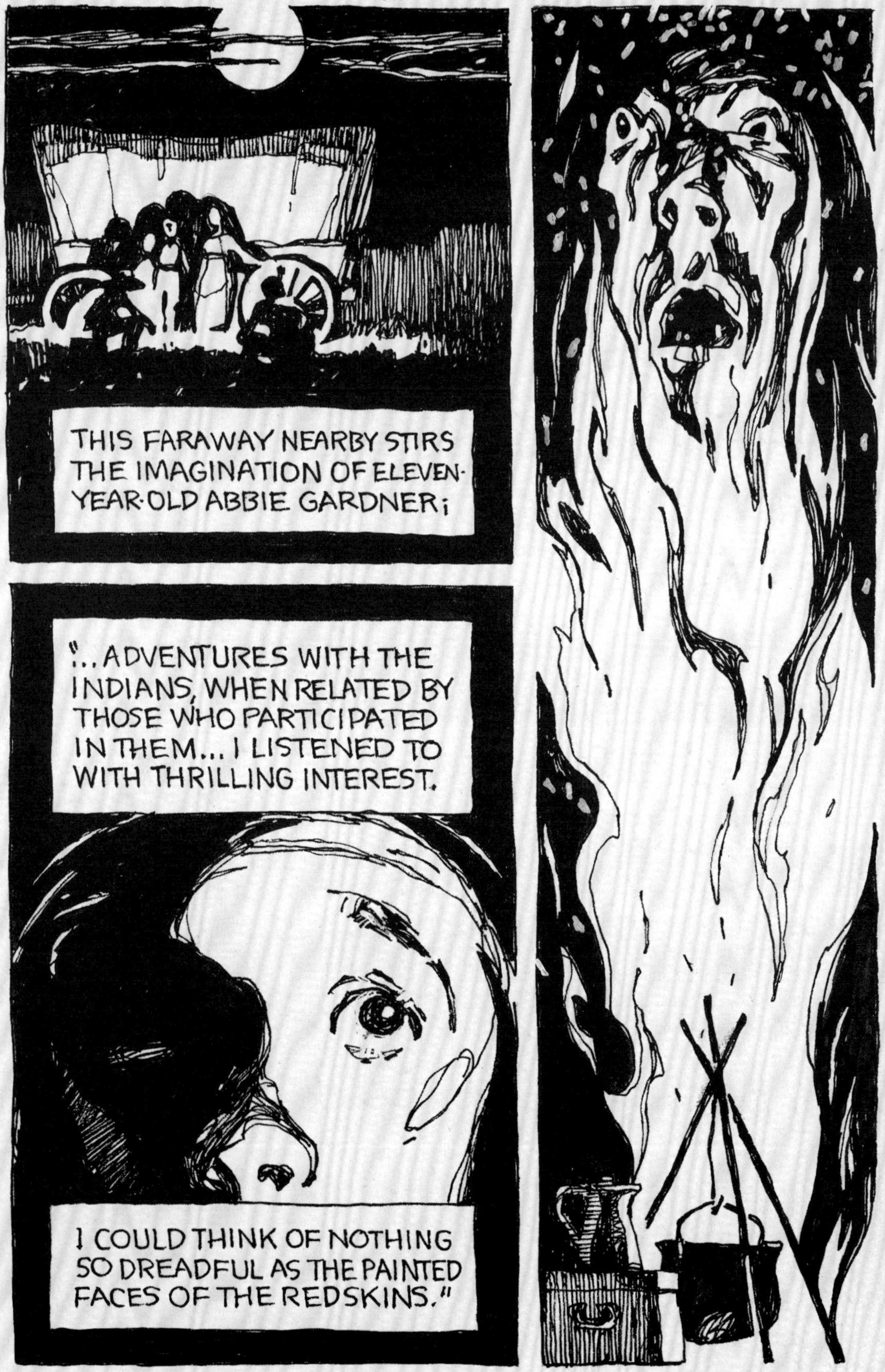
THIS FARAWAY NEARBY STIRS THE IMAGINATION OF ELEVEN-YEAR-OLD ABBIE GARDNER;
"...ADVENTURES WITH THE INDIANS, WHEN RELATED BY THOSE WHO PARTICIPATED IN THEM... I LISTENED TO WITH THRILLING INTEREST.
I COULD THINK OF NOTHING SO DREADFUL AS THE PAINTED FACES OF THE REDSKINS."

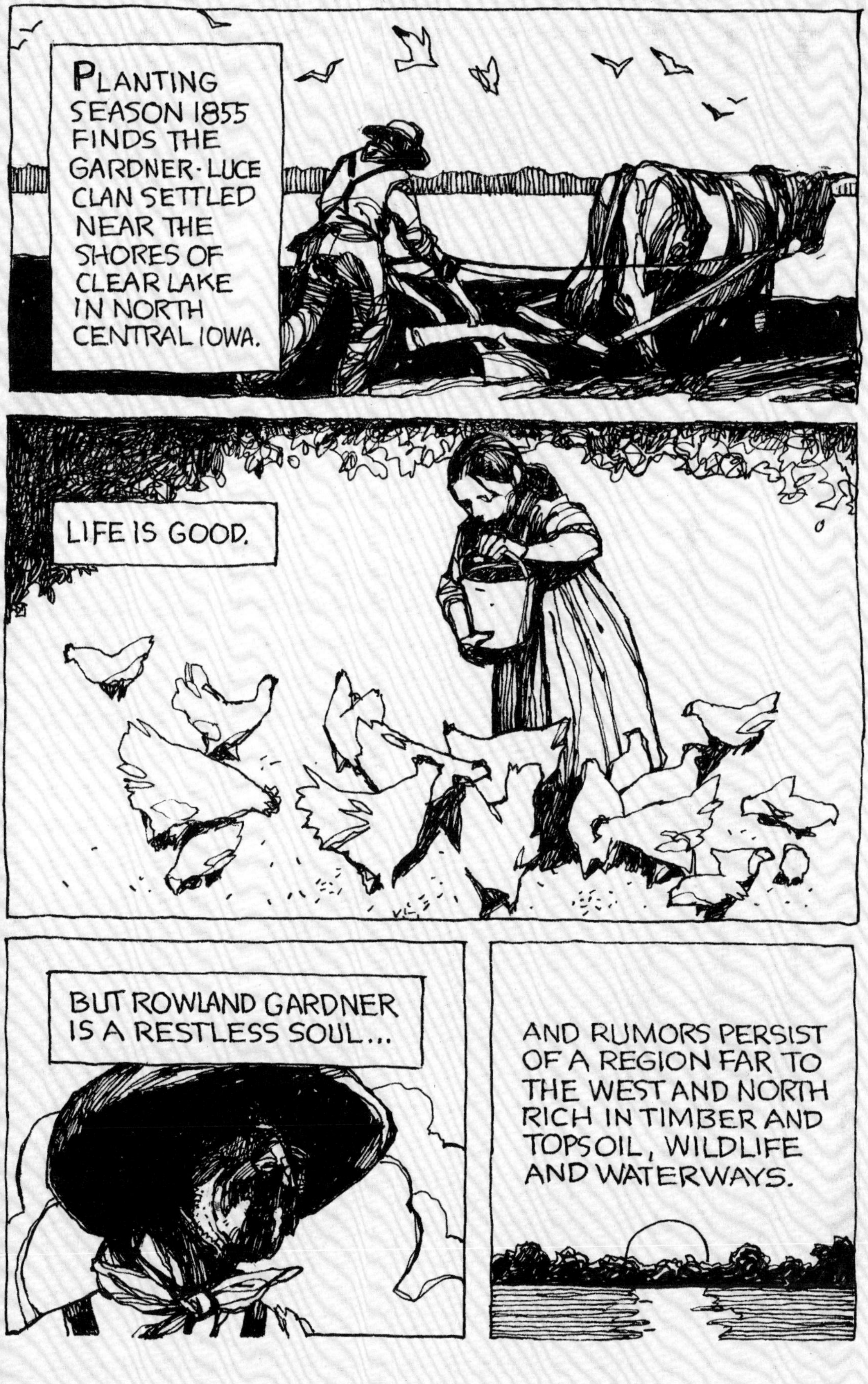
PLANTING SEASON 1855 FINDS THE GARDNER-LUCE CLAN SETTLED NEAR THE SHORES OF CLEAR LAKE IN NORTH CENTRAL IOWA.
LIFE IS GOOD.
BUT ROWLAND GARDNER IS A RESTLESS SOUL...
AND RUMORS PERSIST OF A REGION FAR TO THE WEST AND NORTH RICH IN TIMBER AND TOPSOIL, WILDLIFE AND WATERWAYS.

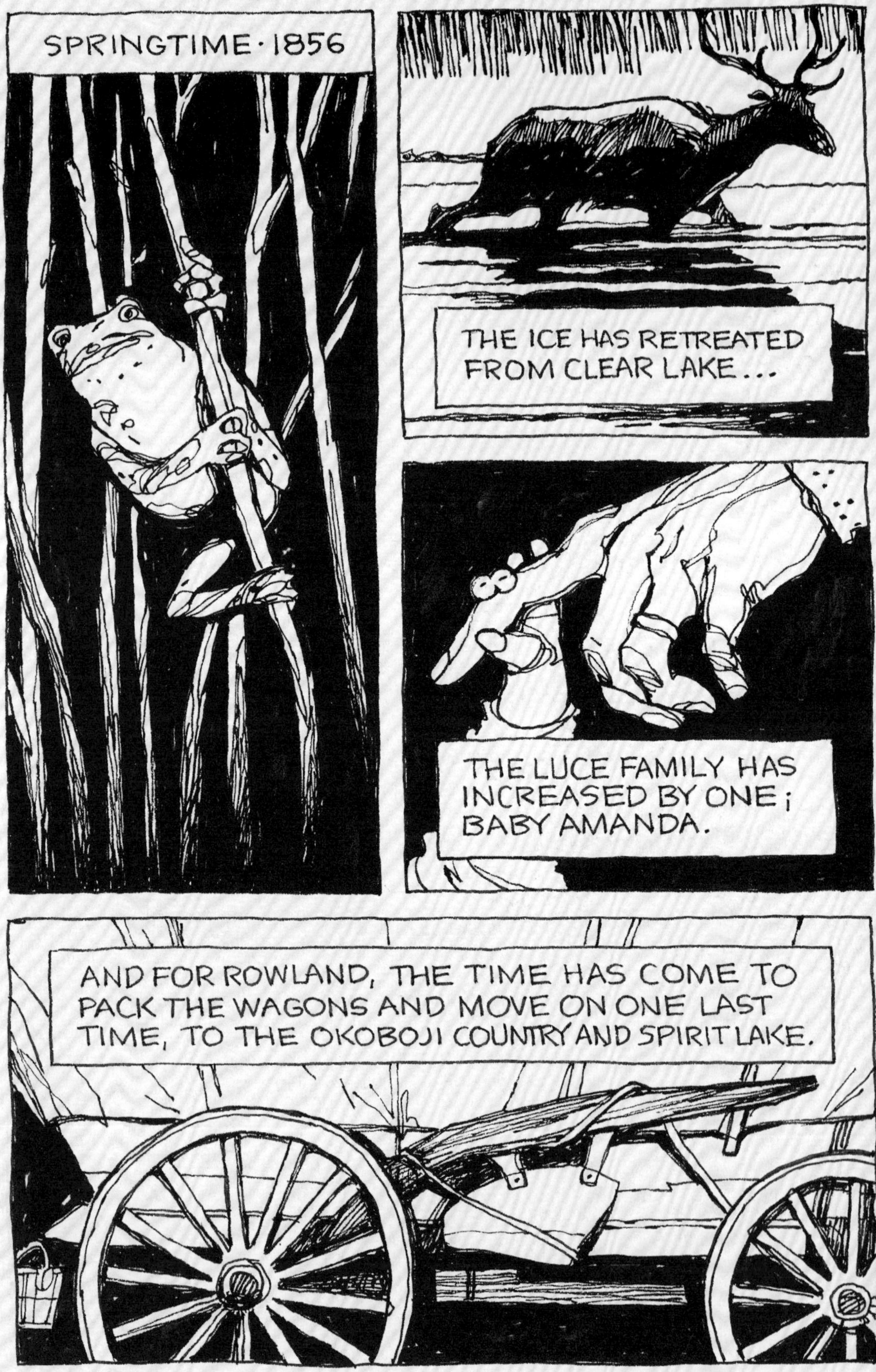
SPRINGTIME · 1856
THE ICE HAS RETREATED FROM CLEAR LAKE...
THE LUCE FAMILY HAS INCREASED BY ONE; BABY AMANDA.
AND FOR ROWLAND, THE TIME HAS COME TO PACK THE WAGONS AND MOVE ON ONE LAST TIME, TO THE OKOBOJI COUNTRY AND SPIRIT LAKE.

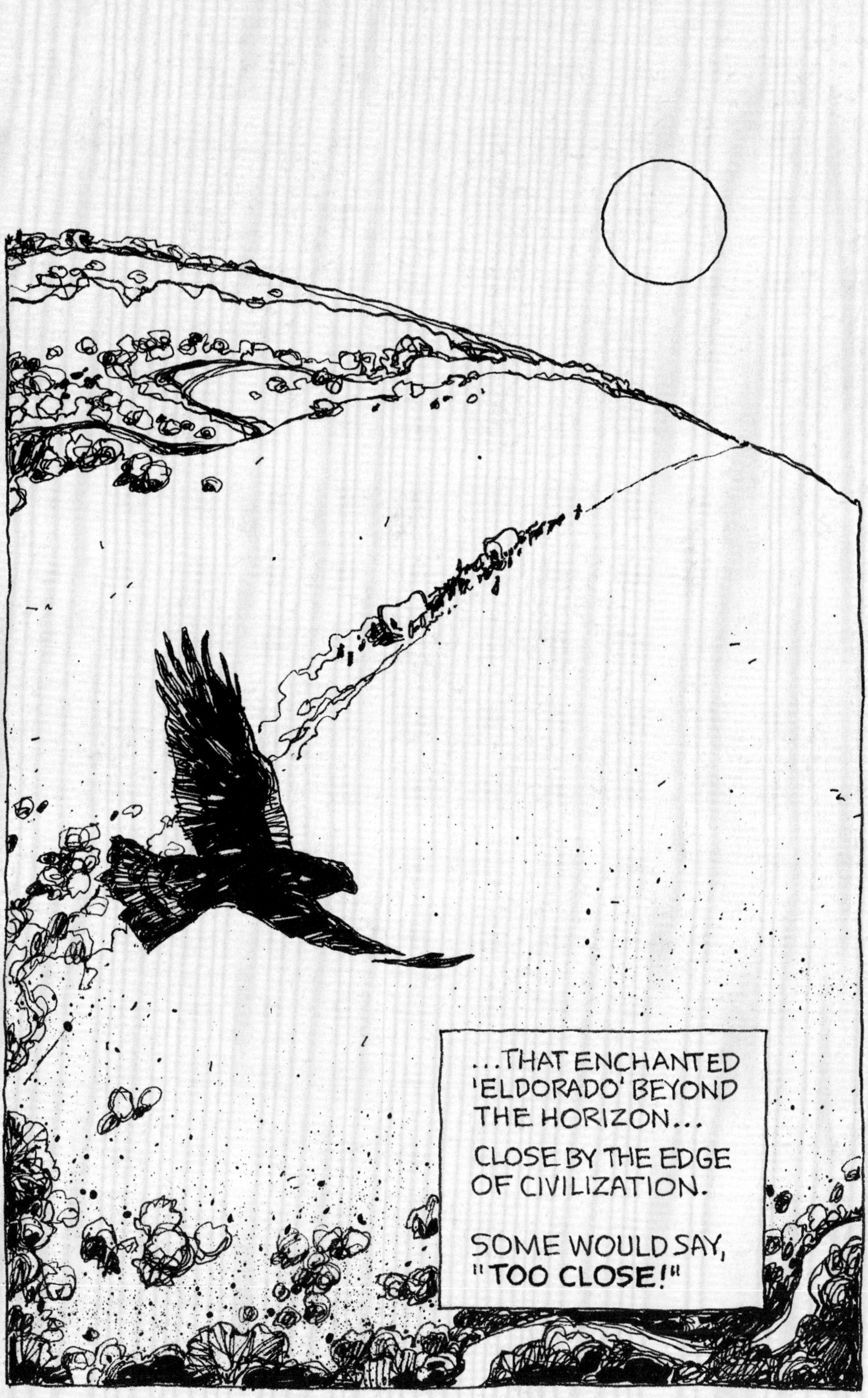
...THAT ENCHANTED 'ELDORADO' BEYOND THE HORIZON...
CLOSE BY THE EDGE OF CIVILIZATION.
SOME WOULD SAY, "TOO CLOSE!"

JUNE 1856

THE MOON OF
RED STRAWBERRIES

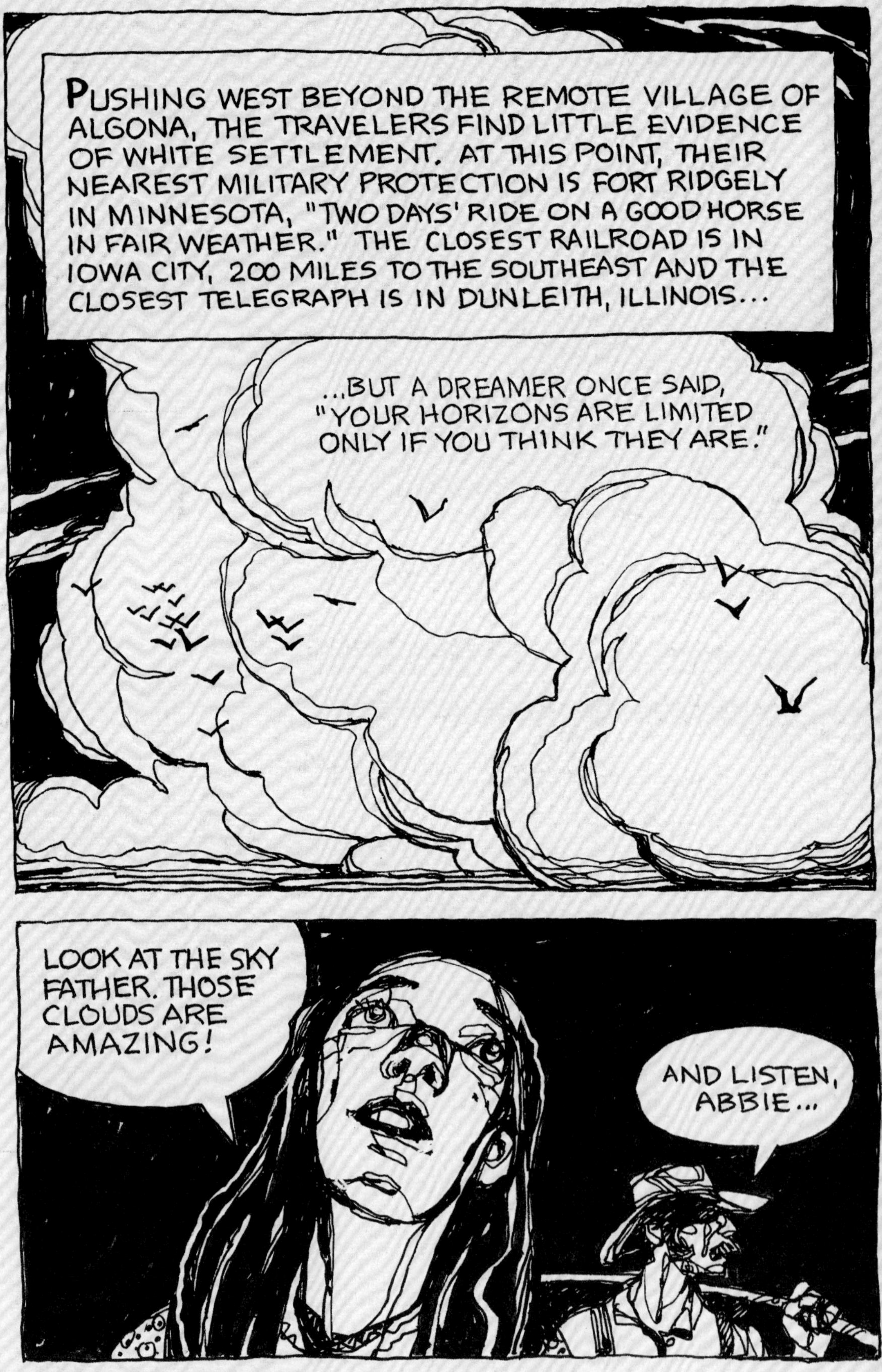
PUSHING WEST BEYOND THE REMOTE VILLAGE OF ALGONA, THE TRAVELERS FIND LITTLE EVIDENCE OF WHITE SETTLEMENT. AT THIS POINT, THEIR NEAREST MILITARY PROTECTION IS FORT RIDGELY IN MINNESOTA, "TWO DAYS' RIDE ON A GOOD HORSE IN FAIR WEATHER." THE CLOSEST RAILROAD IS IN IOWA CITY, 200 MILES TO THE SOUTHEAST AND THE CLOSEST TELEGRAPH IS IN DUNLEITH, ILLINOIS...
...BUT A DREAMER ONCE SAID, "YOUR HORIZONS ARE LIMITED ONLY IF YOU THINK THEY ARE."
LOOK AT THE SKY FATHER. THOSE CLOUDS ARE AMAZING!
AND LISTEN, ABBIE...

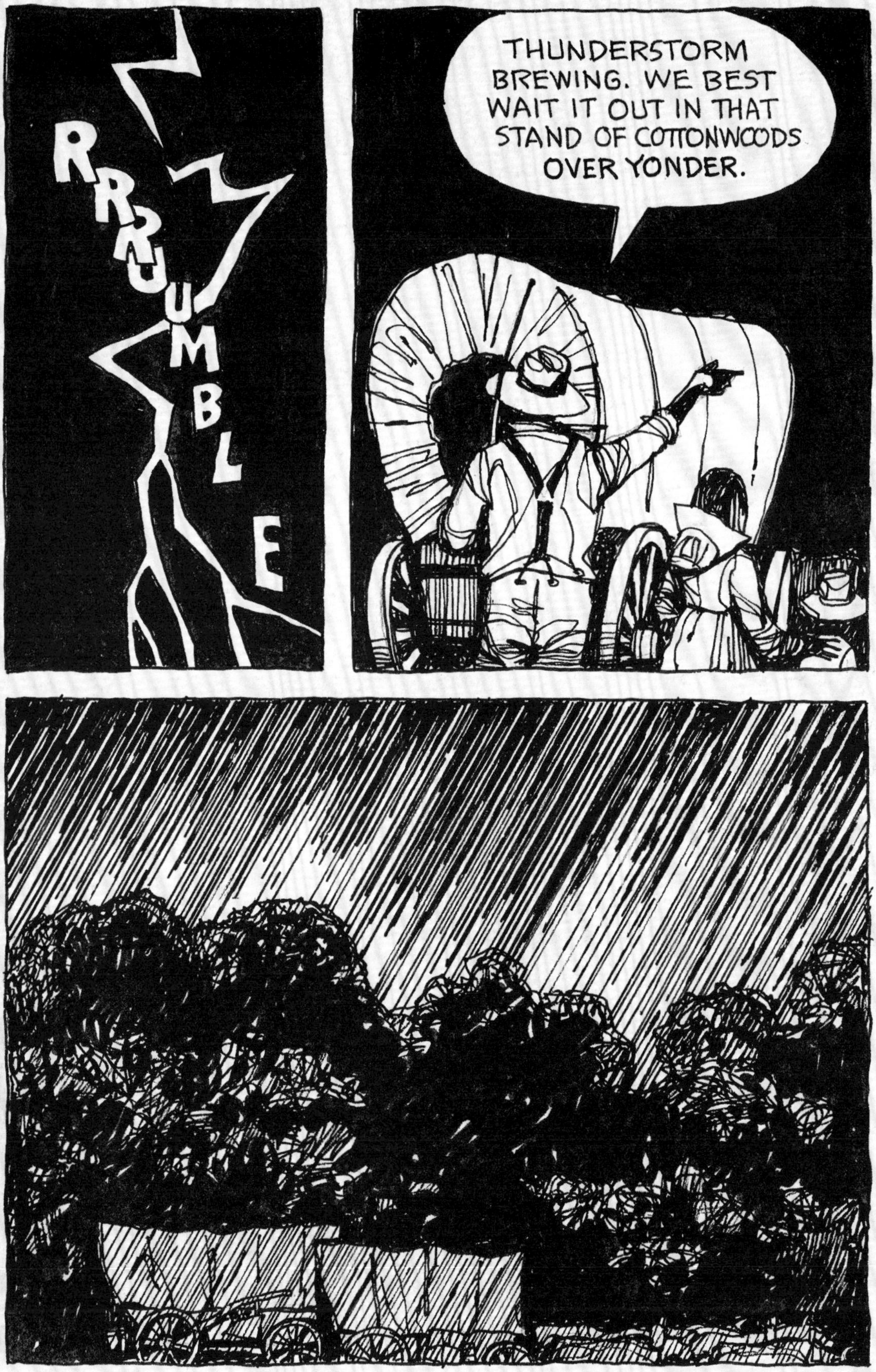
RRRUMBLE
THUNDERSTORM BREWING. WE BEST WAIT IT OUT IN THAT STAND OF COTTONWOODS OVER YONDER.

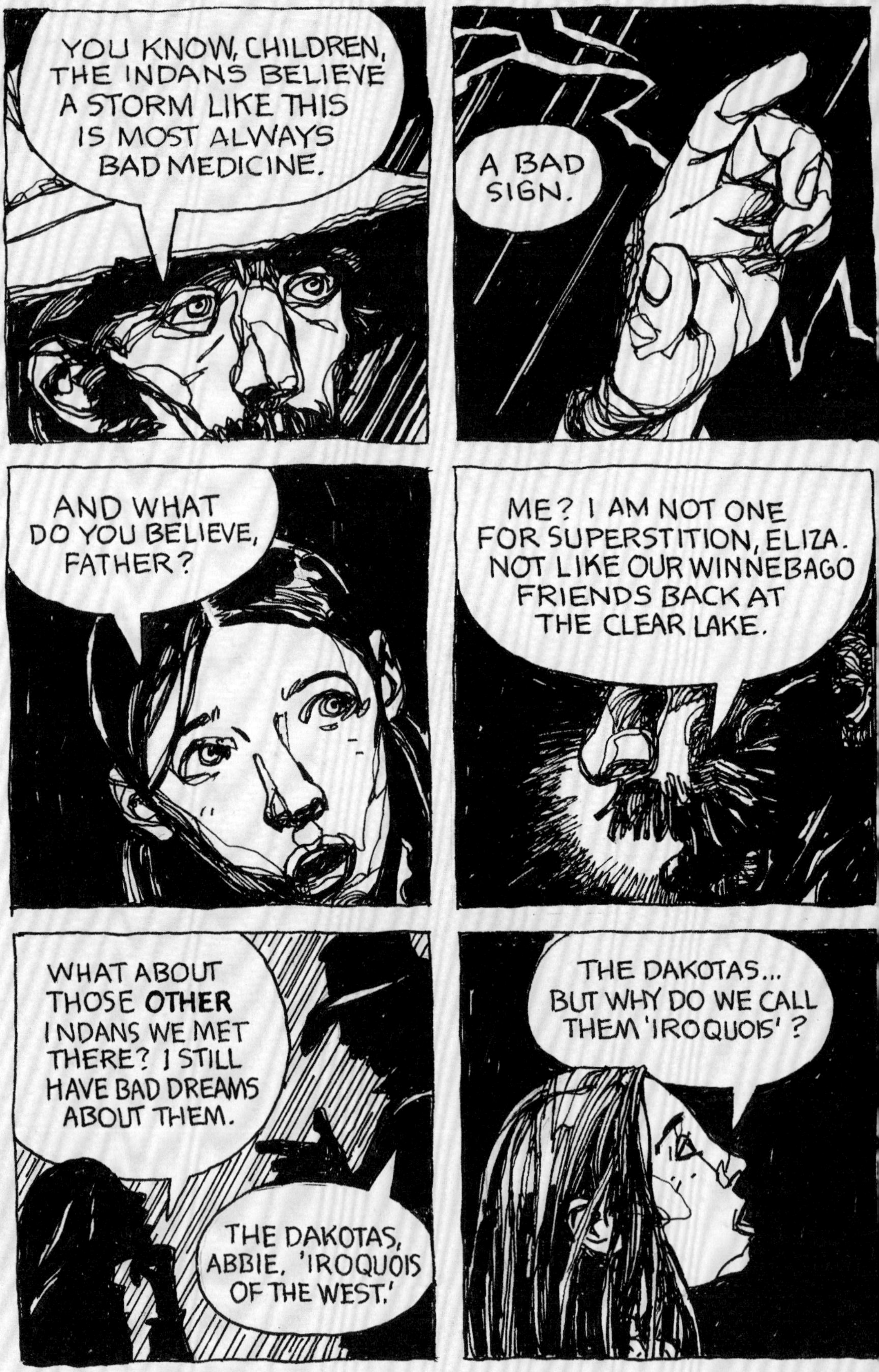
YOU KNOW, CHILDREN, THE INDANS BELIEVE A STORM LIKE THIS IS MOST ALWAYS BAD MEDICINE.
A BAD SIGN.
AND WHAT DO YOU BELIEVE, FATHER?
ME? I AM NOT ONE FOR SUPERSTITION, ELIZA. NOT LIKE OUR WINNEBAGO FRIENDS BACK AT THE CLEAR LAKE.
WHAT ABOUT THOSE **OTHER** INDANS WE MET THERE? I STILL HAVE BAD DREAMS ABOUT THEM.
THE DAKOTAS, ABBIE. 'IROQUOIS OF THE WEST.'
THE DAKOTAS... BUT WHY DO WE CALL THEM 'IROQUOIS'?

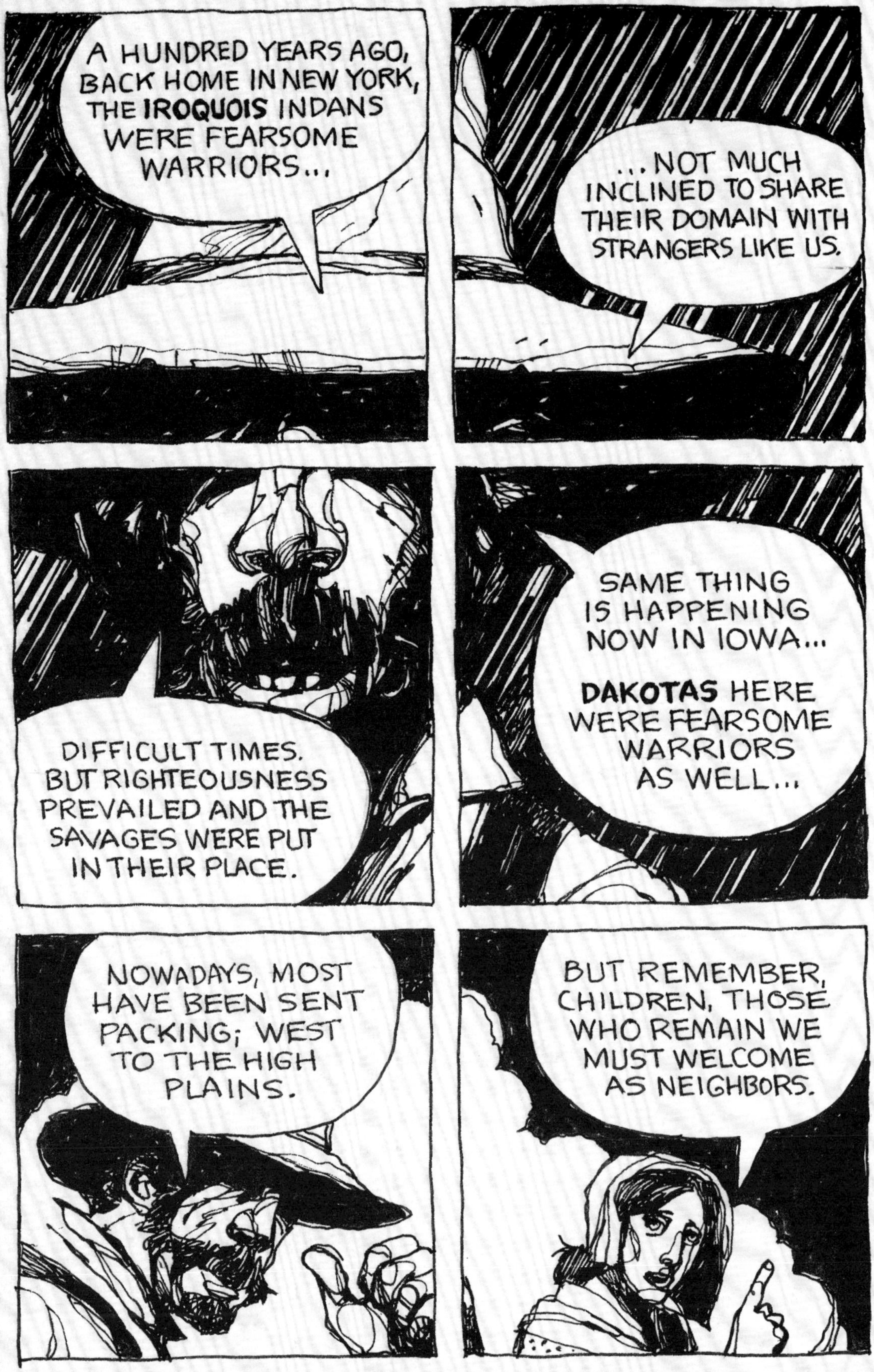
A HUNDRED YEARS AGO, BACK HOME IN NEW YORK, THE **IROQUOIS** INDANS WERE FEARSOME WARRIORS...
...NOT MUCH INCLINED TO SHARE THEIR DOMAIN WITH STRANGERS LIKE US.
DIFFICULT TIMES. BUT RIGHTEOUSNESS PREVAILED AND THE SAVAGES WERE PUT IN THEIR PLACE.
SAME THING IS HAPPENING NOW IN IOWA... **DAKOTAS** HERE WERE FEARSOME WARRIORS AS WELL...
NOWADAYS, MOST HAVE BEEN SENT PACKING; WEST TO THE HIGH PLAINS.
BUT REMEMBER, CHILDREN, THOSE WHO REMAIN WE MUST WELCOME AS NEIGHBORS.

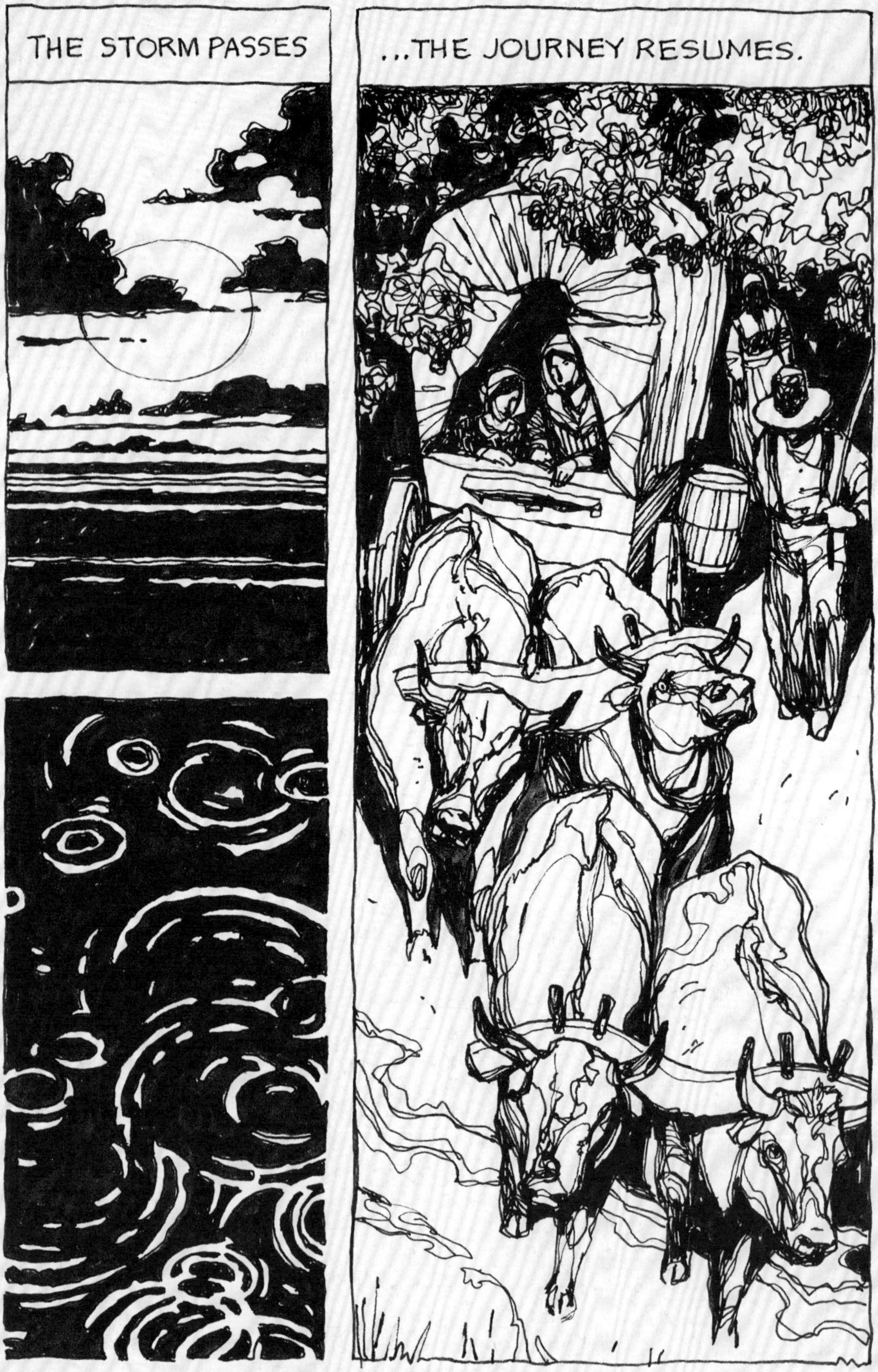
THE STORM PASSES
...THE JOURNEY RESUMES.

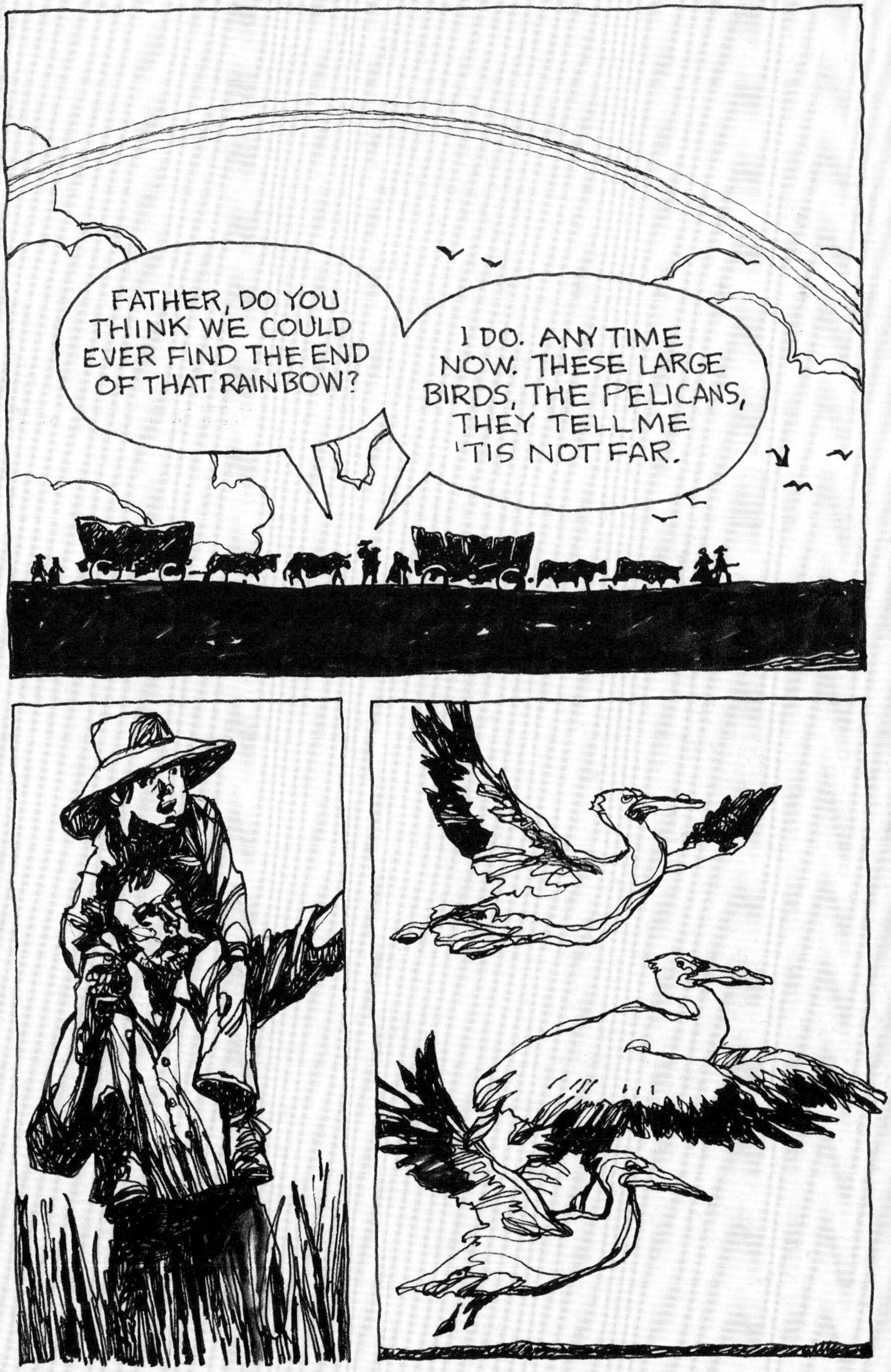
FATHER, DO YOU THINK WE COULD EVER FIND THE END OF THAT RAINBOW?
I DO. ANY TIME NOW. THESE LARGE BIRDS, THE PELICANS, THEY TELL ME 'TIS NOT FAR.

JULY 1856

THE MOON OF RED CHERRIES

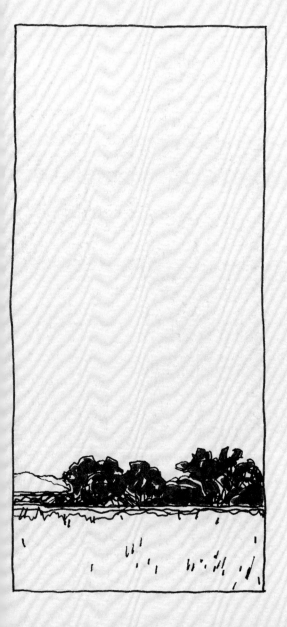

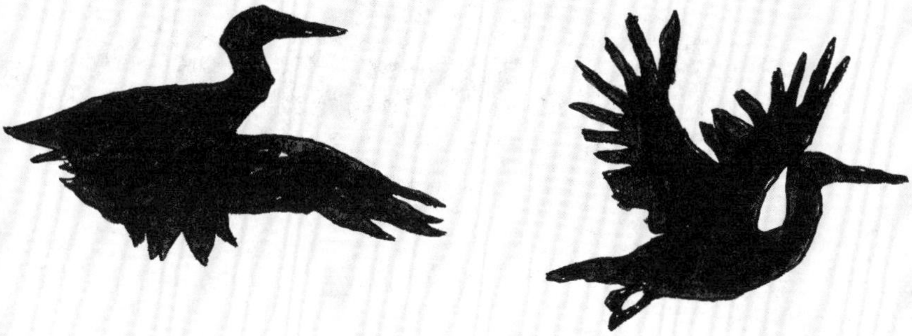

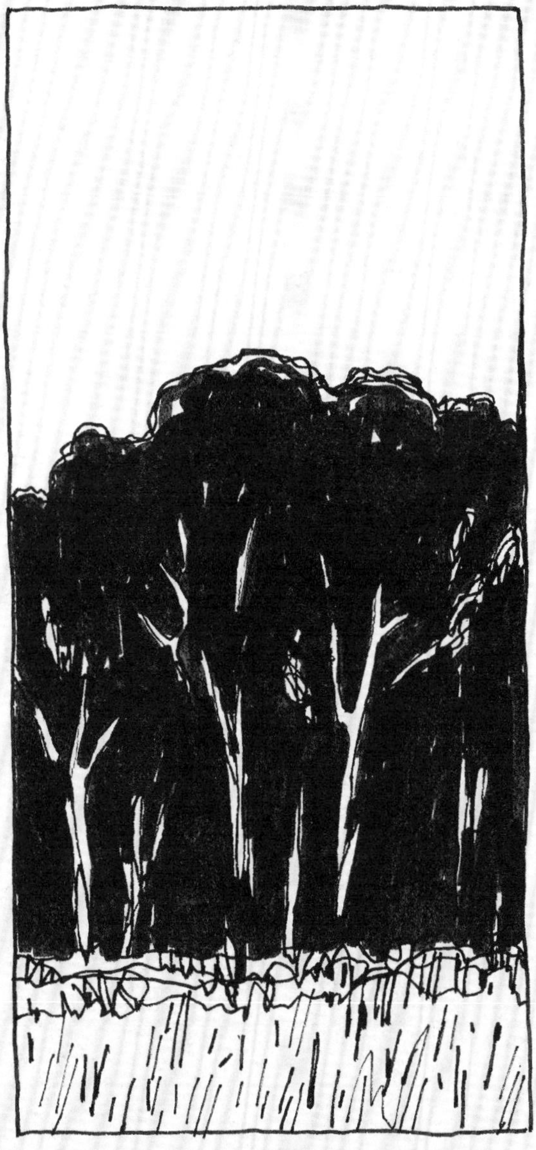

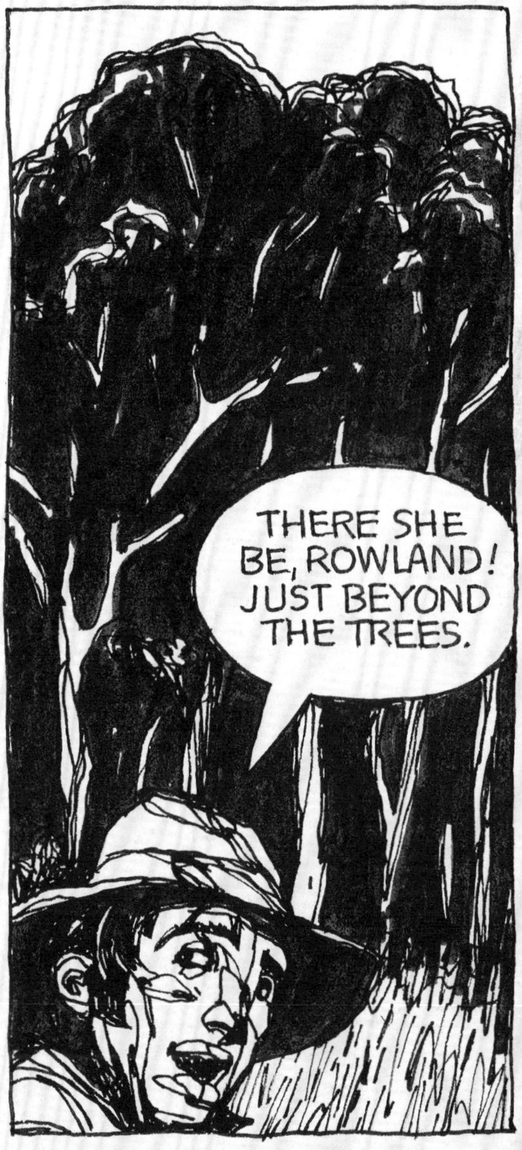
THERE SHE BE, ROWLAND! JUST BEYOND THE TREES.

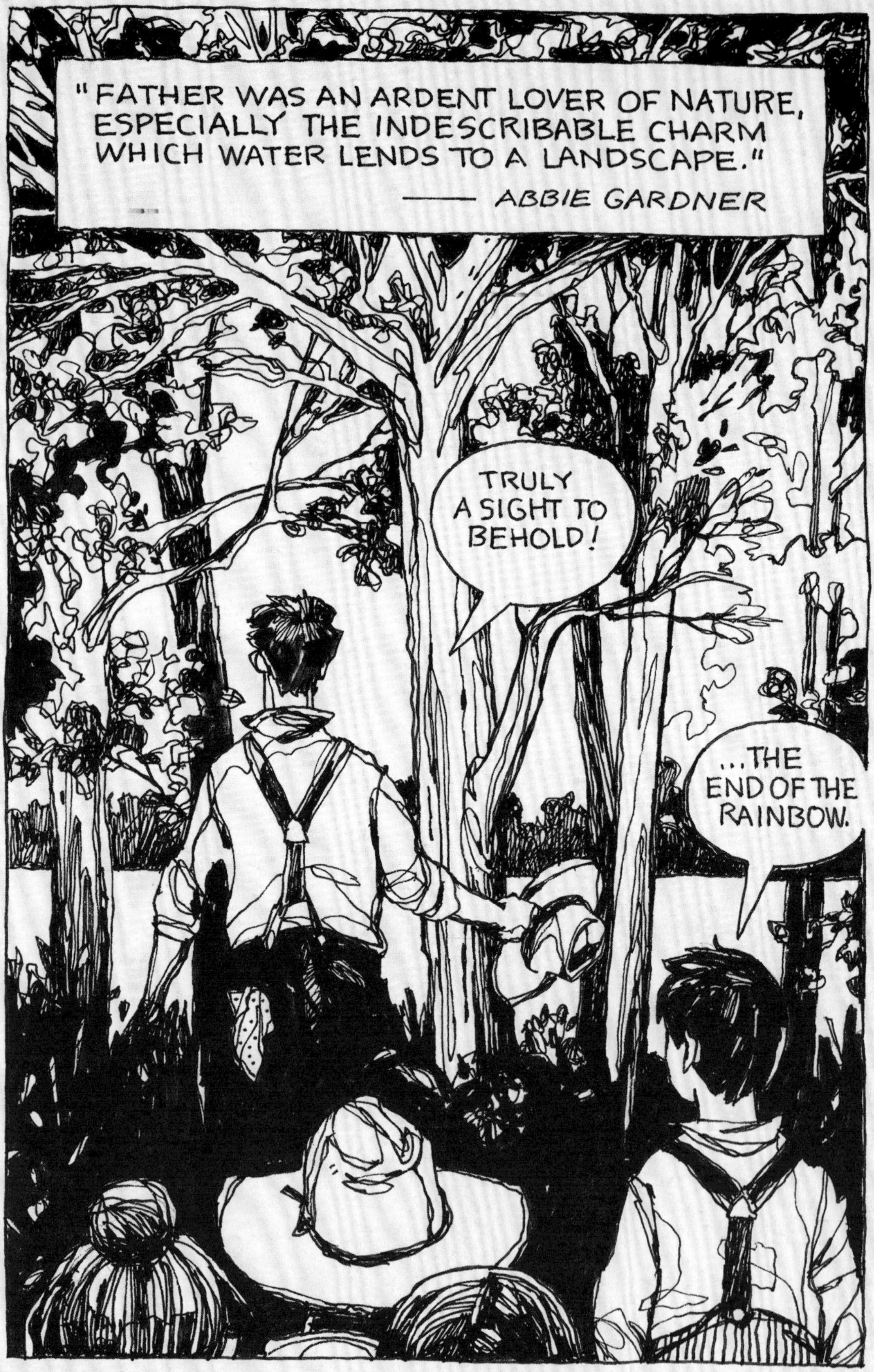
"FATHER WAS AN ARDENT LOVER OF NATURE, ESPECIALLY THE INDESCRIBABLE CHARM WHICH WATER LENDS TO A LANDSCAPE."
—— ABBIE GARDNER
TRULY A SIGHT TO BEHOLD!
...THE END OF THE RAINBOW.

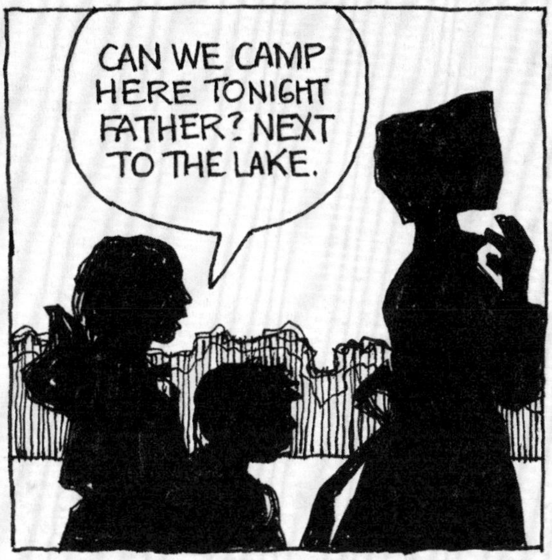
CAN WE CAMP HERE TONIGHT FATHER? NEXT TO THE LAKE.

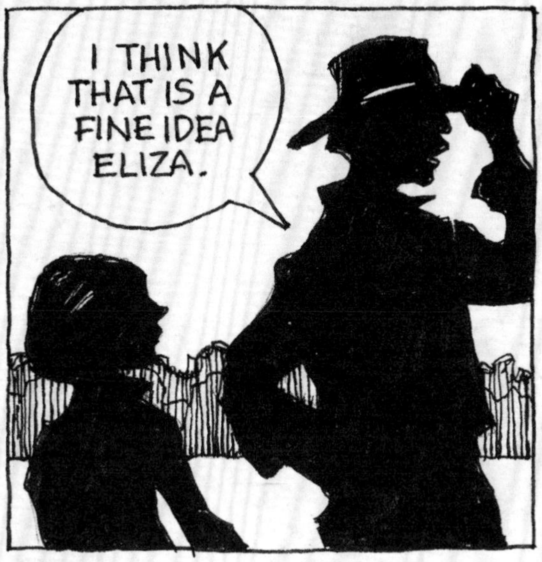
I THINK THAT IS A FINE IDEA ELIZA.

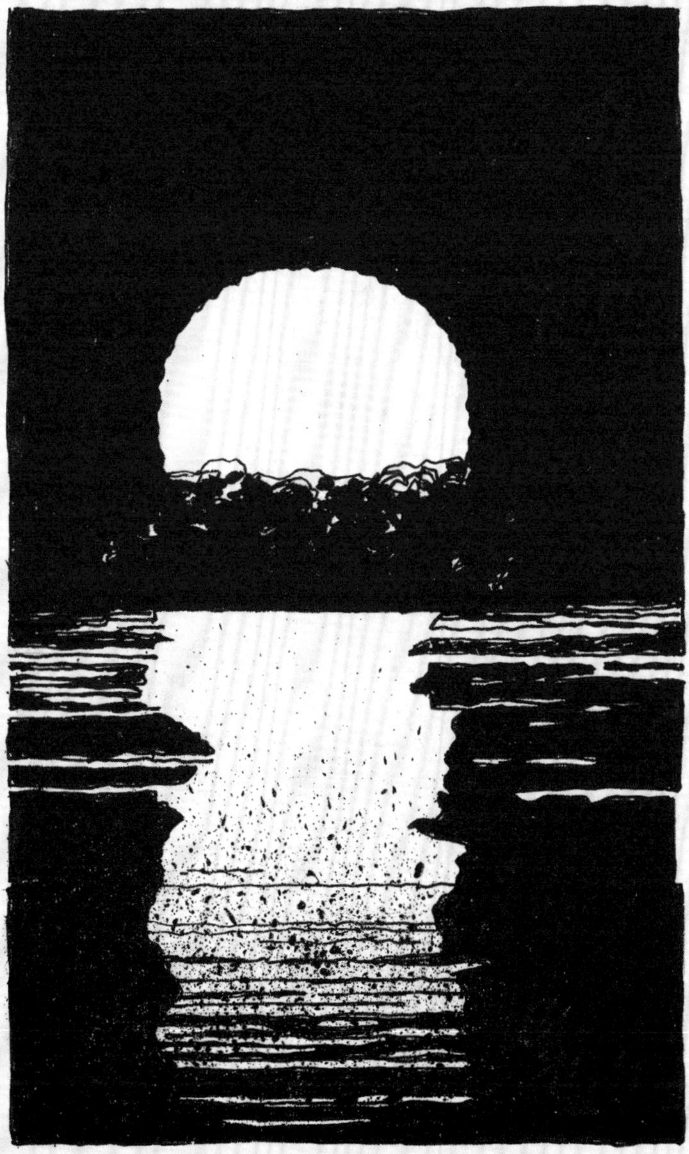

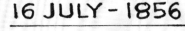

16 JULY - 1856

A SOFT TWILIGHT FADES TO BLACK, THE QUIET OF THIS REMOTE SHORE CHECKED ONLY BY THE SLAP OF A BEAVER TAIL

... AND BY THE SOUND OF VOICES AROUND A CAMP-FIRE, SPEAKING IN A STRANGE LANGUAGE:

ENGLISH.

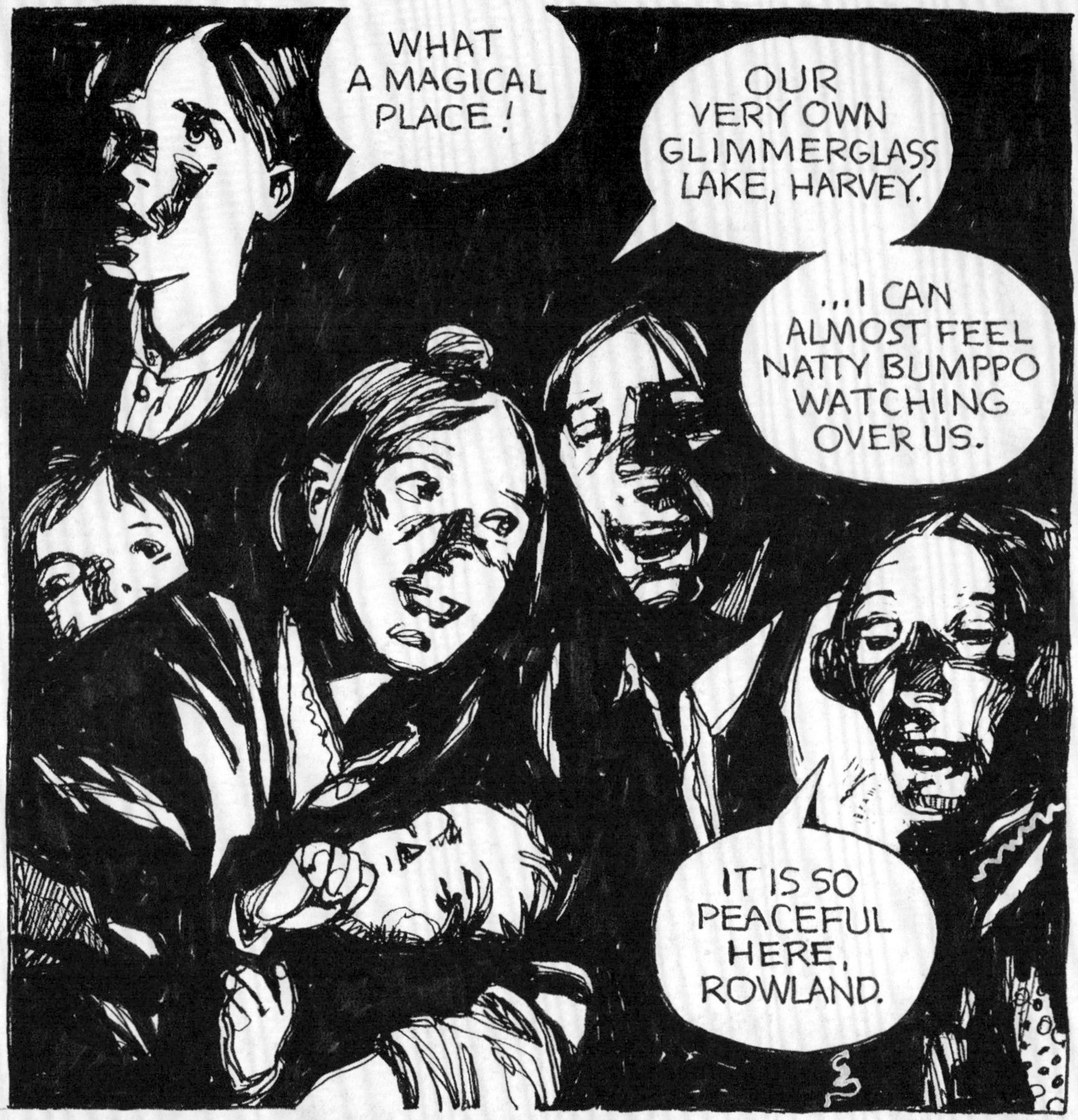
WHAT A MAGICAL PLACE!
OUR VERY OWN GLIMMERGLASS LAKE, HARVEY.
...I CAN ALMOST FEEL NATTY BUMPPO WATCHING OVER US.
IT IS SO PEACEFUL HERE, ROWLAND.

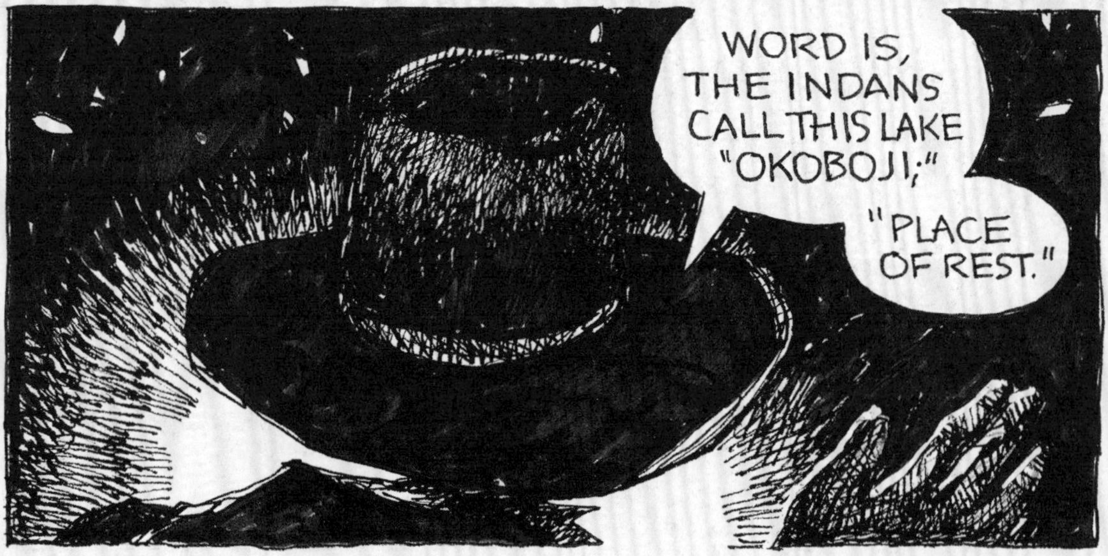
WORD IS, THE INDANS CALL THIS LAKE "OKOBOJI;"
"PLACE OF REST."

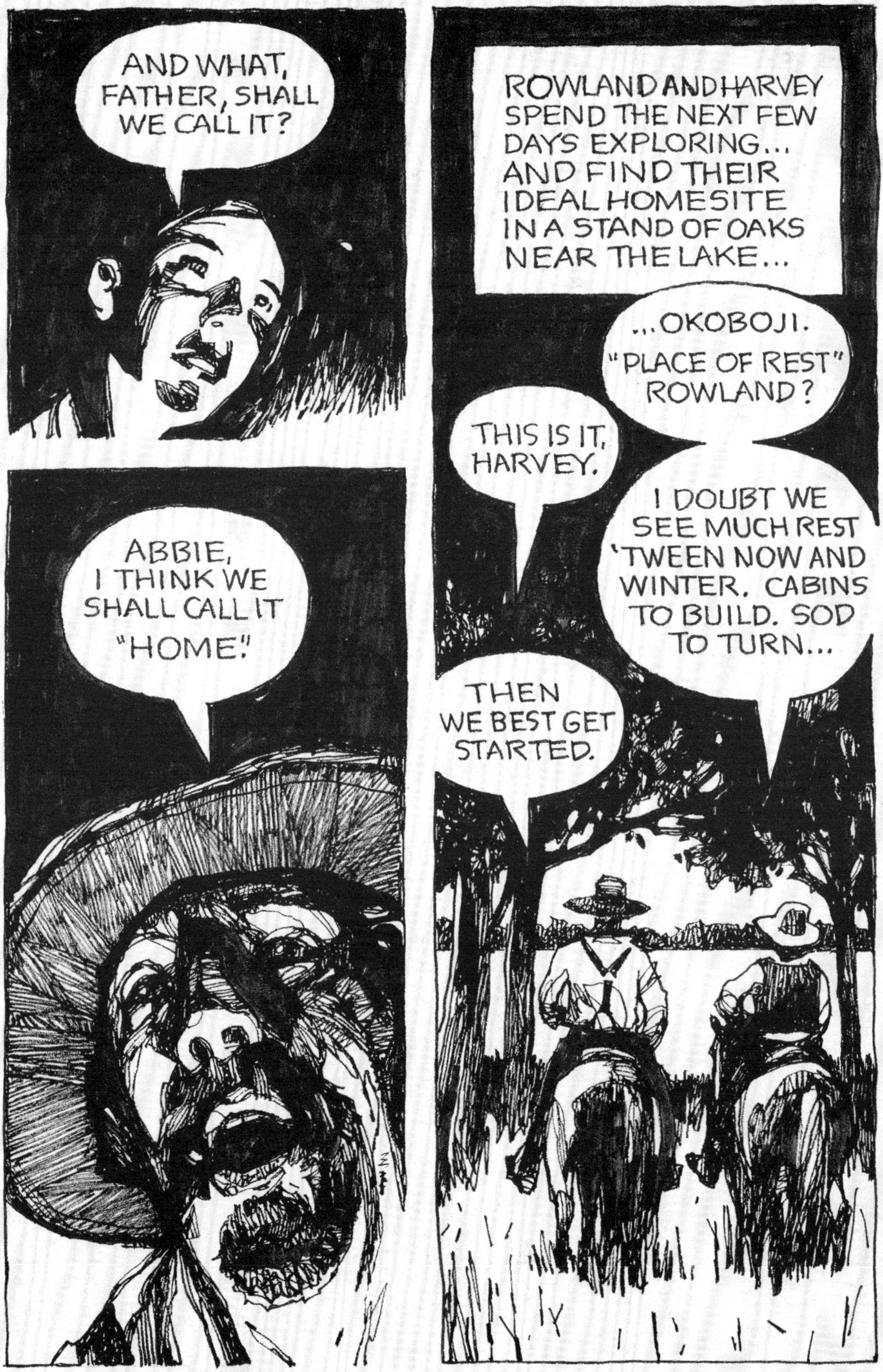
AND WHAT, FATHER, SHALL WE CALL IT?
ABBIE, I THINK WE SHALL CALL IT "HOME."
ROWLAND AND HARVEY SPEND THE NEXT FEW DAYS EXPLORING... AND FIND THEIR IDEAL HOMESITE IN A STAND OF OAKS NEAR THE LAKE...
...OKOBOJI. "PLACE OF REST" ROWLAND?
THIS IS IT, HARVEY.
I DOUBT WE SEE MUCH REST 'TWEEN NOW AND WINTER. CABINS TO BUILD. SOD TO TURN...
THEN WE BEST GET STARTED.

AUGUST 1856

THE MOON WHEN CHERRIES TURN BLACK

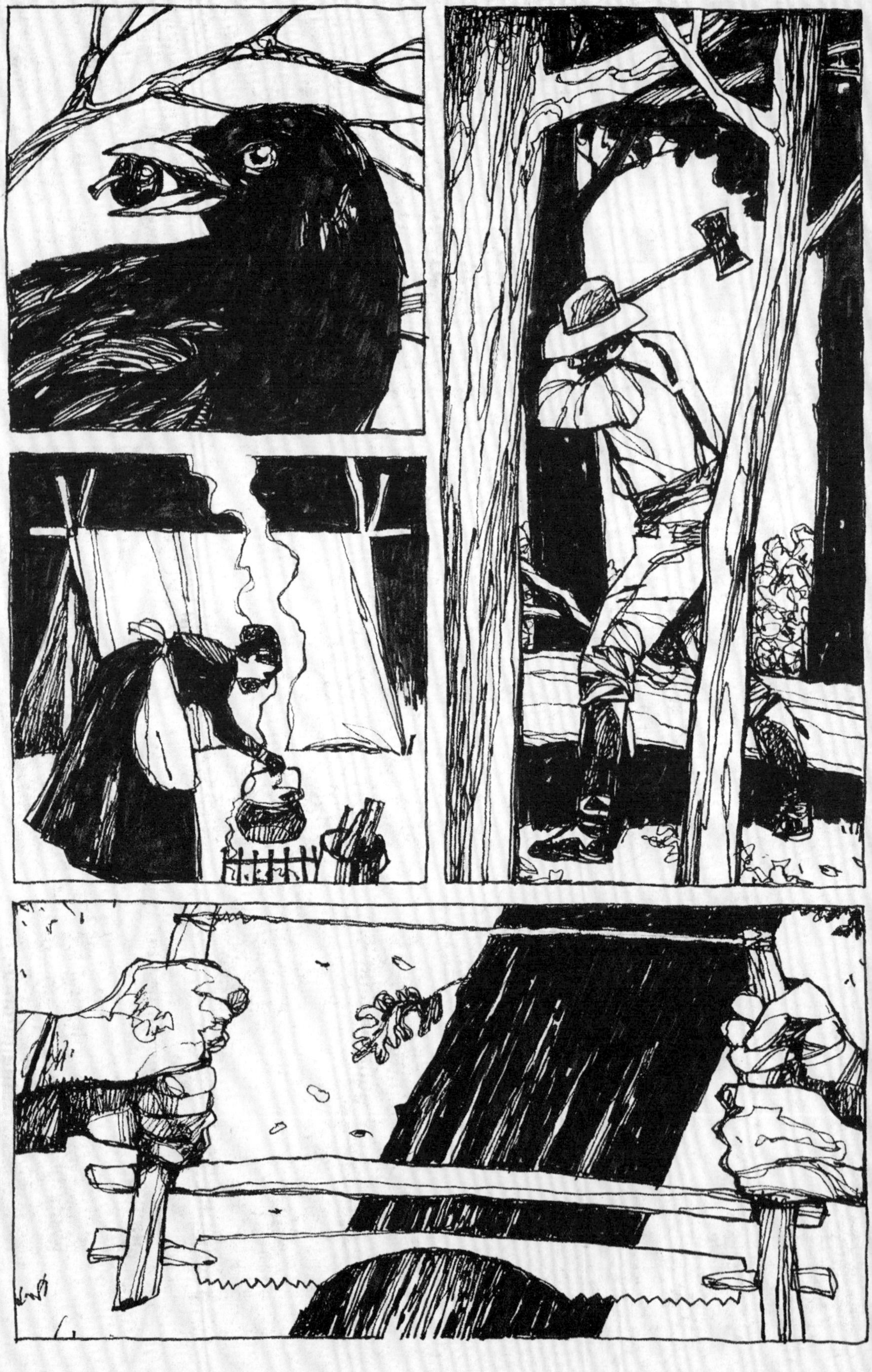

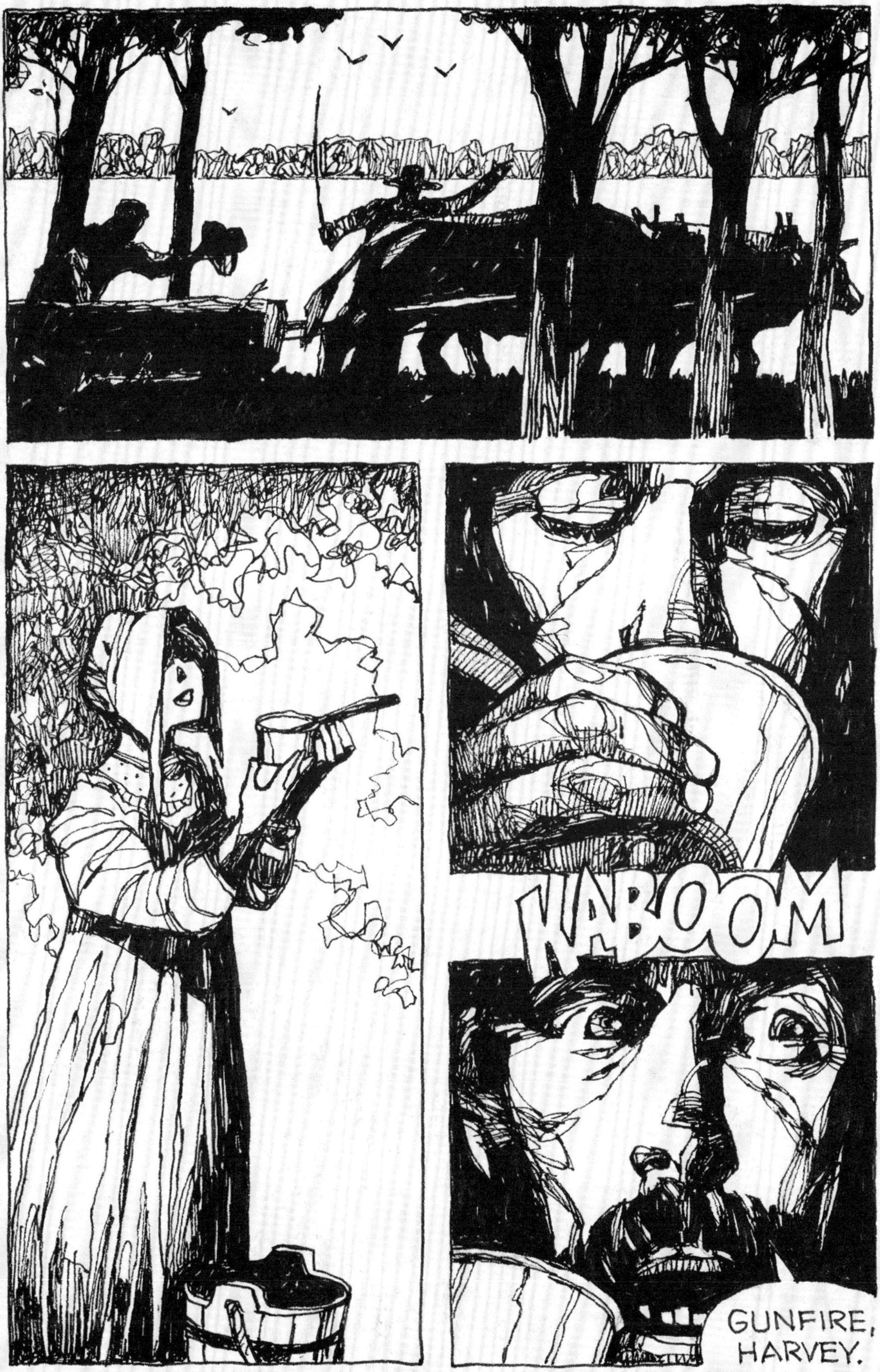
KABOOM
GUNFIRE, HARVEY.

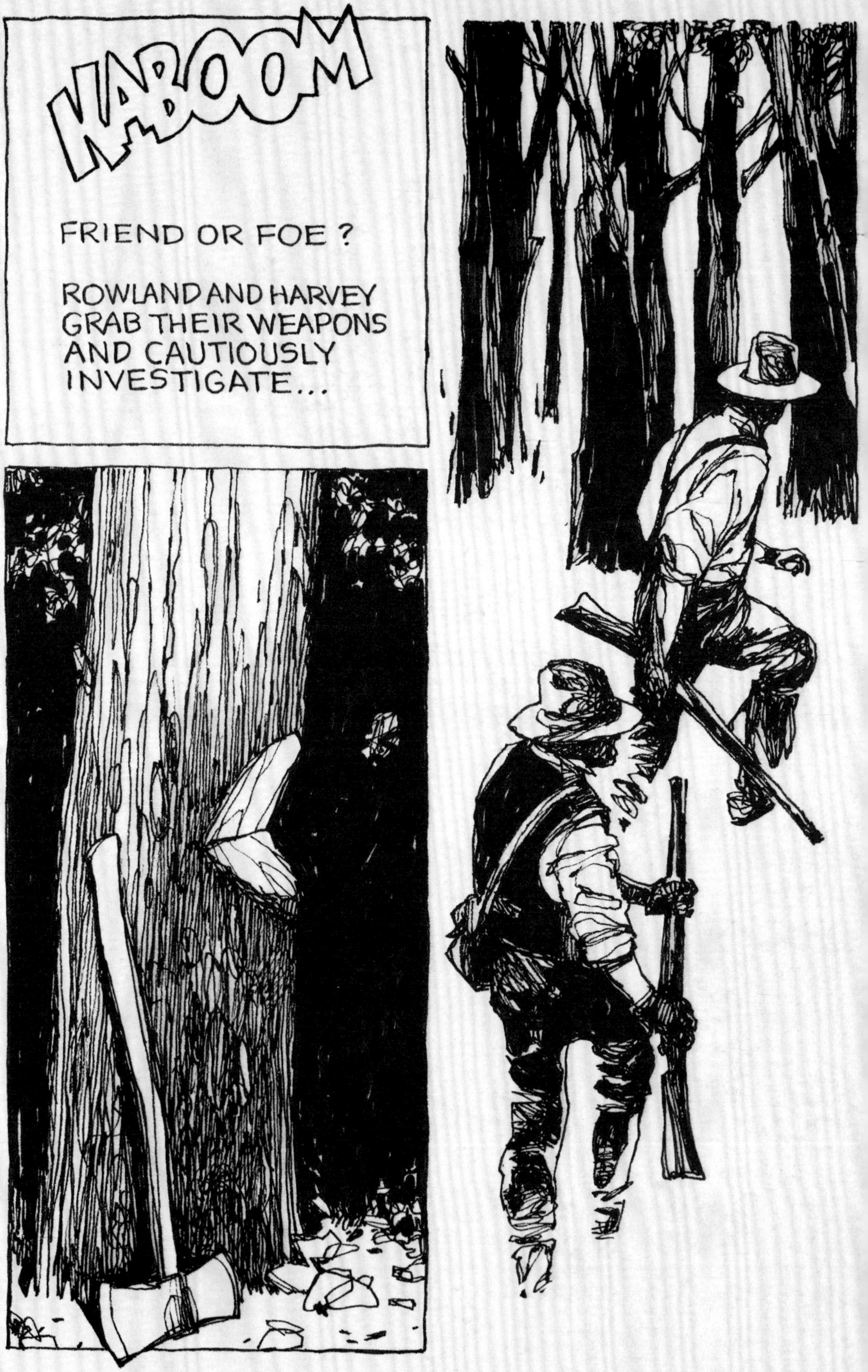
HABOOM
FRIEND OR FOE?
ROWLAND AND HARVEY GRAB THEIR WEAPONS AND CAUTIOUSLY INVESTIGATE...

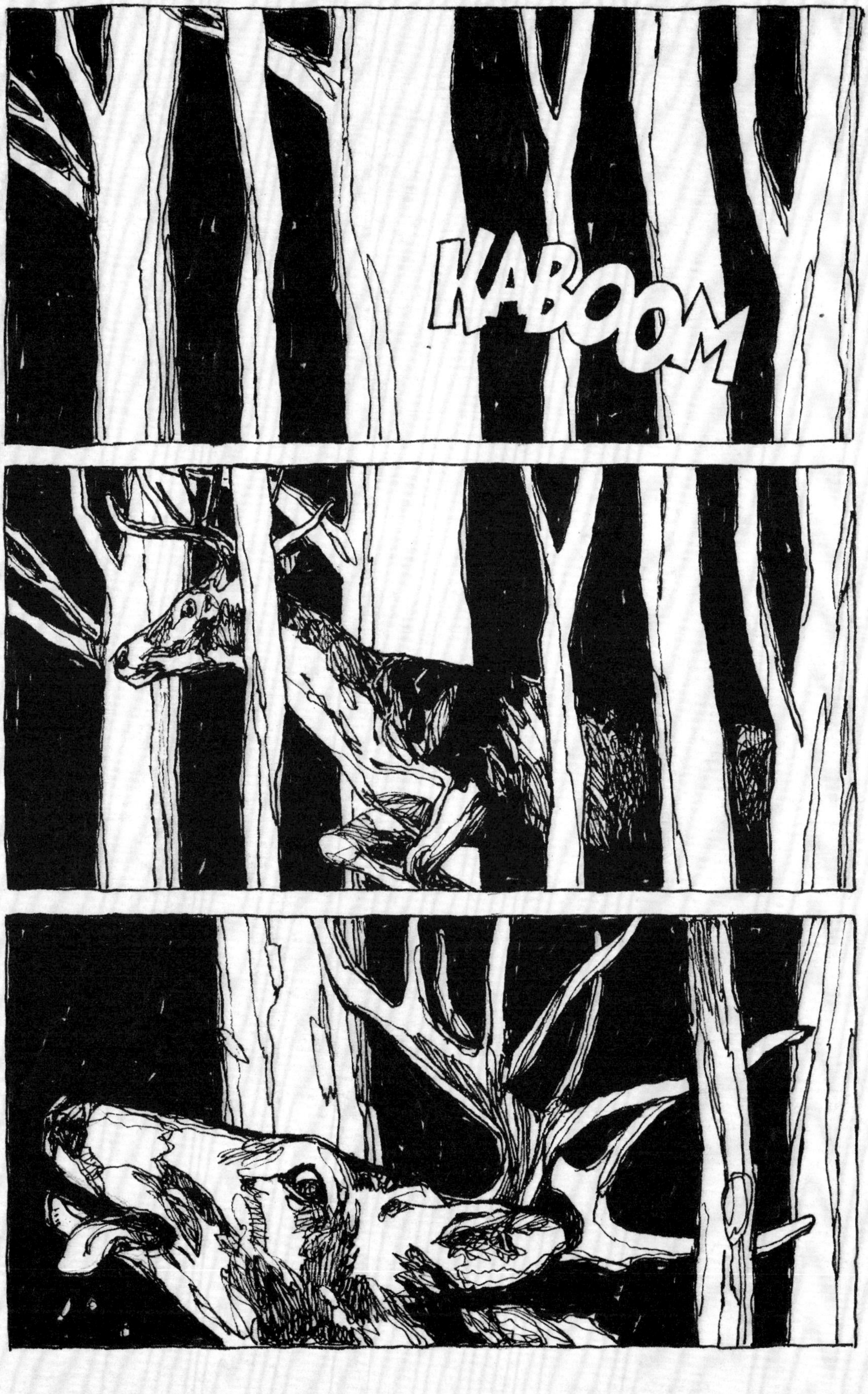
KABOOM

A MORTALLY WOUNDED BUCK STUMBLES INTO VIEW, FOLLOWED BY FOUR HUNTERS; WILLIAM AND CARL GRANGER, BERT SNYDER AND DR. I.H. HARRIOTT.

ABBIE RECALLS, "THEY CAME FROM RED WING, MINNESOTA, TO SEEK FOR THEMSELVES HOMES IN THIS FOREST PRIMEVAL".

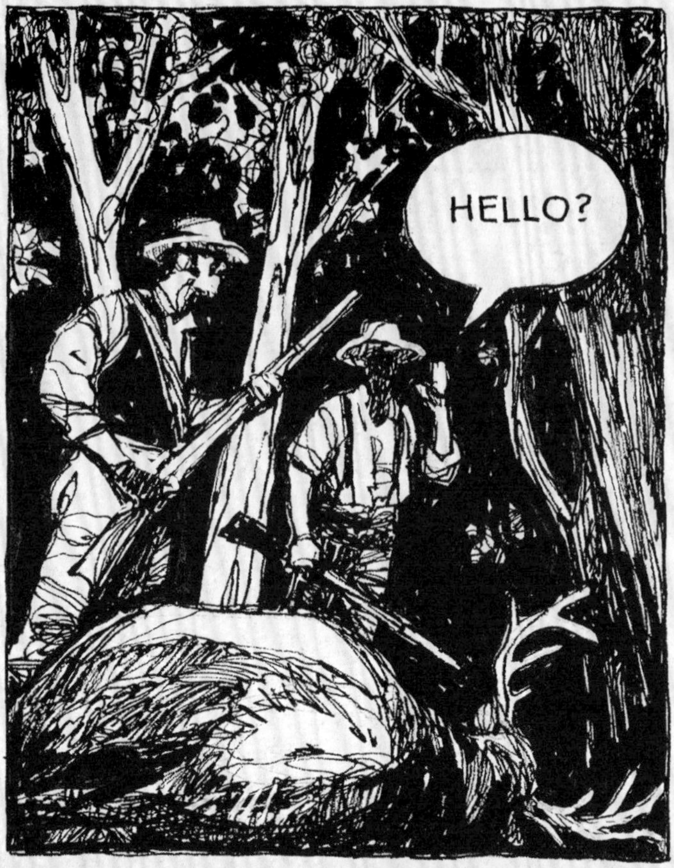
HELLO?

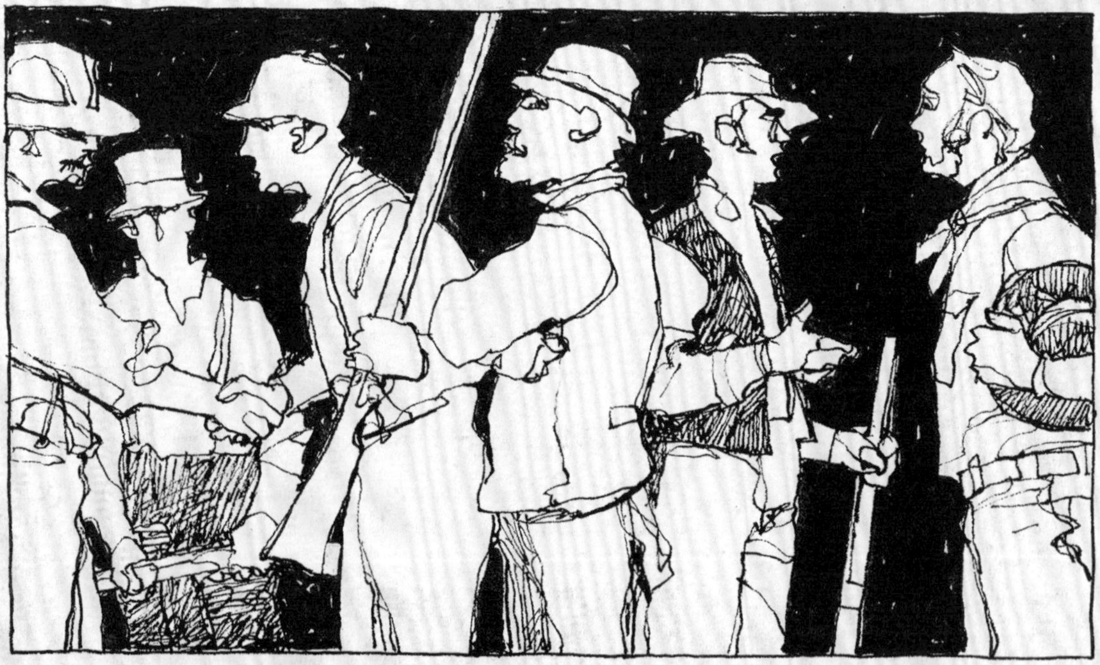

AS SUMMER CREEPS TOWARD AUTUMN, THE TIDE OF CIVILIZATION CREEPS INTO NORTHWEST IOWA.

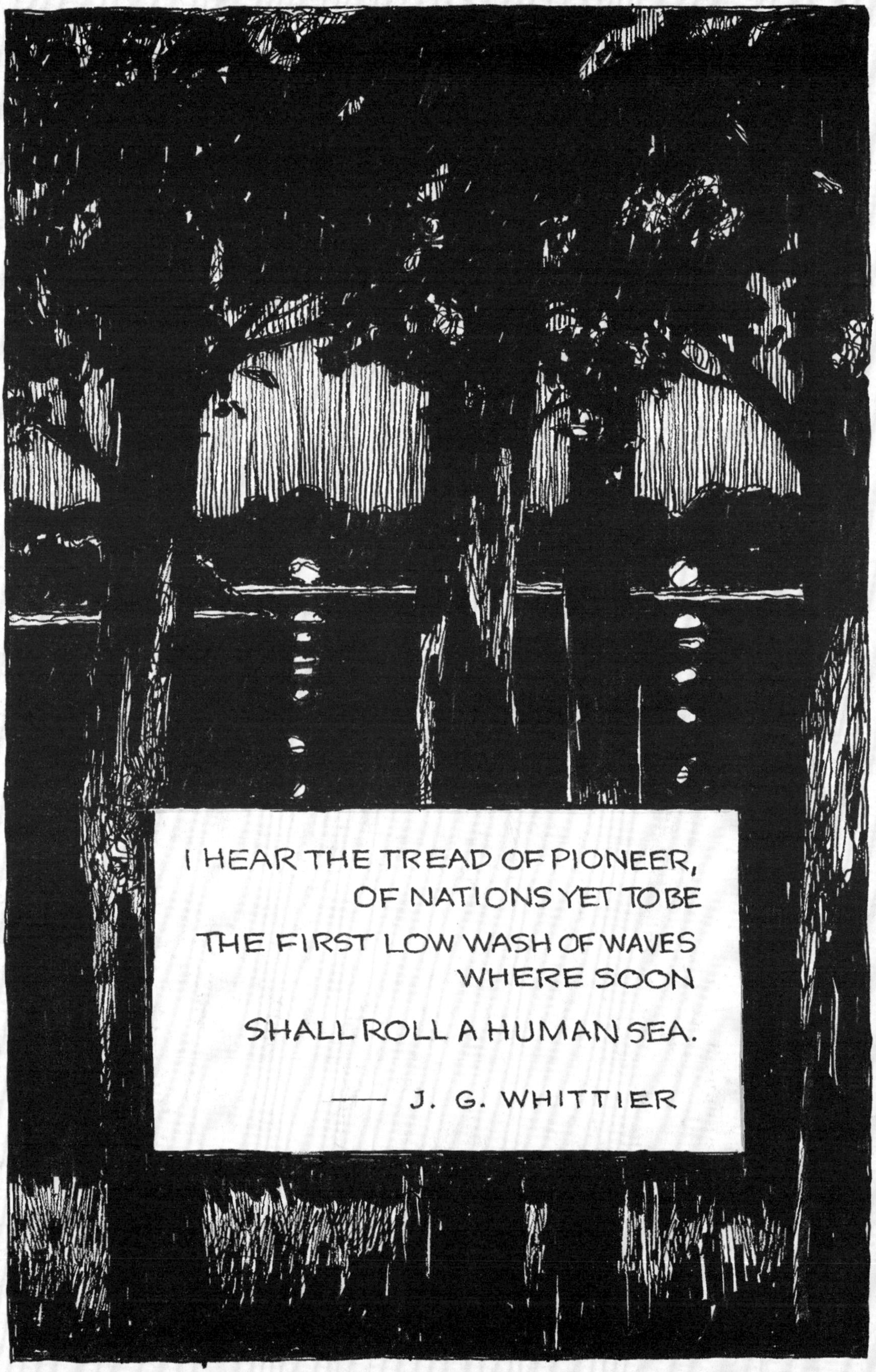
I HEAR THE TREAD OF PIONEER,
OF NATIONS YET TO BE
THE FIRST LOW WASH OF WAVES
WHERE SOON
SHALL ROLL A HUMAN SEA.
— J. G. WHITTIER

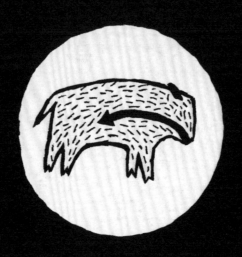

SEPTEMBER 1856

THE MOON WHEN CALVES GROW HAIR

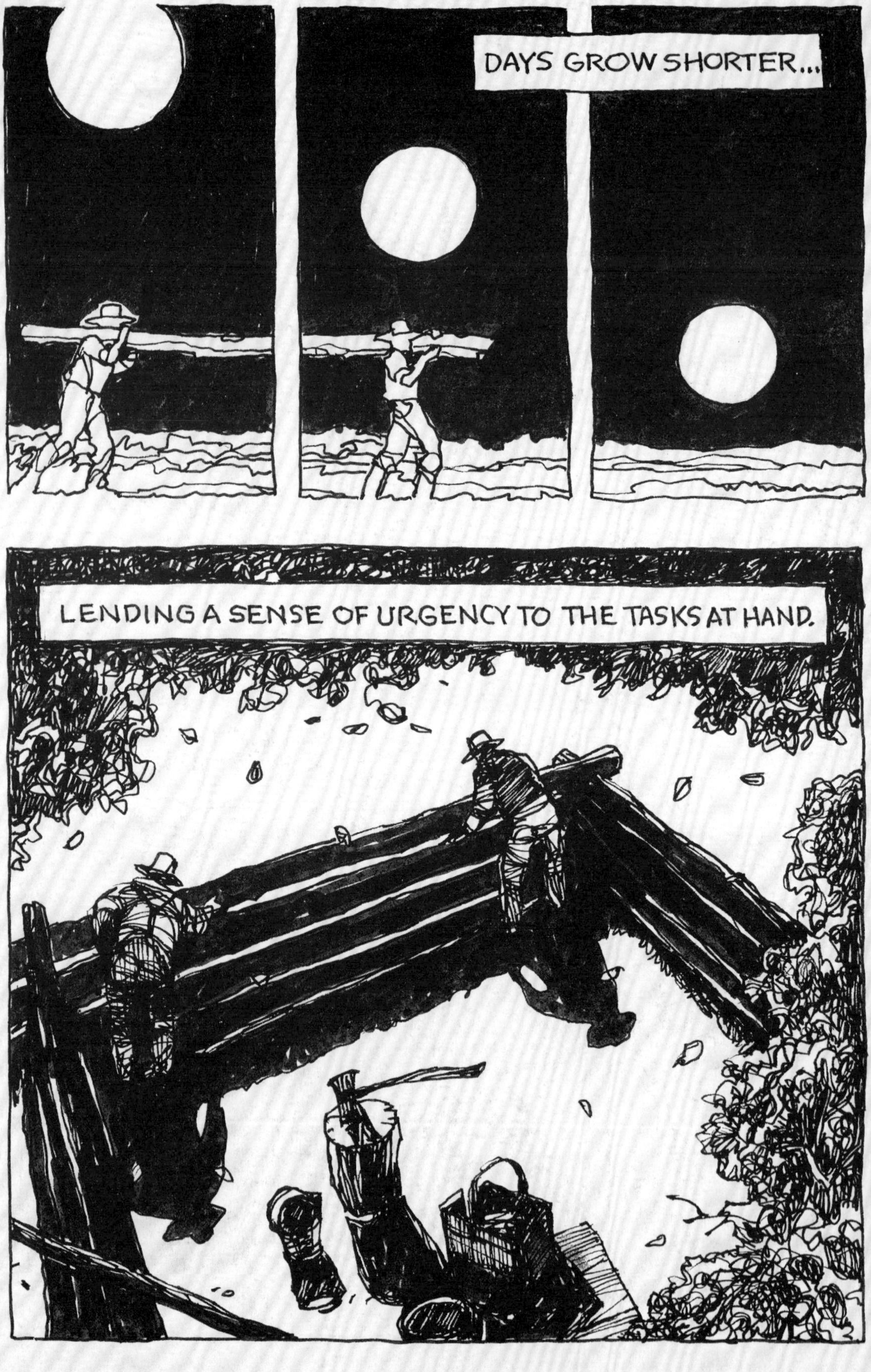
DAYS GROW SHORTER...
LENDING A SENSE OF URGENCY TO THE TASKS AT HAND.

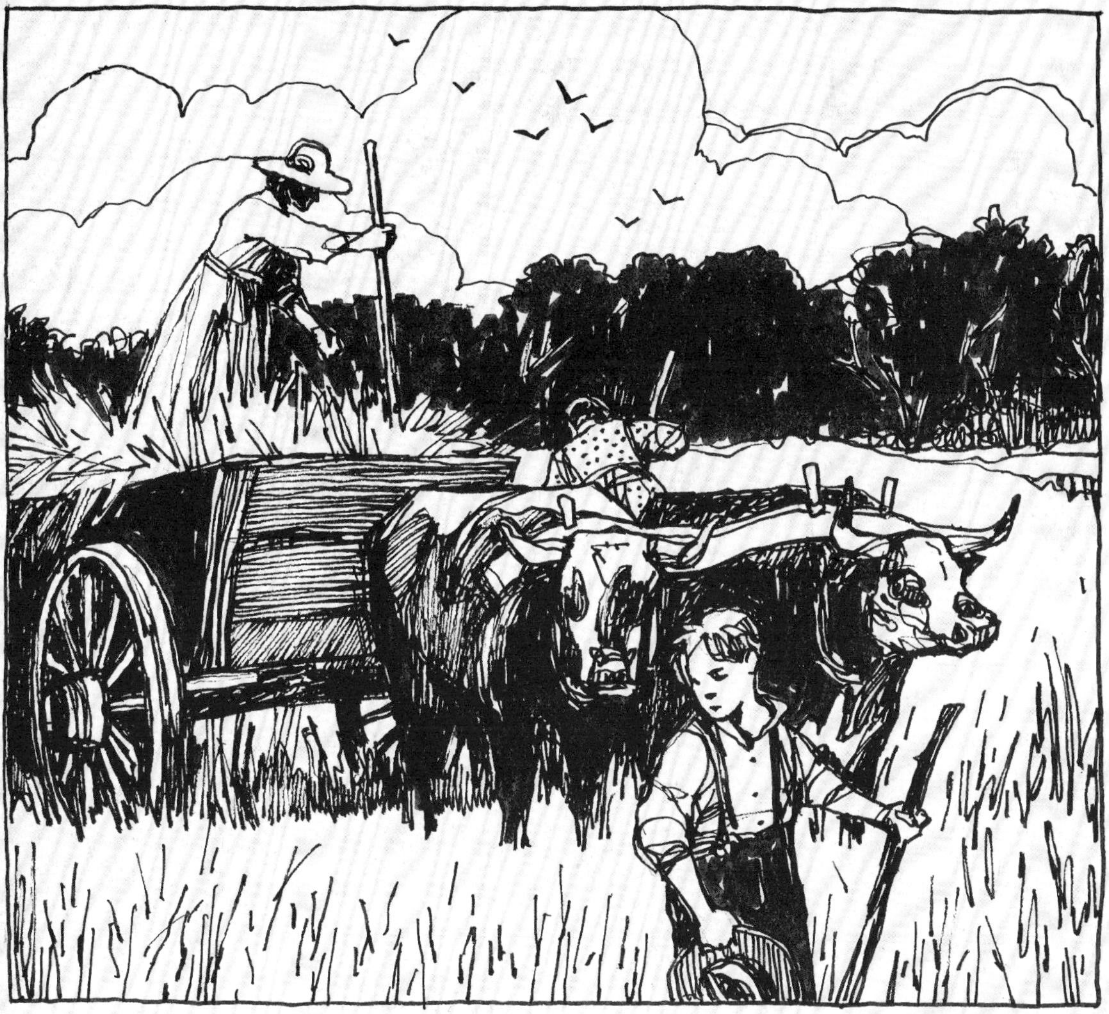

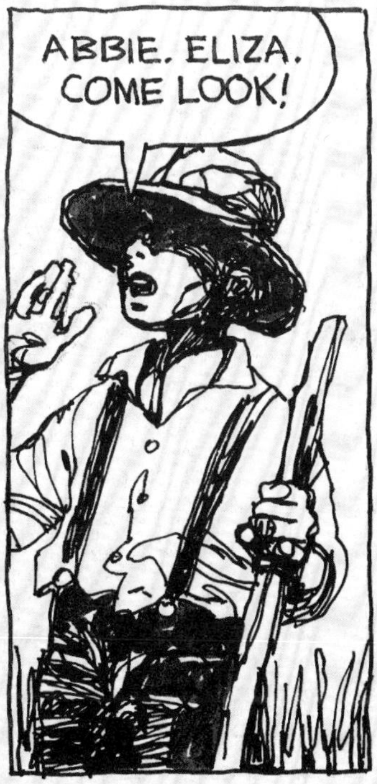
ABBIE. ELIZA.
COME LOOK!

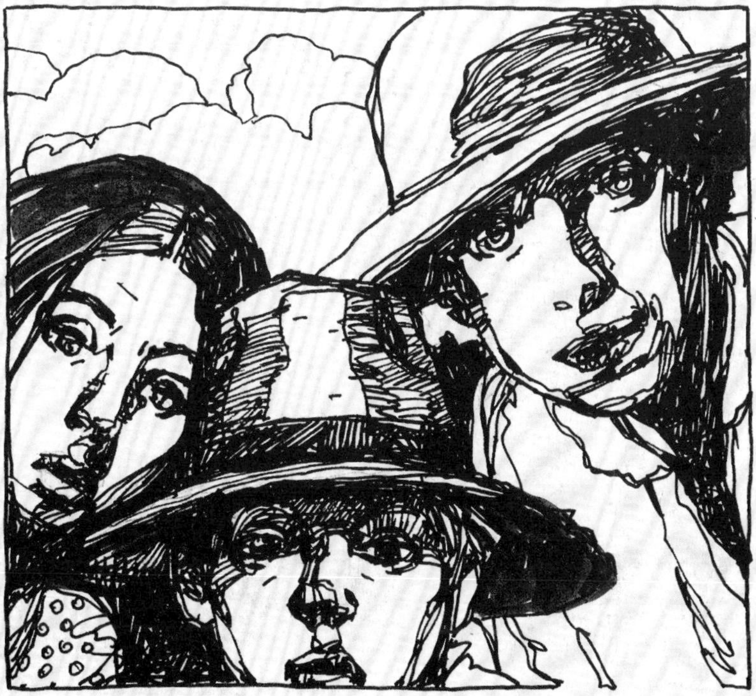

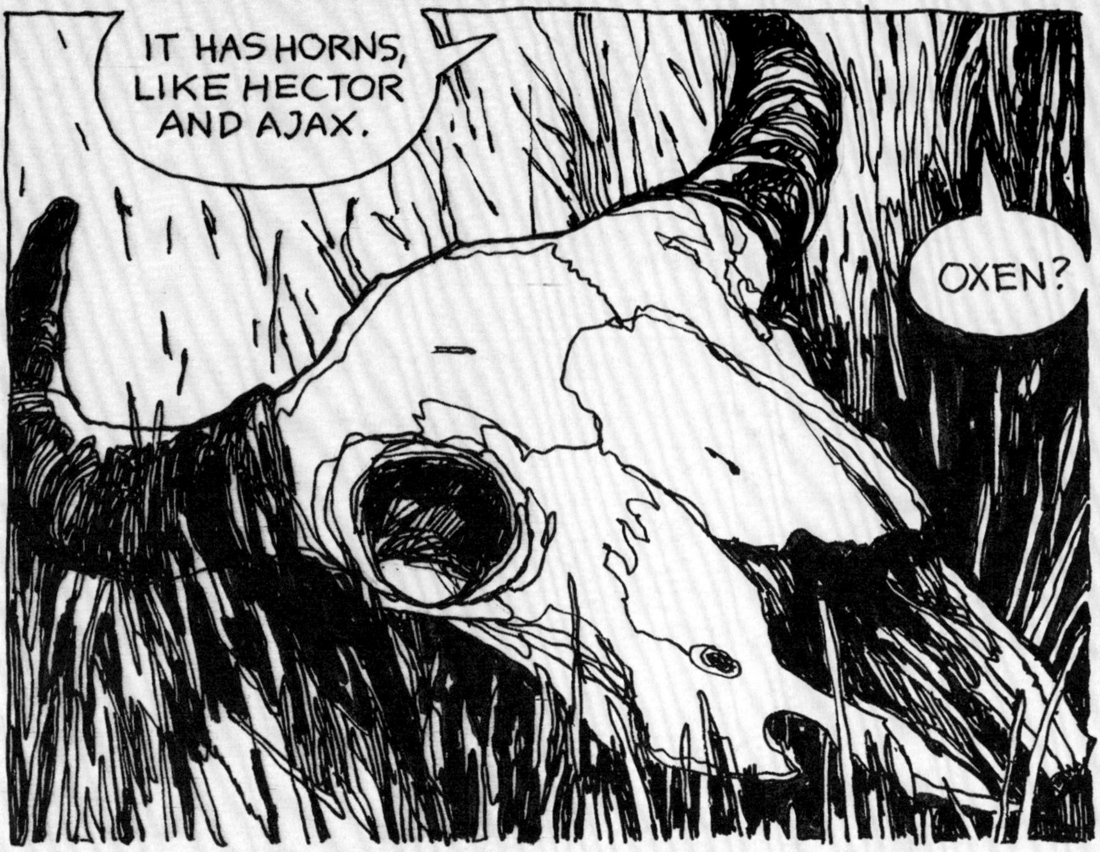
IT HAS HORNS, LIKE HECTOR AND AJAX.
OXEN?

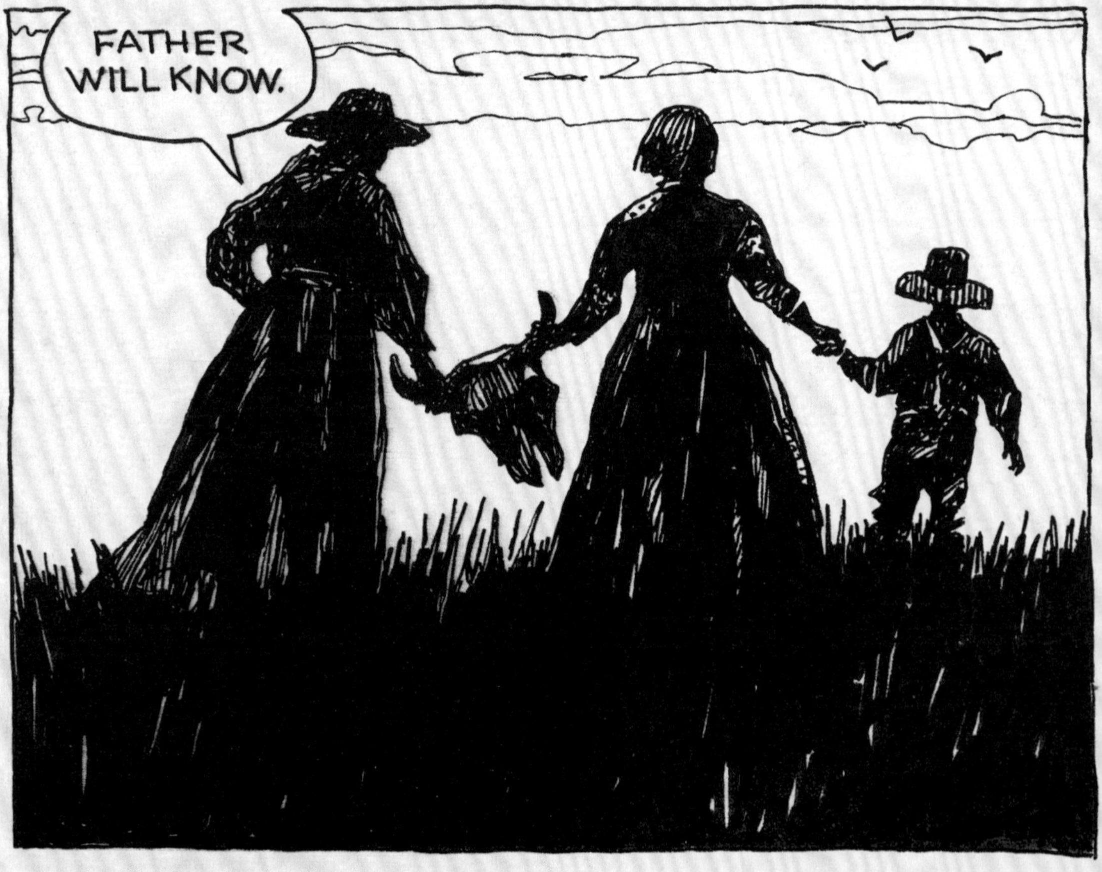
FATHER WILL KNOW.

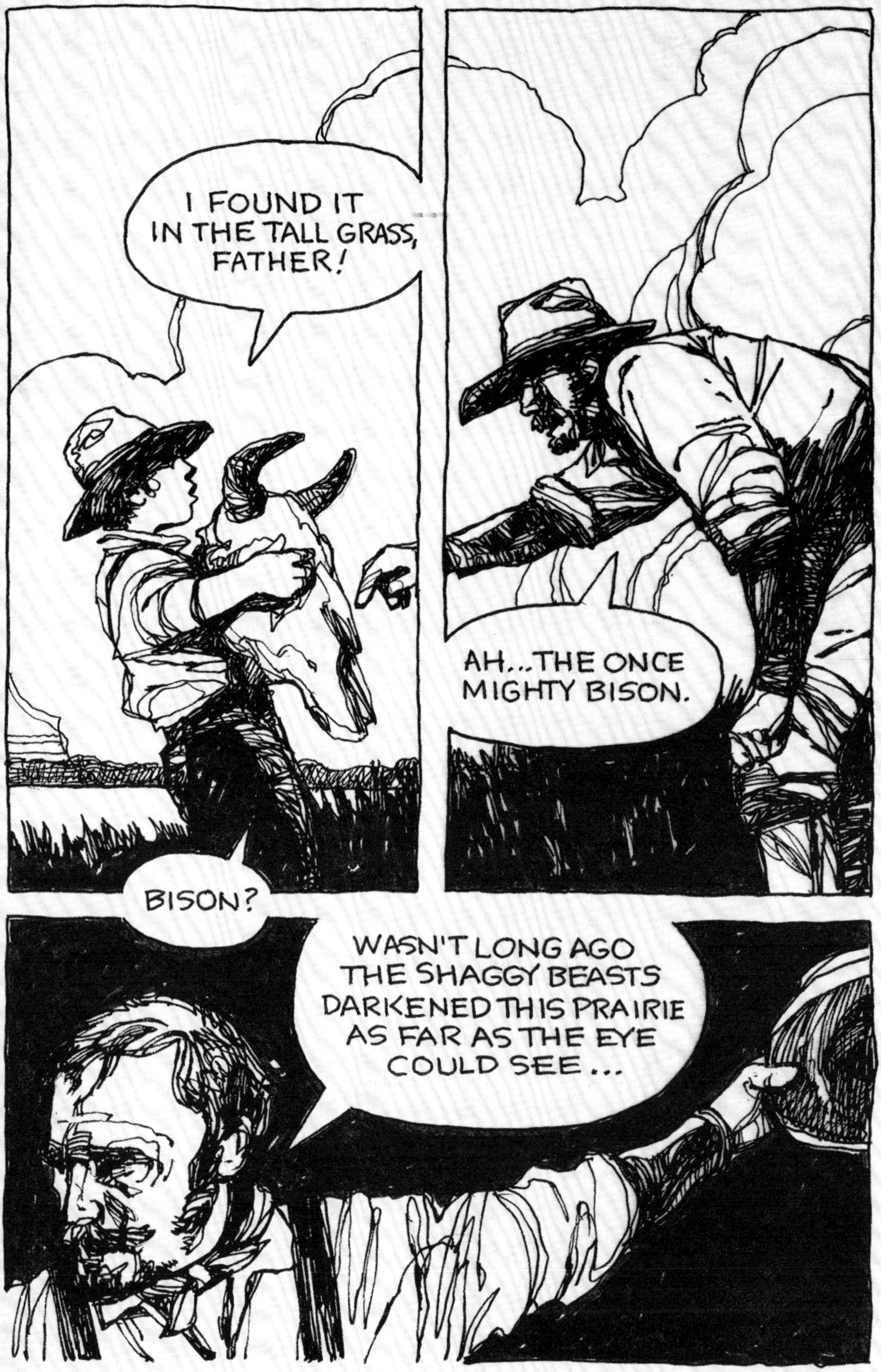
I FOUND IT IN THE TALL GRASS, FATHER!
AH...THE ONCE MIGHTY BISON.
BISON?
WASN'T LONG AGO THE SHAGGY BEASTS DARKENED THIS PRAIRIE AS FAR AS THE EYE COULD SEE...

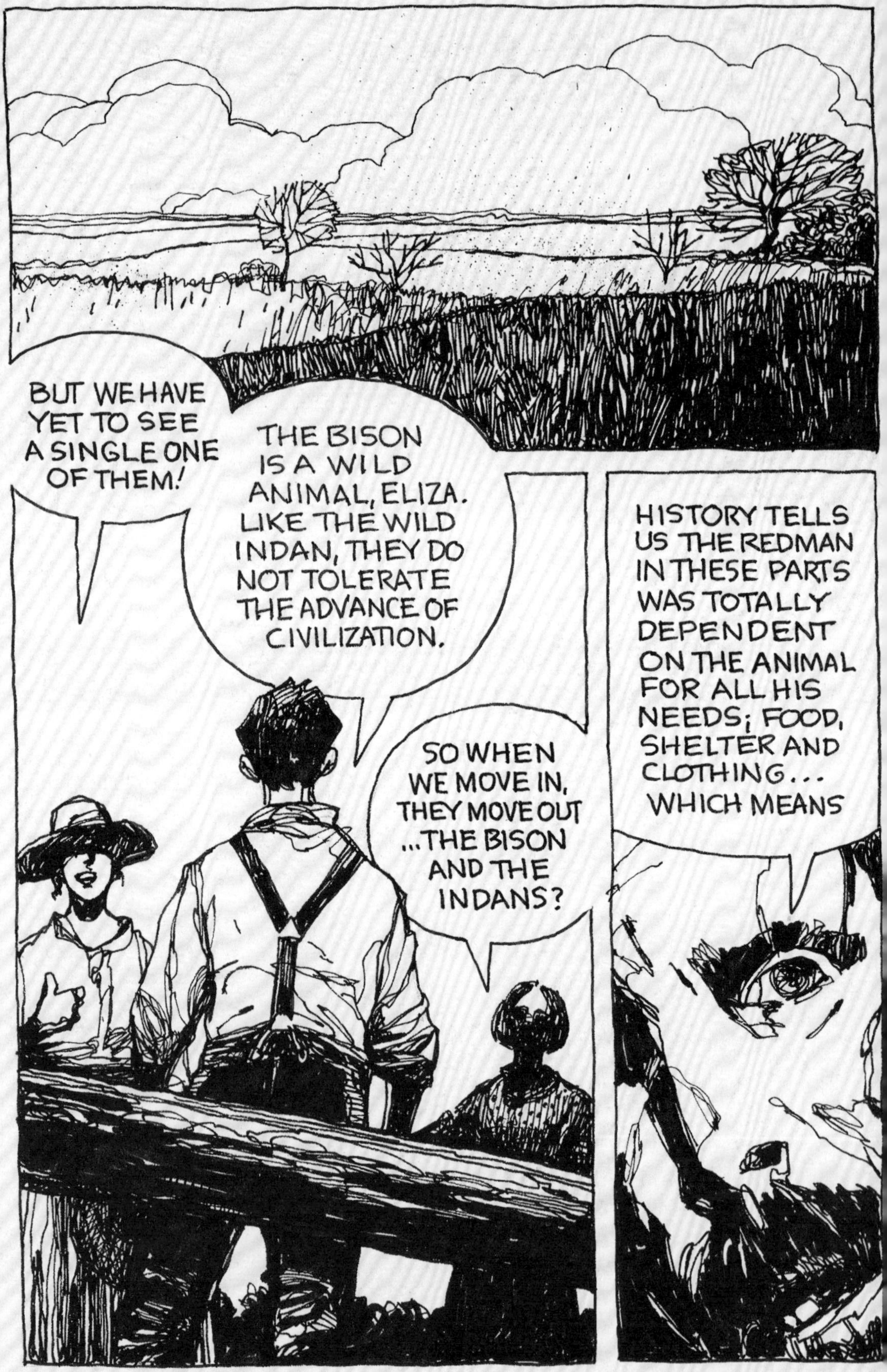
BUT WE HAVE YET TO SEE A SINGLE ONE OF THEM!
THE BISON IS A WILD ANIMAL, ELIZA. LIKE THE WILD INDAN, THEY DO NOT TOLERATE THE ADVANCE OF CIVILIZATION.
SO WHEN WE MOVE IN, THEY MOVE OUT ...THE BISON AND THE INDANS?
HISTORY TELLS US THE REDMAN IN THESE PARTS WAS TOTALLY DEPENDENT ON THE ANIMAL FOR ALL HIS NEEDS; FOOD, SHELTER AND CLOTHING... WHICH MEANS

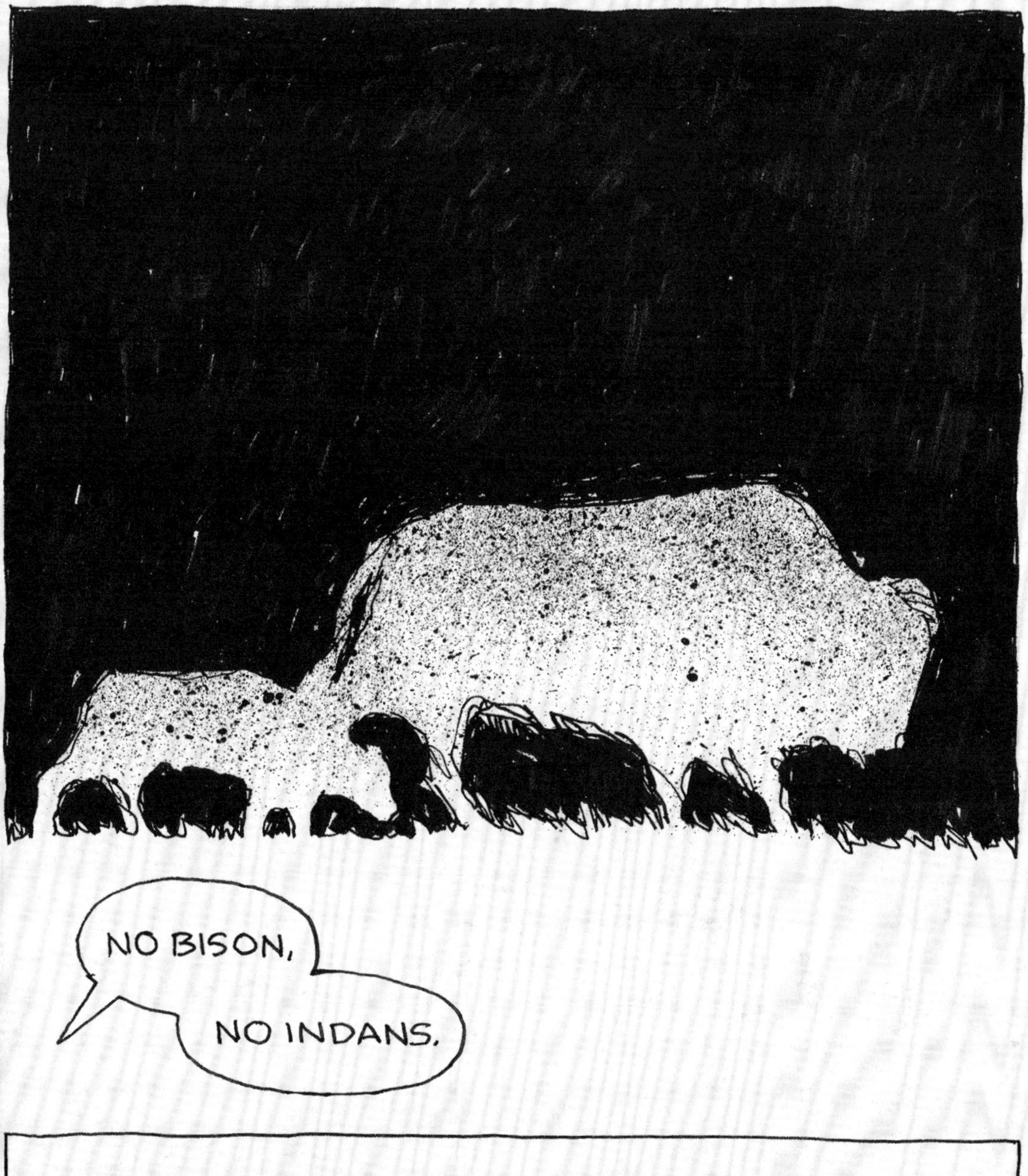
NO BISON,
NO INDANS.

...NO QUESTION, THAT SO LONG AS THERE ARE MILLIONS OF BISON IN THE WEST, THE INDIANS CANNOT BE CONTROLLED, EVEN BY THE STRONG ARM OF THE GOVERNMENT. I BELIEVE IT WOULD BE A GREAT STEP FORWARD IN THE CIVILIZATION OF INDIANS AND THE PRESERVATION OF PEACE IF THERE WAS NOT A BISON IN EXISTENCE.

— *CONGRESSMAN JAMES THROCKMORTON*

OCTOBER 1856

THE MOON OF CHANGING SEASONS

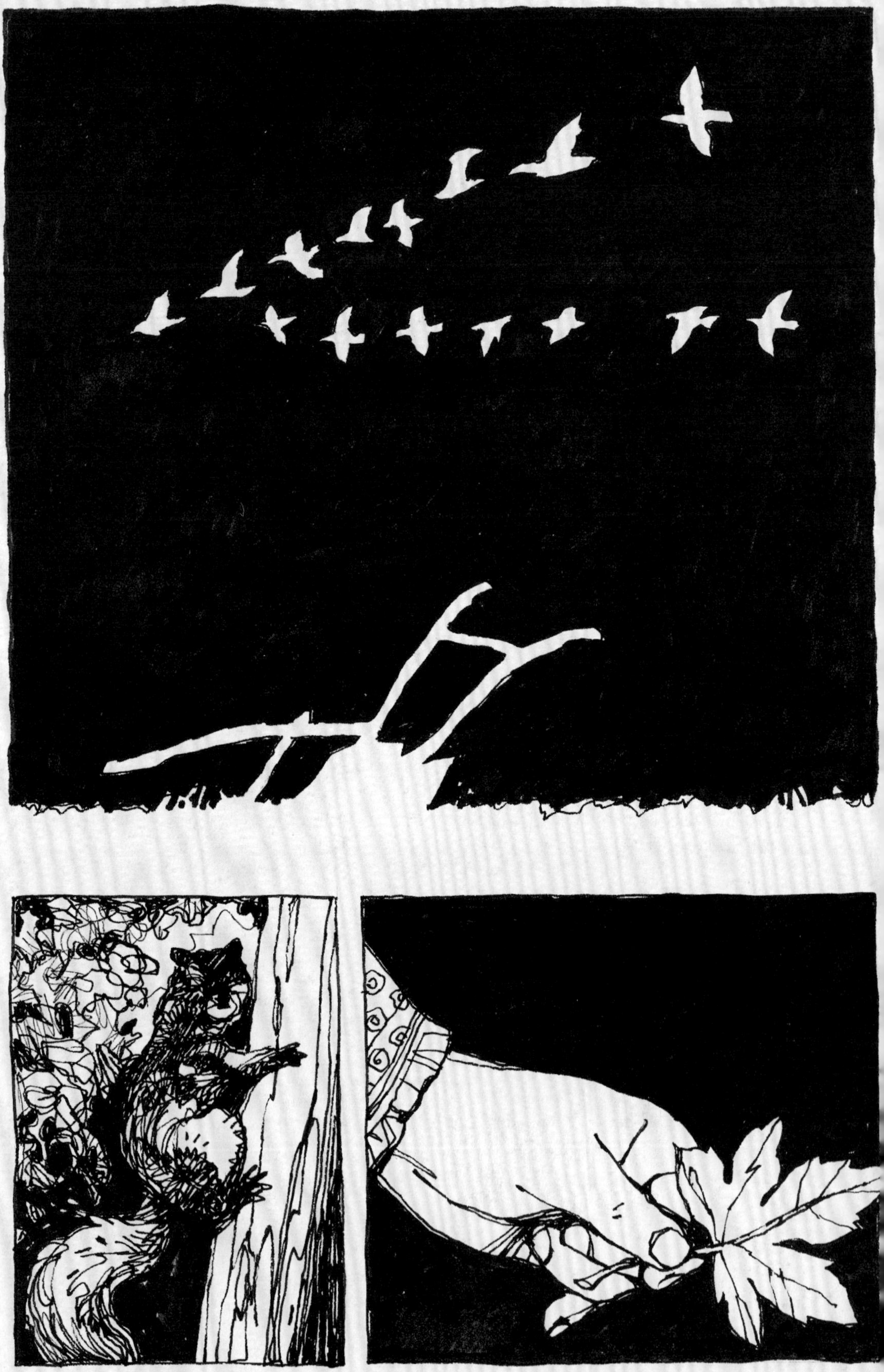

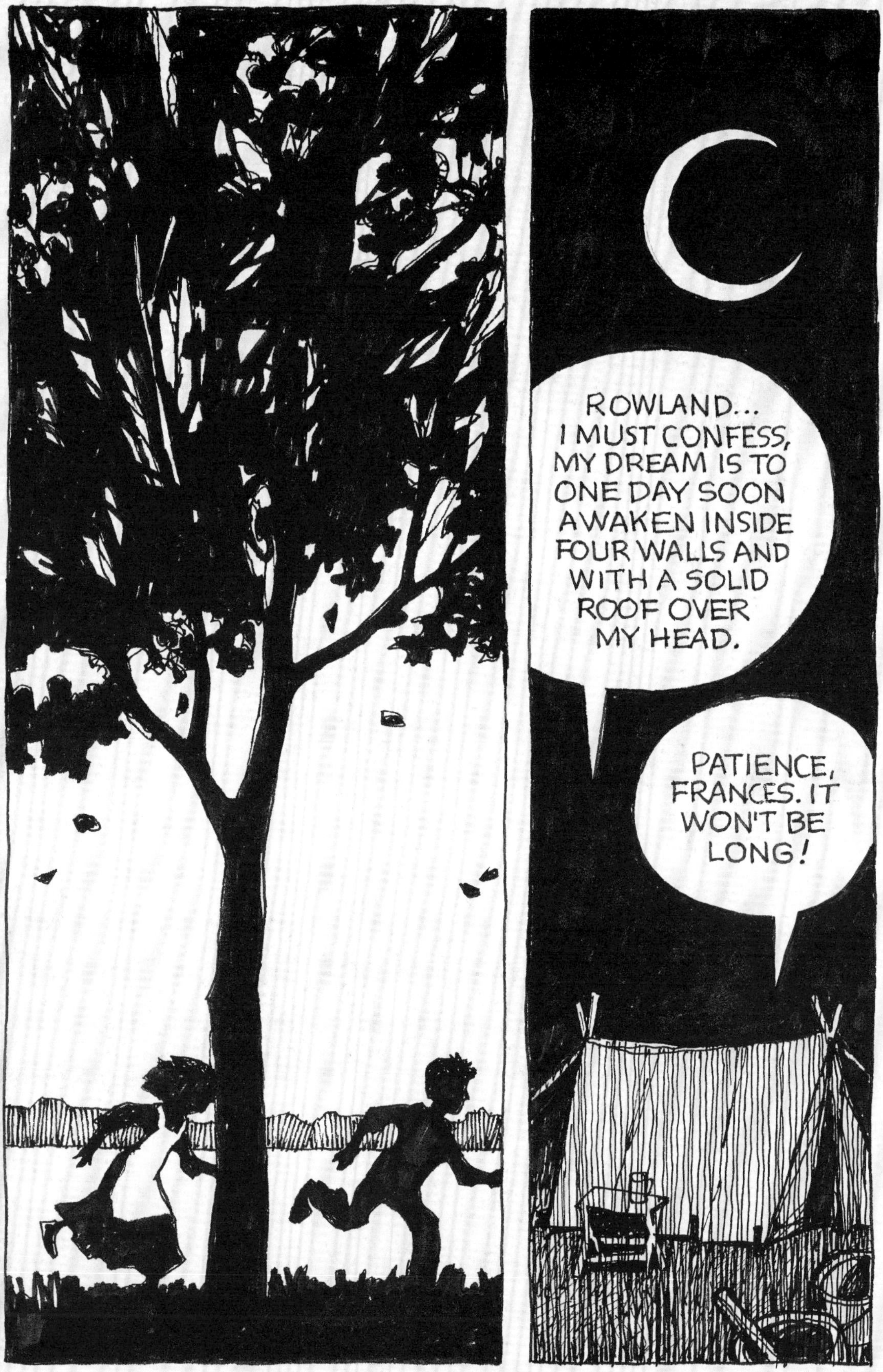
ROWLAND... I MUST CONFESS, MY DREAM IS TO ONE DAY SOON AWAKEN INSIDE FOUR WALLS AND WITH A SOLID ROOF OVER MY HEAD.
PATIENCE, FRANCES. IT WON'T BE LONG!

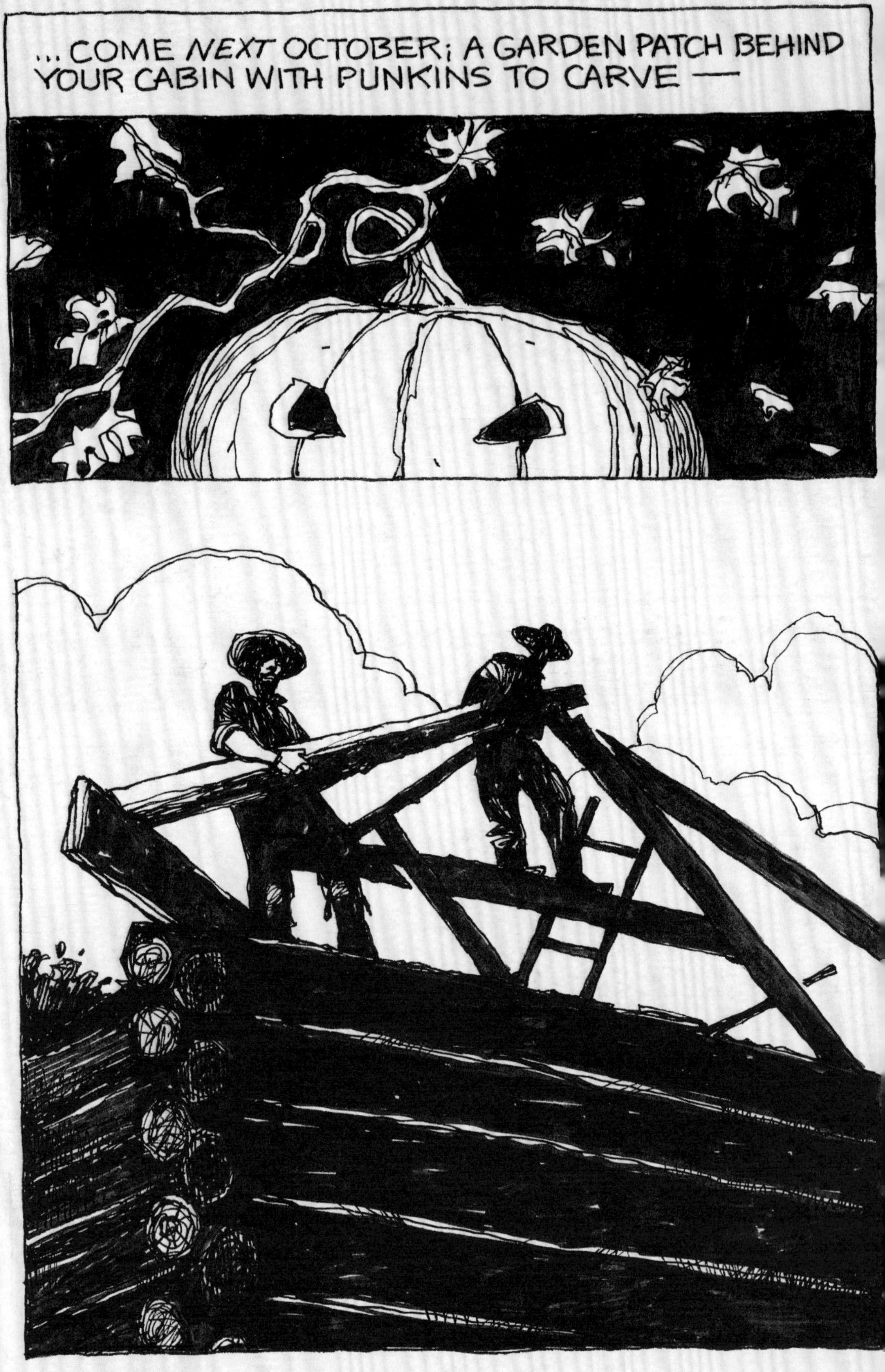
...COME *NEXT* OCTOBER; A GARDEN PATCH BEHIND YOUR CABIN WITH PUNKINS TO CARVE —

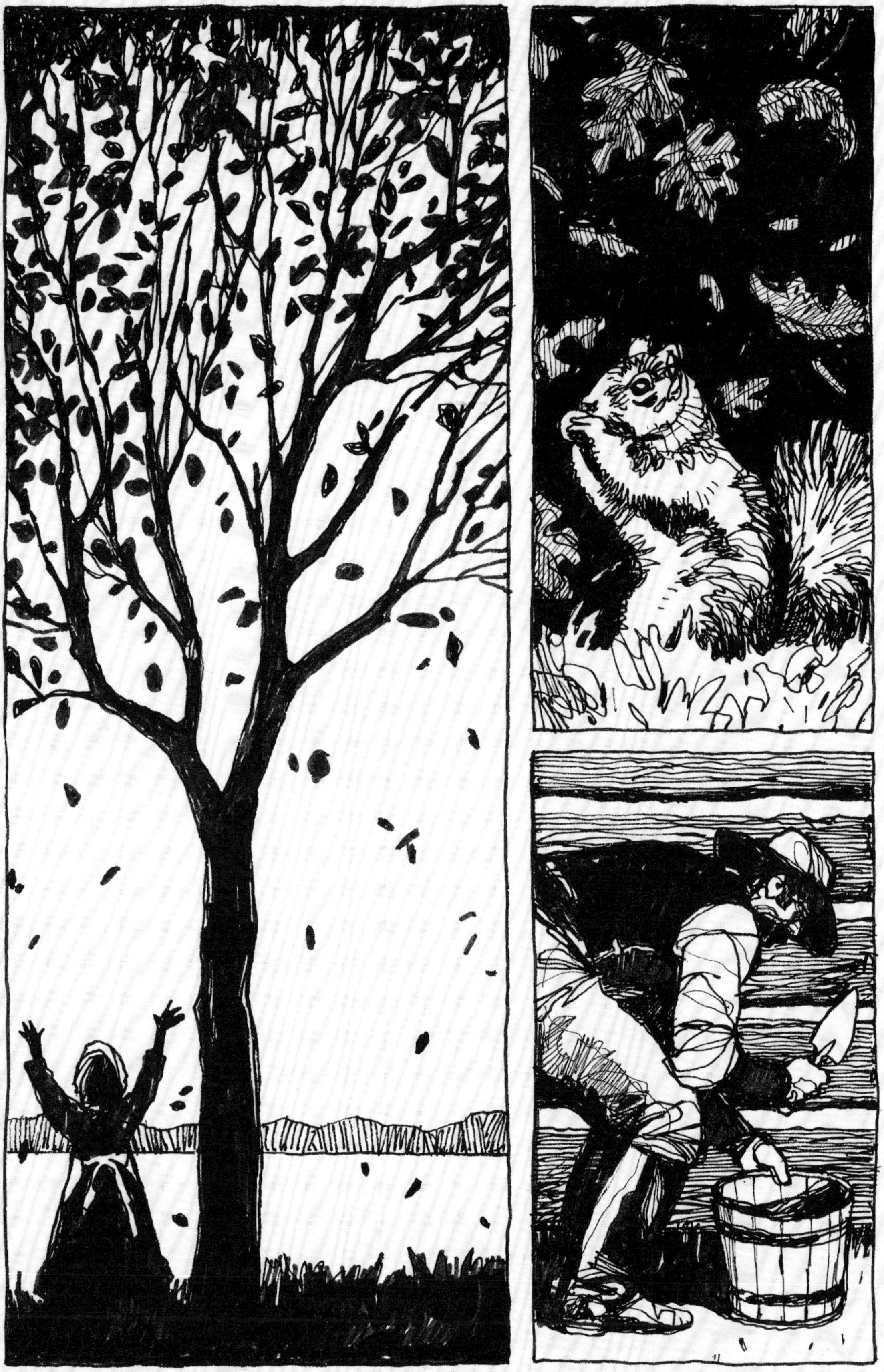

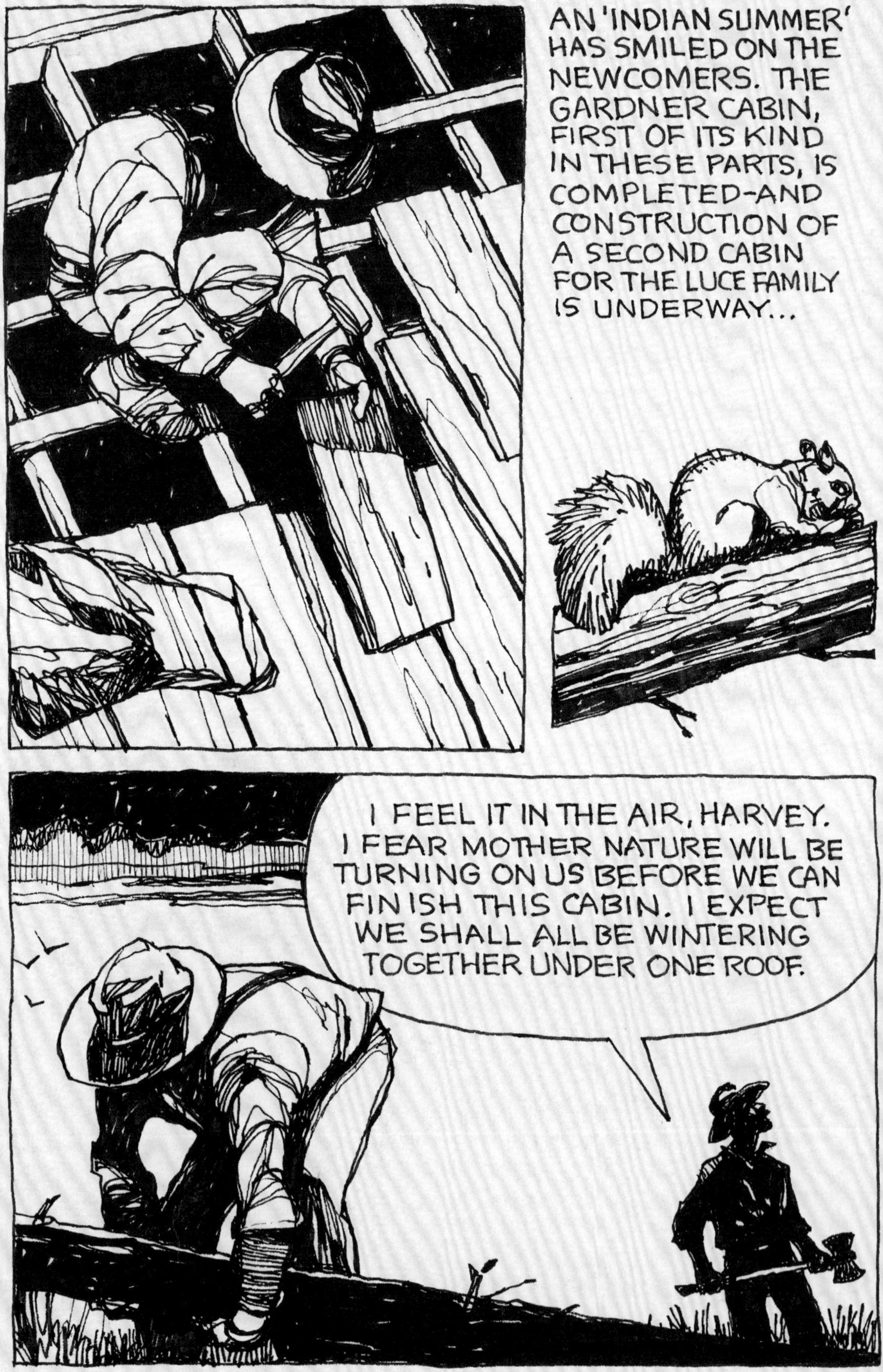
AN 'INDIAN SUMMER' HAS SMILED ON THE NEWCOMERS. THE GARDNER CABIN, FIRST OF ITS KIND IN THESE PARTS, IS COMPLETED-AND CONSTRUCTION OF A SECOND CABIN FOR THE LUCE FAMILY IS UNDERWAY...
I FEEL IT IN THE AIR, HARVEY. I FEAR MOTHER NATURE WILL BE TURNING ON US BEFORE WE CAN FINISH THIS CABIN. I EXPECT WE SHALL ALL BE WINTERING TOGETHER UNDER ONE ROOF.

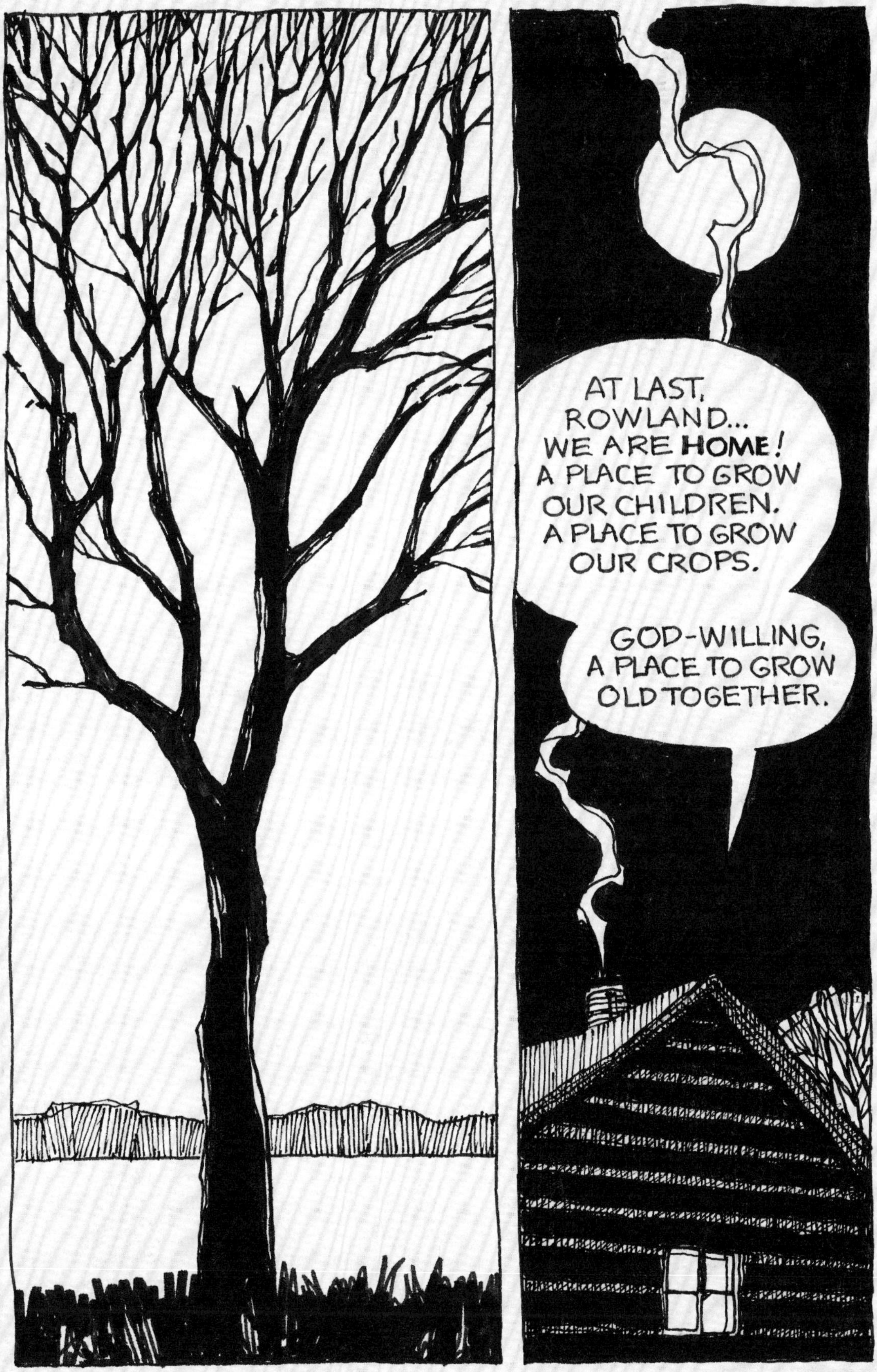
AT LAST, ROWLAND... WE ARE **HOME**! A PLACE TO GROW OUR CHILDREN. A PLACE TO GROW OUR CROPS.
GOD-WILLING, A PLACE TO GROW OLD TOGETHER.

NOVEMBER 1856

THE MOON WHEN DEER RUT

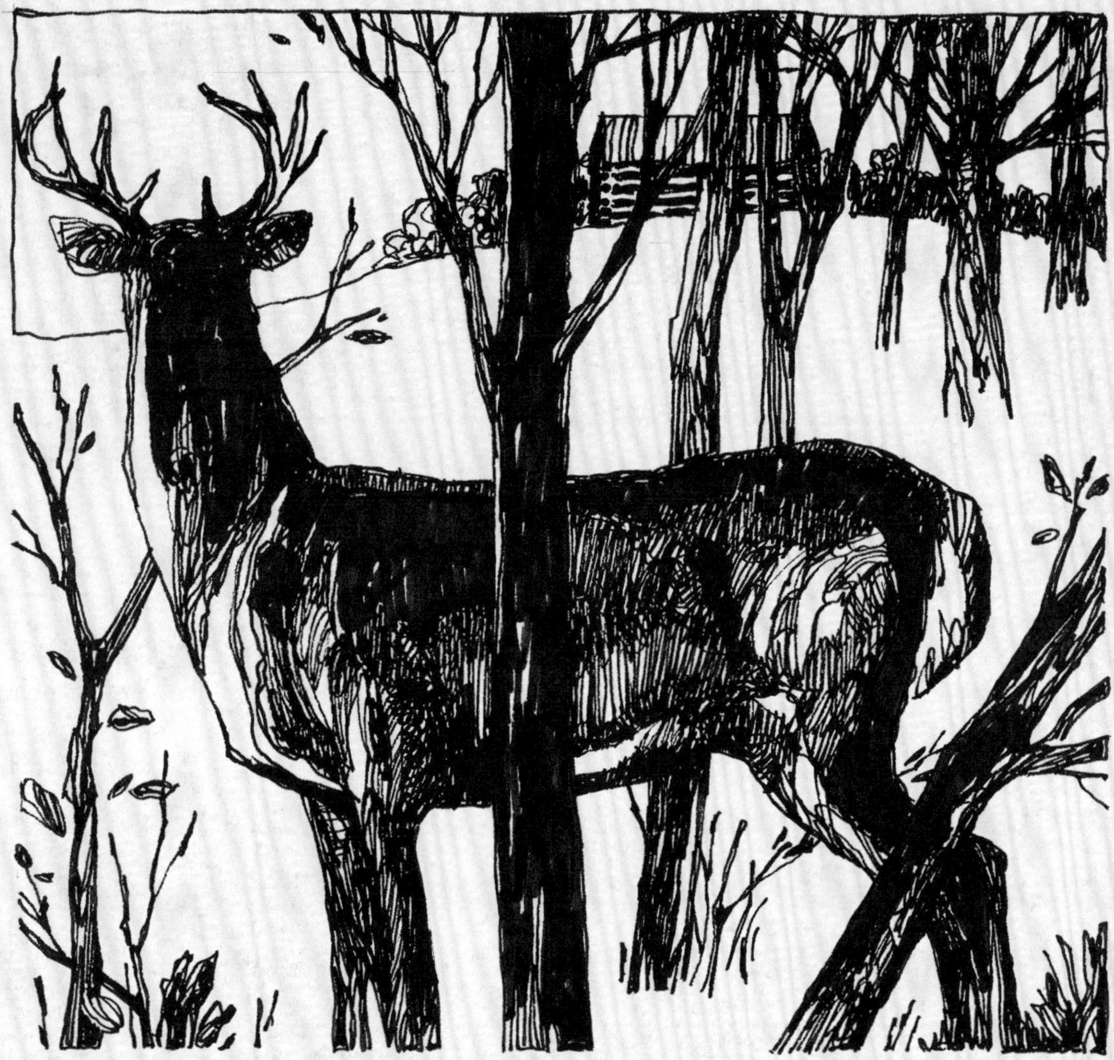

NOT LONG WERE WE ALONE IN THIS NEW-FOUND 'ELDORADO.' KNOWLEDGE OF ITS RICH LANDS, LUXURIANT GROVES, ABUNDANT GAME AND FISH, ITS BEAUTIFUL SCENERY AND HEALTHFUL CLIMATE, SOON REACHED MANY WHO HAD A LOVE FOR ADVENTURE;

SO THAT BY THE FIRST OF NOVEMBER SIX FAMILIES WERE SNUGLY HOUSED IN LOG CABINS WITHIN SIX MILES OF US; BESIDES SEVERAL SINGLE MEN IN THE SETTLEMENT.

— *ABBIE GARDNER*

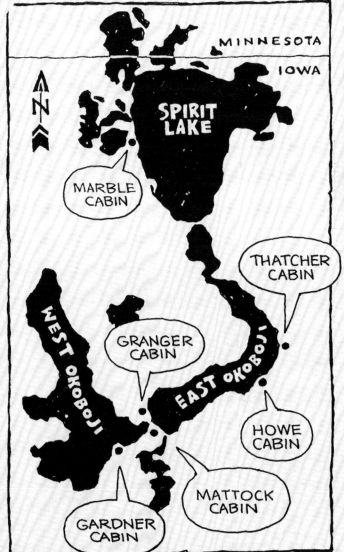

MINNESOTA

IOWA

SPIRIT LAKE

MARBLE CABIN

THATCHER CABIN

WEST OKOBOJI

GRANGER CABIN

EAST OKOBOJI

HOWE CABIN

MATTOCK CABIN

GARDNER CABIN

THE 'WASICHUS' HAD ARRIVED.

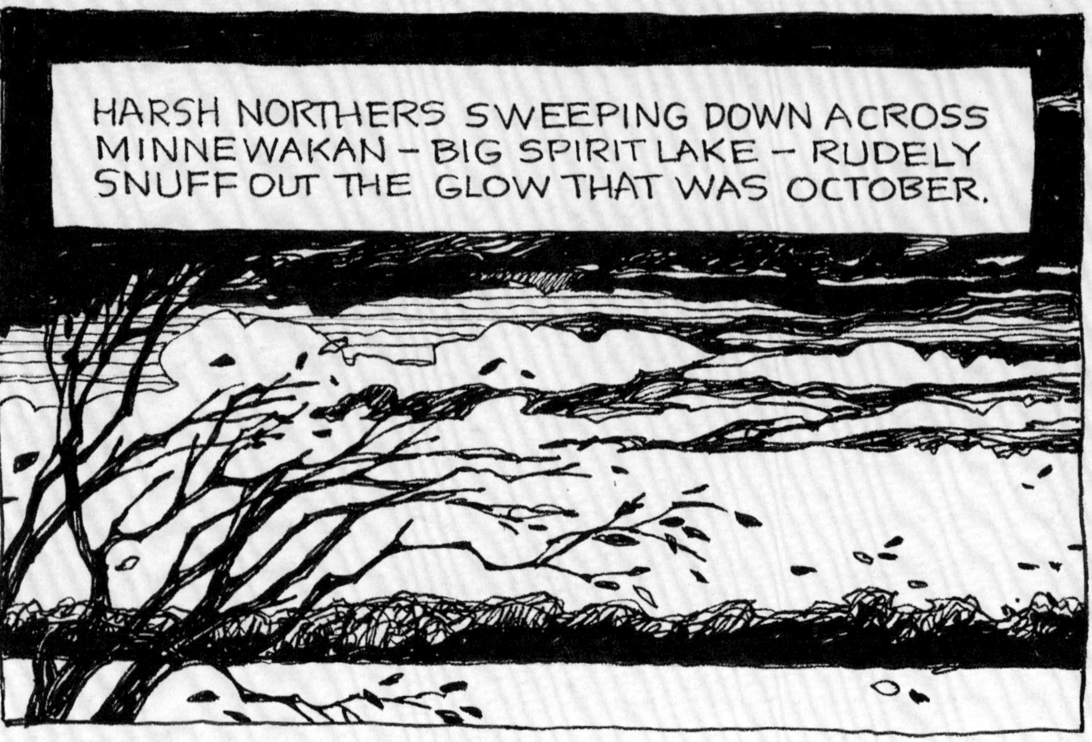
HARSH NORTHERS SWEEPING DOWN ACROSS MINNEWAKAN – BIG SPIRIT LAKE – RUDELY SNUFF OUT THE GLOW THAT WAS OCTOBER.

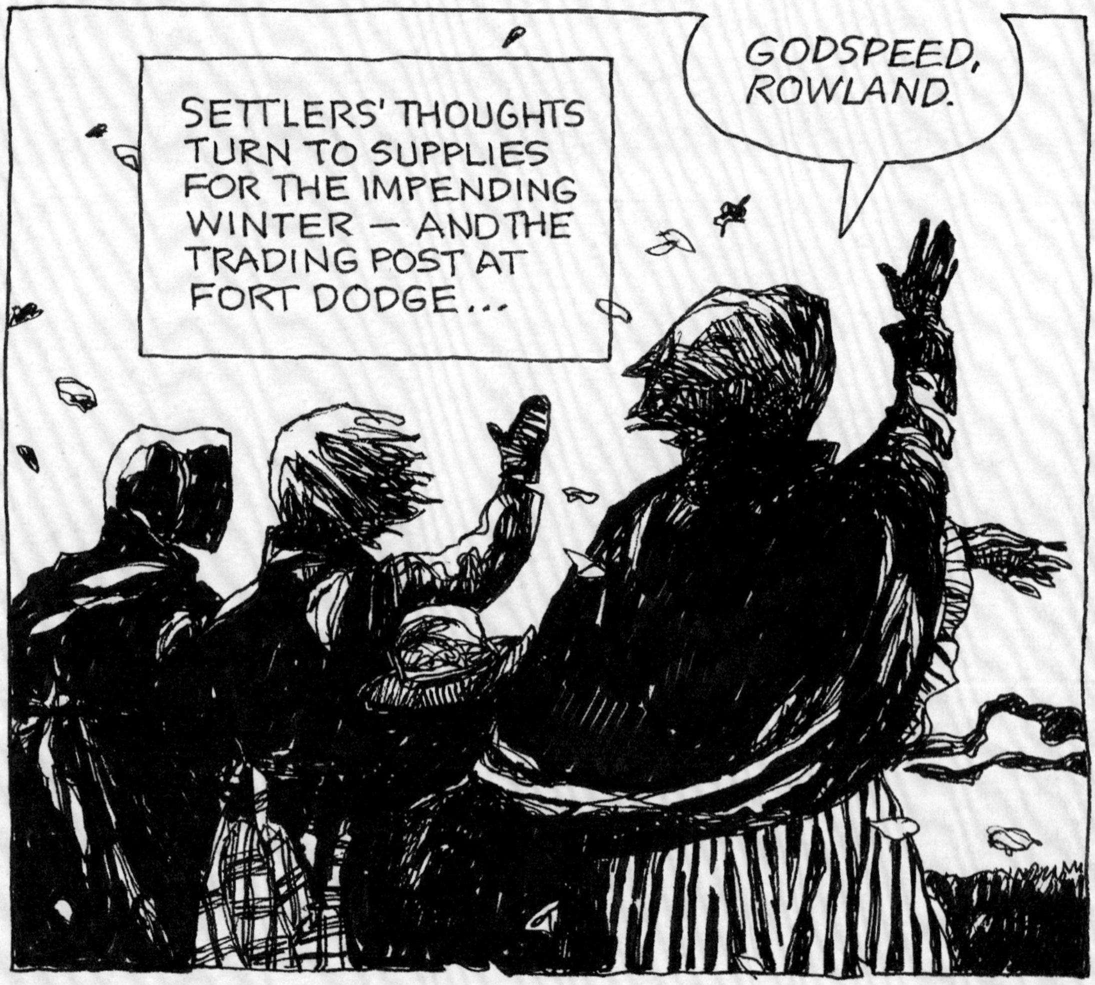
SETTLERS' THOUGHTS TURN TO SUPPLIES FOR THE IMPENDING WINTER – AND THE TRADING POST AT FORT DODGE...
GODSPEED, ROWLAND.

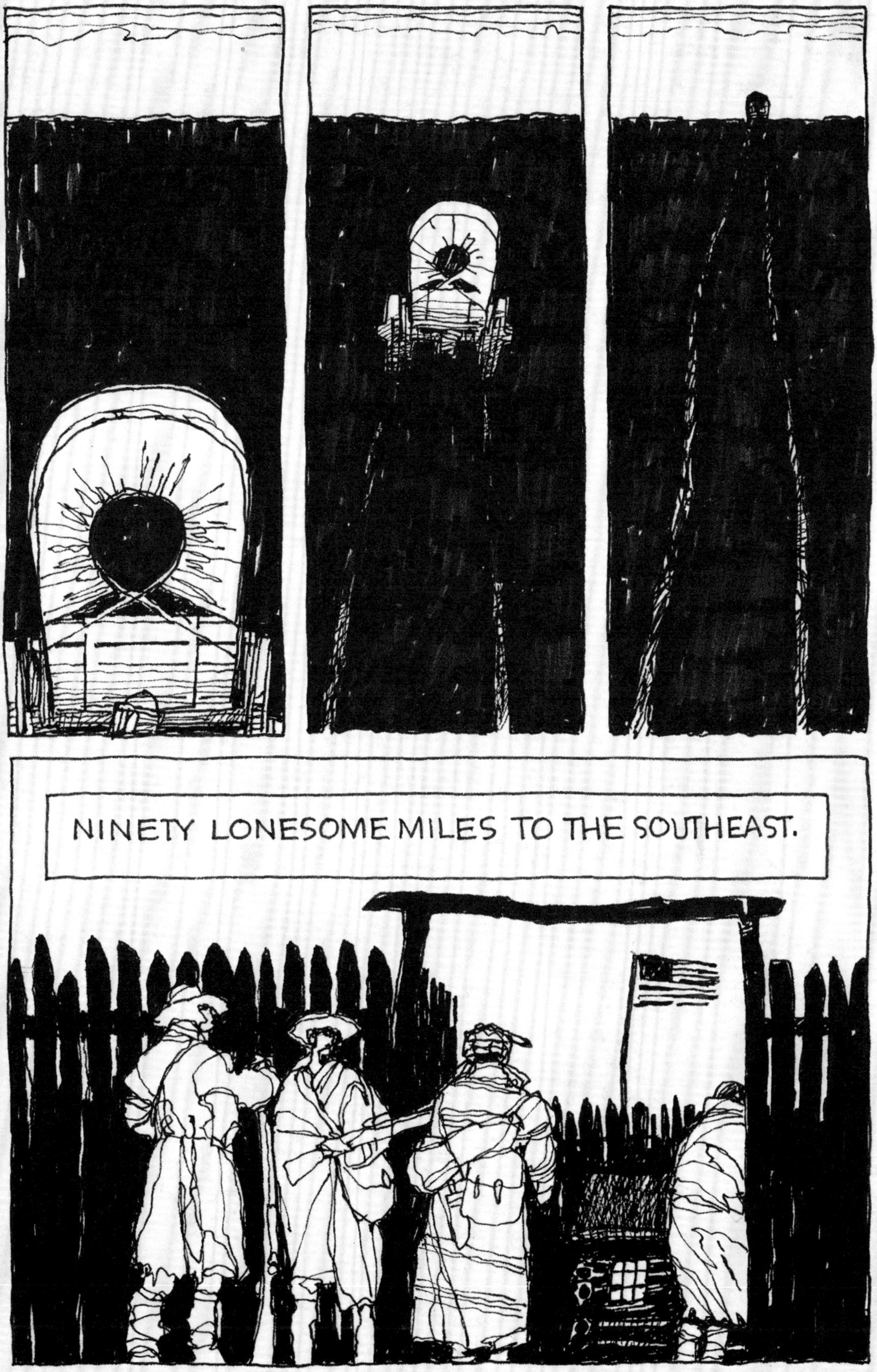
NINETY LONESOME MILES TO THE SOUTHEAST.

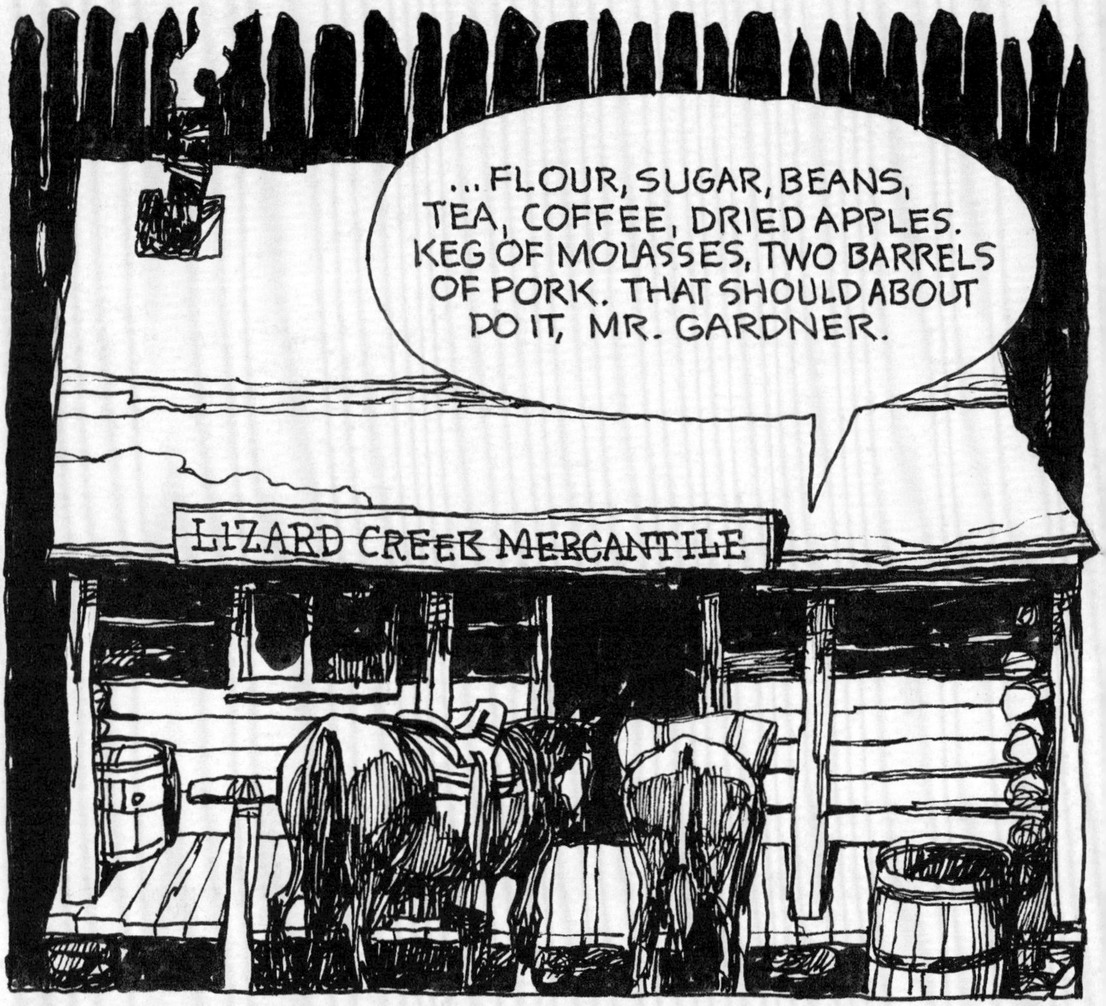
...FLOUR, SUGAR, BEANS, TEA, COFFEE, DRIED APPLES. KEG OF MOLASSES, TWO BARRELS OF PORK. THAT SHOULD ABOUT DO IT, MR. GARDNER.
LIZARD CREEK MERCANTILE

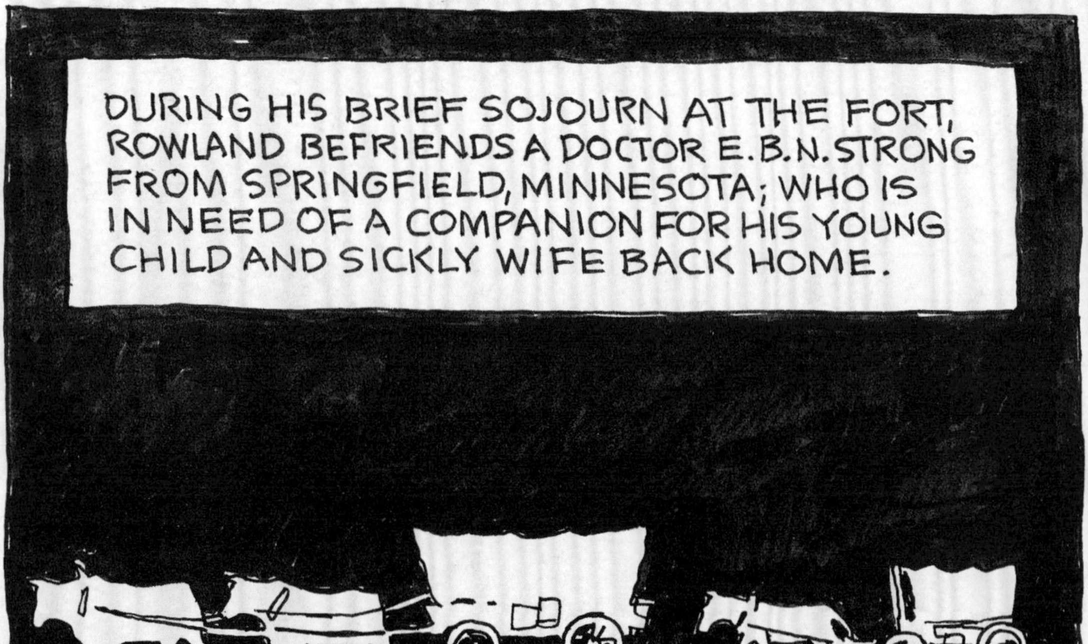
DURING HIS BRIEF SOJOURN AT THE FORT, ROWLAND BEFRIENDS A DOCTOR E.B.N. STRONG FROM SPRINGFIELD, MINNESOTA; WHO IS IN NEED OF A COMPANION FOR HIS YOUNG CHILD AND SICKLY WIFE BACK HOME.

HOPEFULLY, I WILL BE HOME FOR CHRISTMAS.

THE GOOD DOCTOR RETURNS WITH ROWLAND TO OKOBOJI, AND AS FATE WOULD HAVE IT, CONVINCES SIXTEEN-YEAR-OLD ELIZA GARDNER TO JOIN HIS FAMILY IN SPRINGFIELD AS THEIR NANNY.

DECEMBER 1856

THE MOON OF POPPING TREES

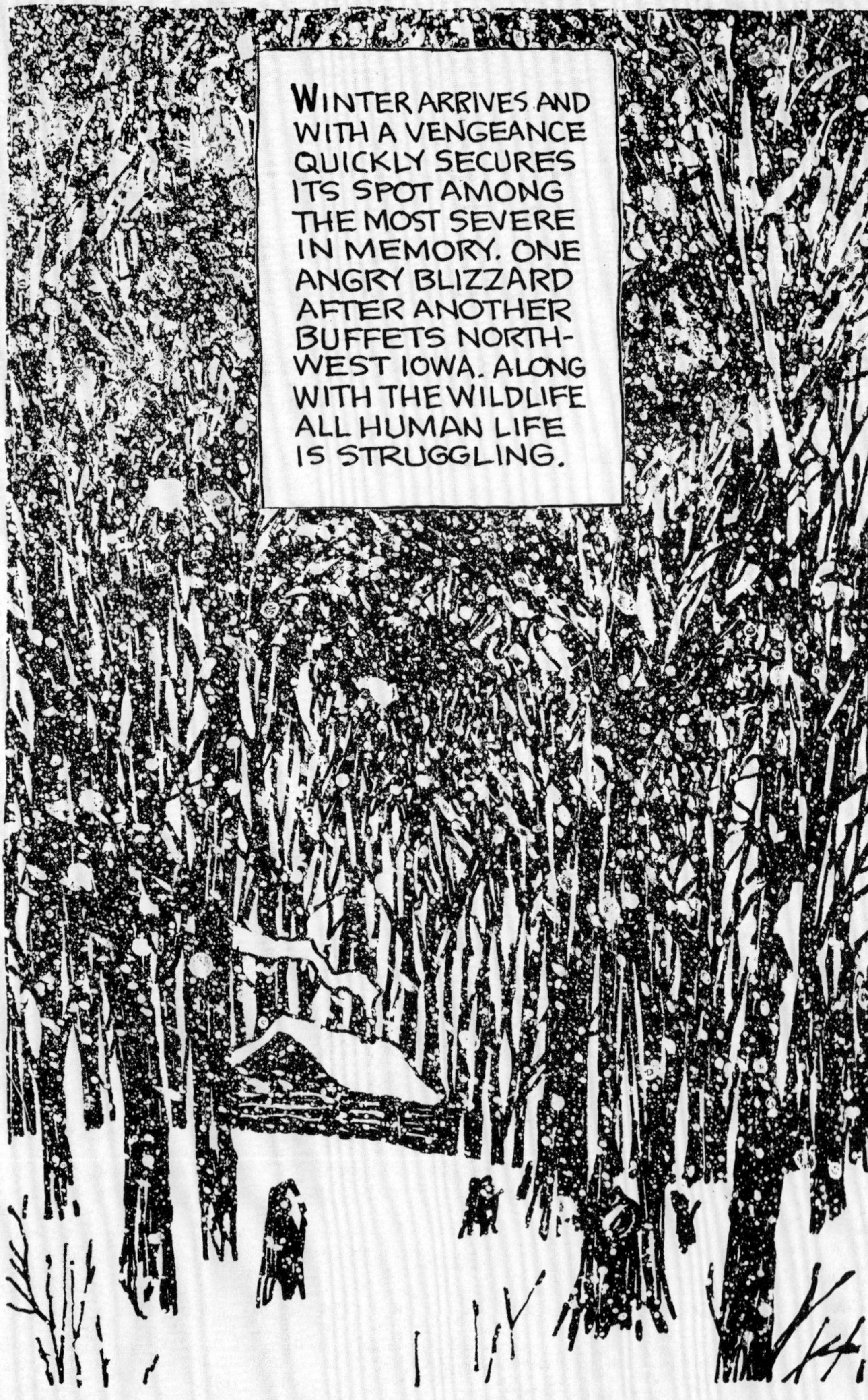
WINTER ARRIVES AND WITH A VENGEANCE QUICKLY SECURES ITS SPOT AMONG THE MOST SEVERE IN MEMORY. ONE ANGRY BLIZZARD AFTER ANOTHER BUFFETS NORTH-WEST IOWA. ALONG WITH THE WILDLIFE ALL HUMAN LIFE IS STRUGGLING.

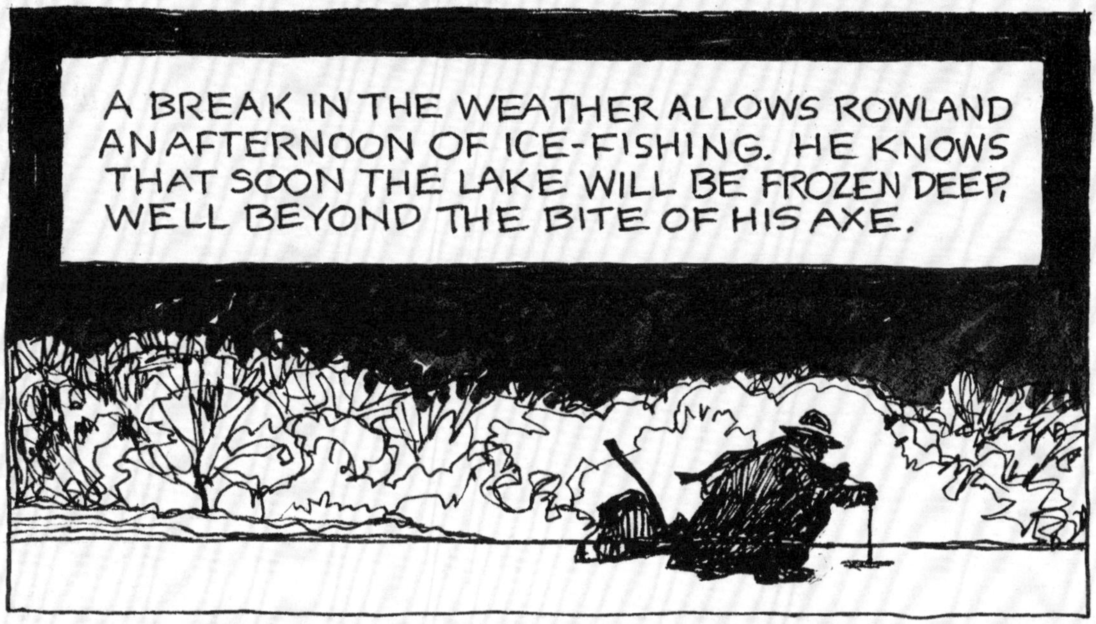
A BREAK IN THE WEATHER ALLOWS ROWLAND AN AFTERNOON OF ICE-FISHING. HE KNOWS THAT SOON THE LAKE WILL BE FROZEN DEEP, WELL BEYOND THE BITE OF HIS AXE.

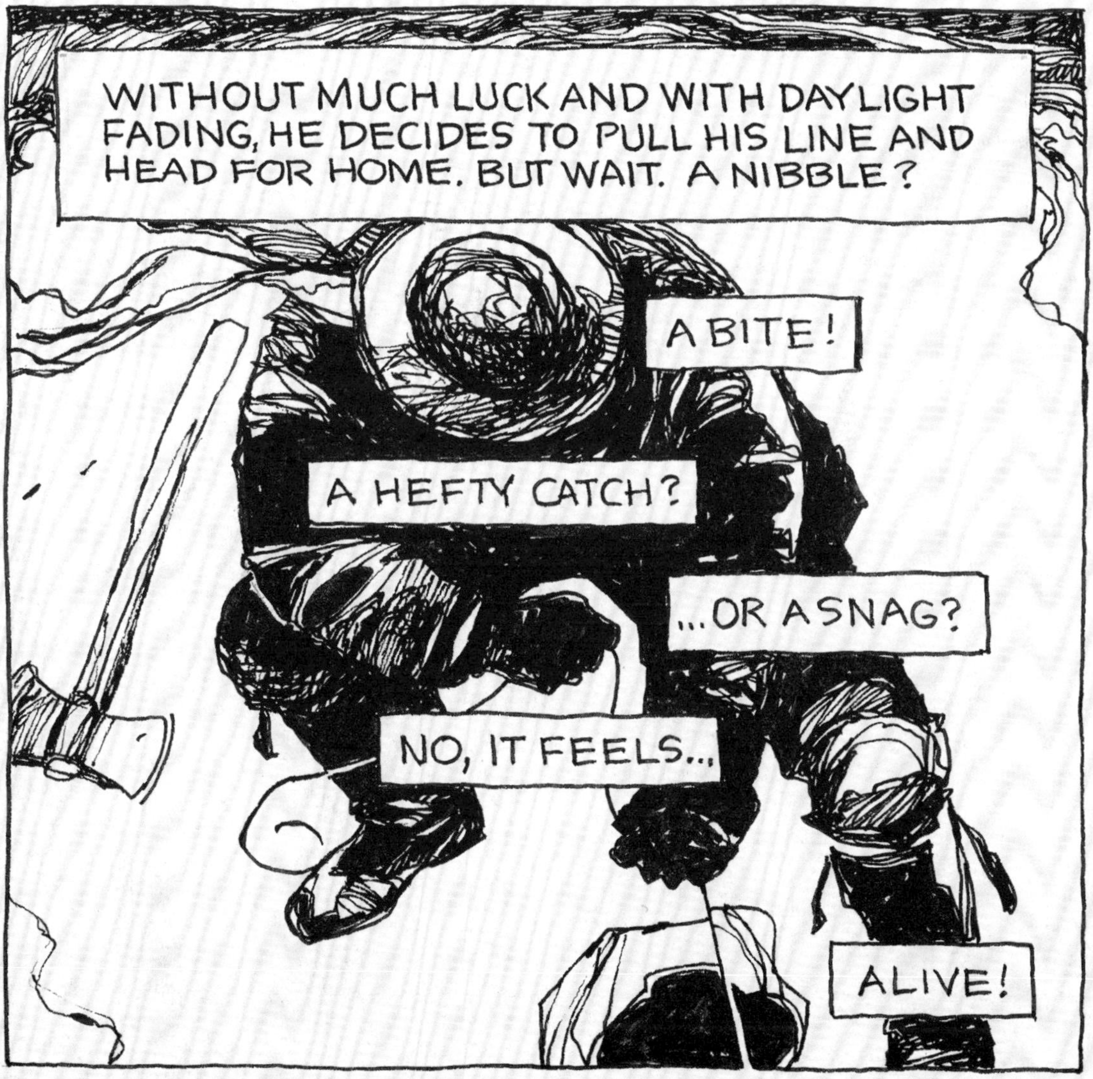
WITHOUT MUCH LUCK AND WITH DAYLIGHT FADING, HE DECIDES TO PULL HIS LINE AND HEAD FOR HOME. BUT WAIT. A NIBBLE?
A BITE!
A HEFTY CATCH?
...OR A SNAG?
NO, IT FEELS...
ALIVE!

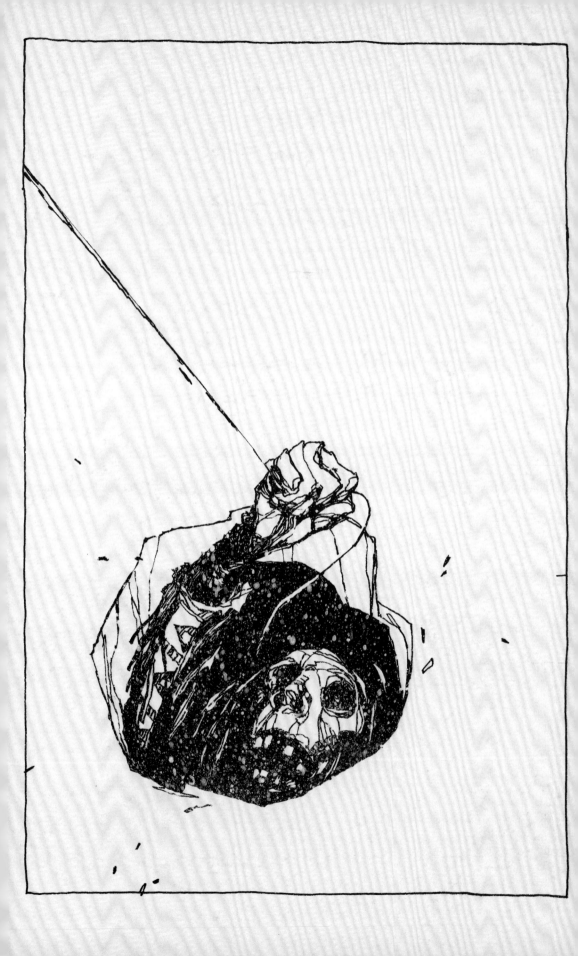

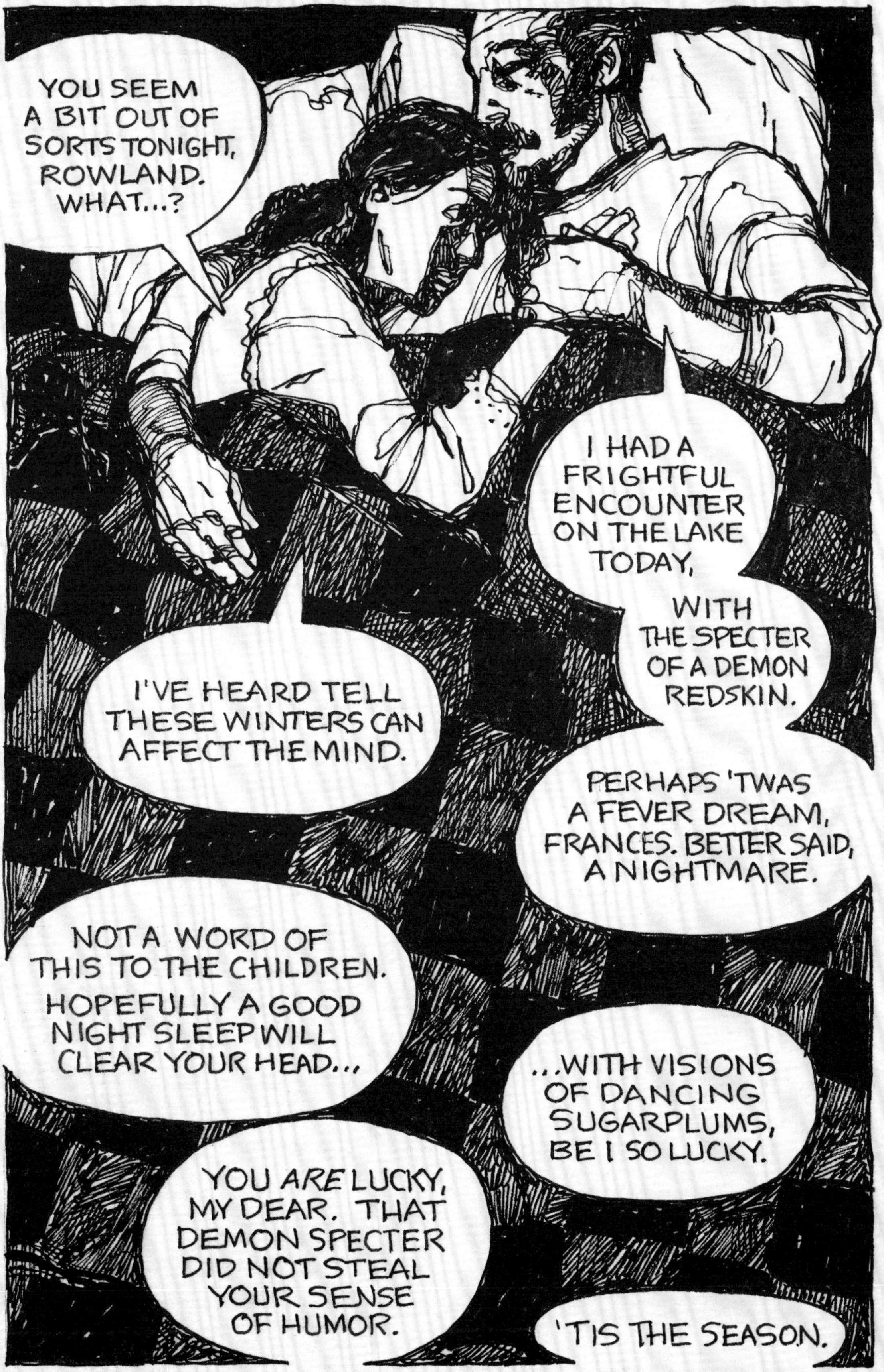
YOU SEEM A BIT OUT OF SORTS TONIGHT, ROWLAND. WHAT...?
I HAD A FRIGHTFUL ENCOUNTER ON THE LAKE TODAY,
WITH THE SPECTER OF A DEMON REDSKIN.
I'VE HEARD TELL THESE WINTERS CAN AFFECT THE MIND.
PERHAPS 'TWAS A FEVER DREAM, FRANCES. BETTER SAID, A NIGHTMARE.
NOT A WORD OF THIS TO THE CHILDREN.
HOPEFULLY A GOOD NIGHT SLEEP WILL CLEAR YOUR HEAD...
...WITH VISIONS OF DANCING SUGARPLUMS, BE I SO LUCKY.
YOU *ARE* LUCKY, MY DEAR. THAT DEMON SPECTER DID NOT STEAL YOUR SENSE OF HUMOR.
'TIS THE SEASON.

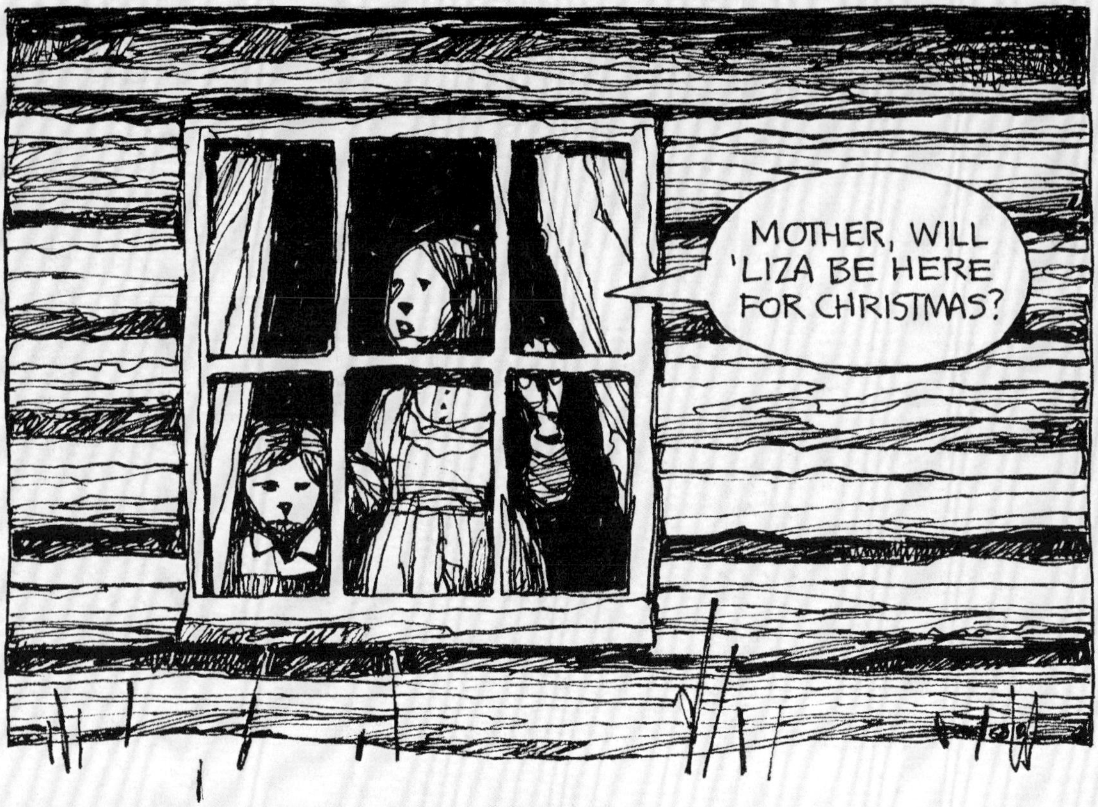
MOTHER, WILL 'LIZA BE HERE FOR CHRISTMAS?

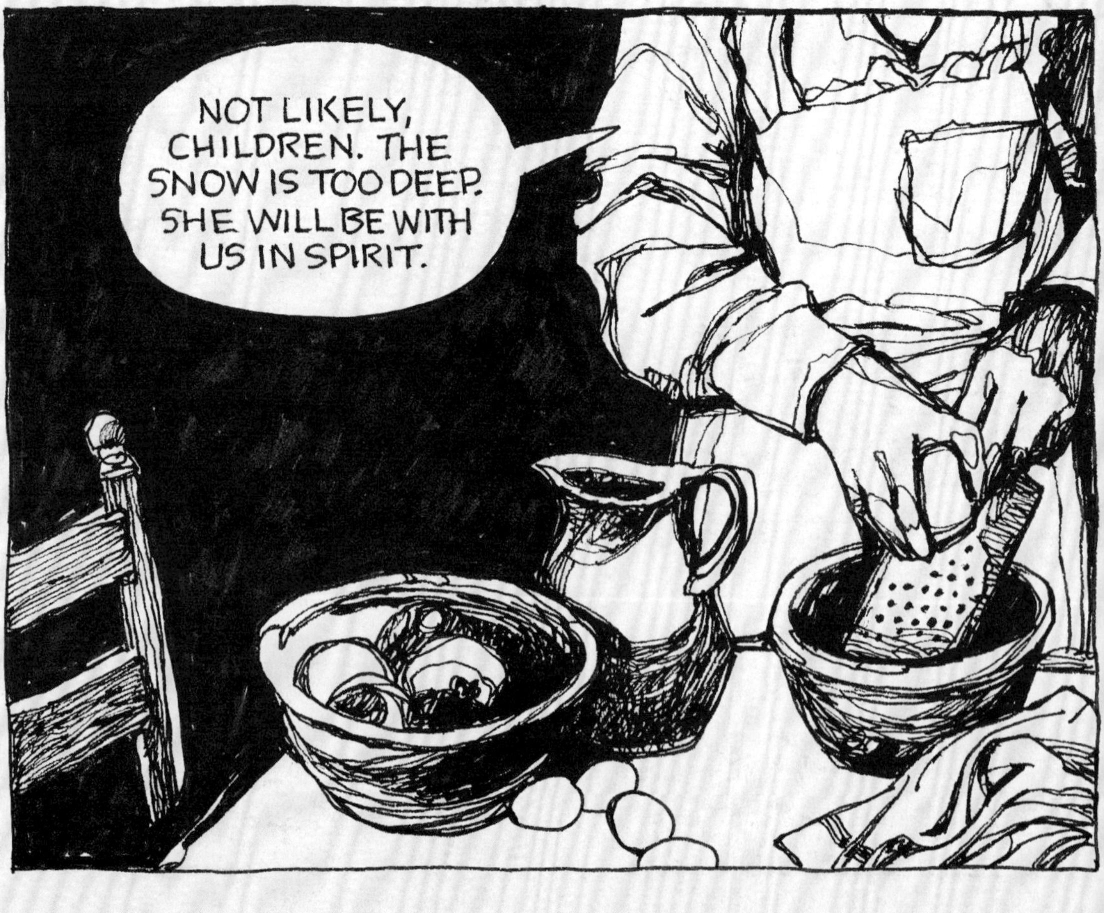
NOT LIKELY, CHILDREN. THE SNOW IS TOO DEEP. SHE WILL BE WITH US IN SPIRIT.

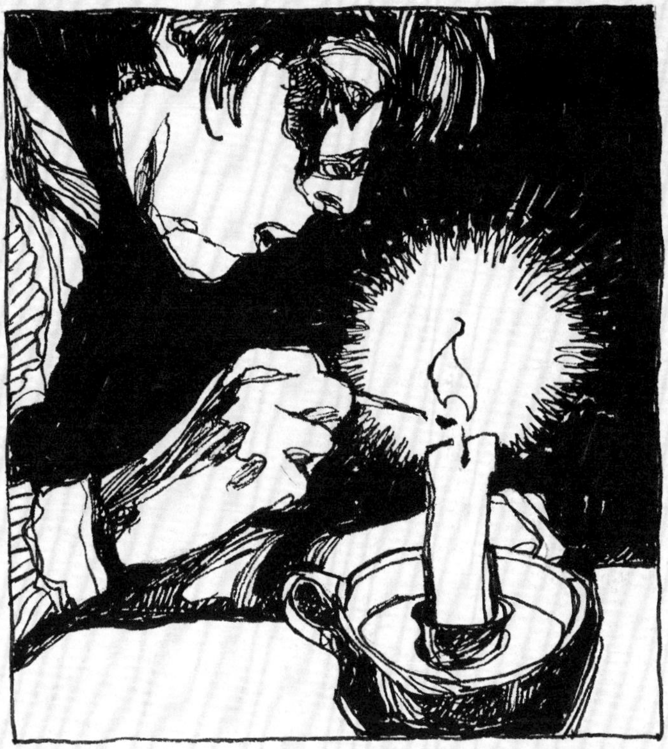

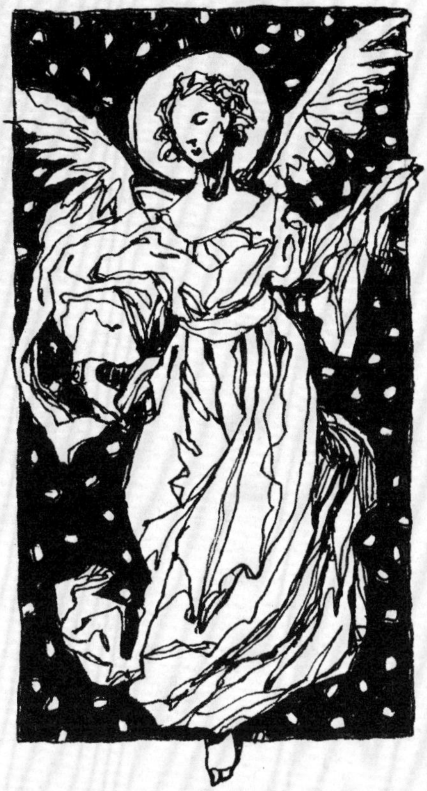

AND SUDDENLY THERE WAS WITH THE ANGEL
A MULTITUDE OF THE HEAVENLY HOST PRAISING GOD,
AND SAYING, GLORY TO GOD IN THE HIGHEST,

AND ON EARTH PEACE, GOOD WILL TOWARD ALL MEN.

— THE GOSPEL OF ST. LUKE

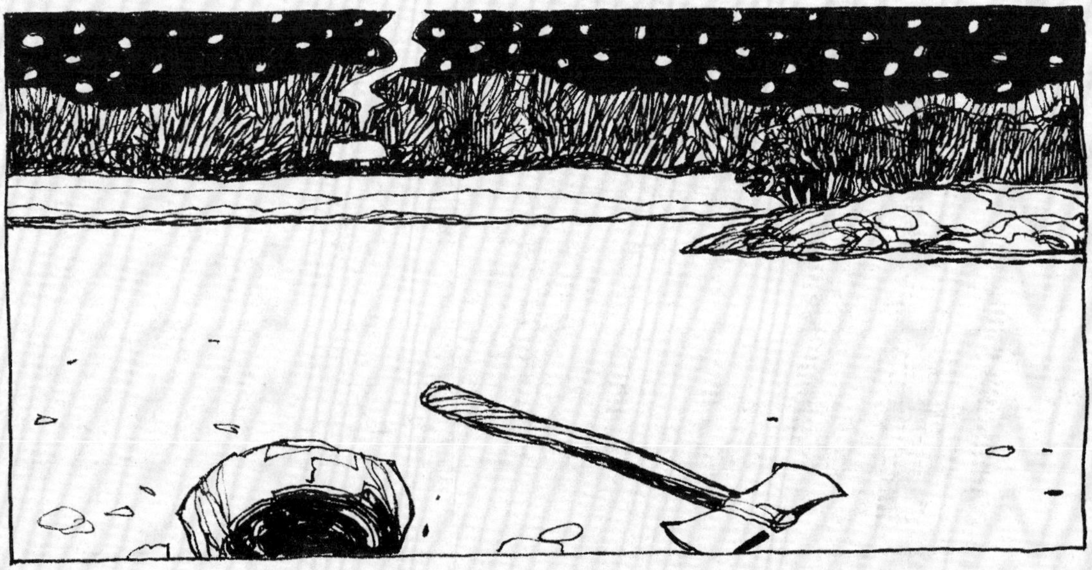

JANUARY 1857

THE MOON OF FROST IN THE TIPI

THE NEW YEAR OFFERS LITTLE RESPITE FROM DECEMBER'S ICY BLASTS...

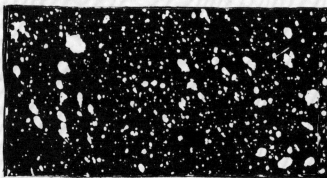

... FOSTERING AN EPIDEMIC OF CABIN FEVER AMONG THE THIRTYSOME HOMESTEADERS SCATTERED ALONG THE LAKESHORES.

THE ONLY CURE:

APRIL.

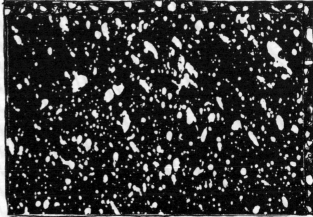

INSIDE THE GARDNER CABIN A TEMPORARY TONIC FOR THE FEVER IS FOUND TUCKED AWAY IN AN OXHIDE TRUNK.

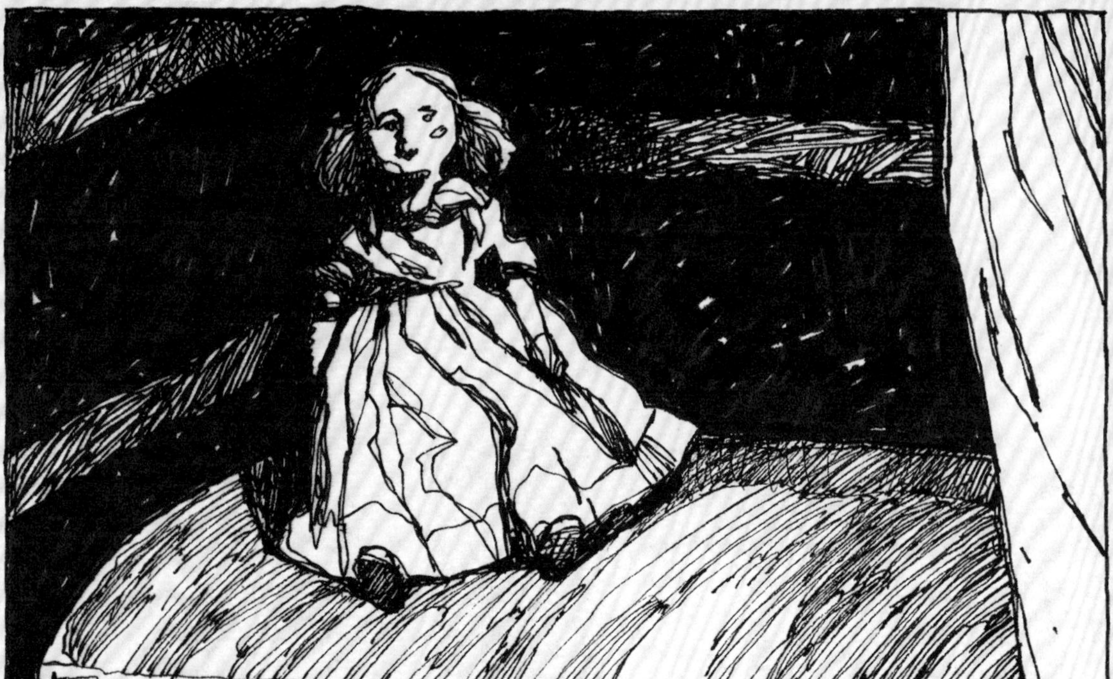

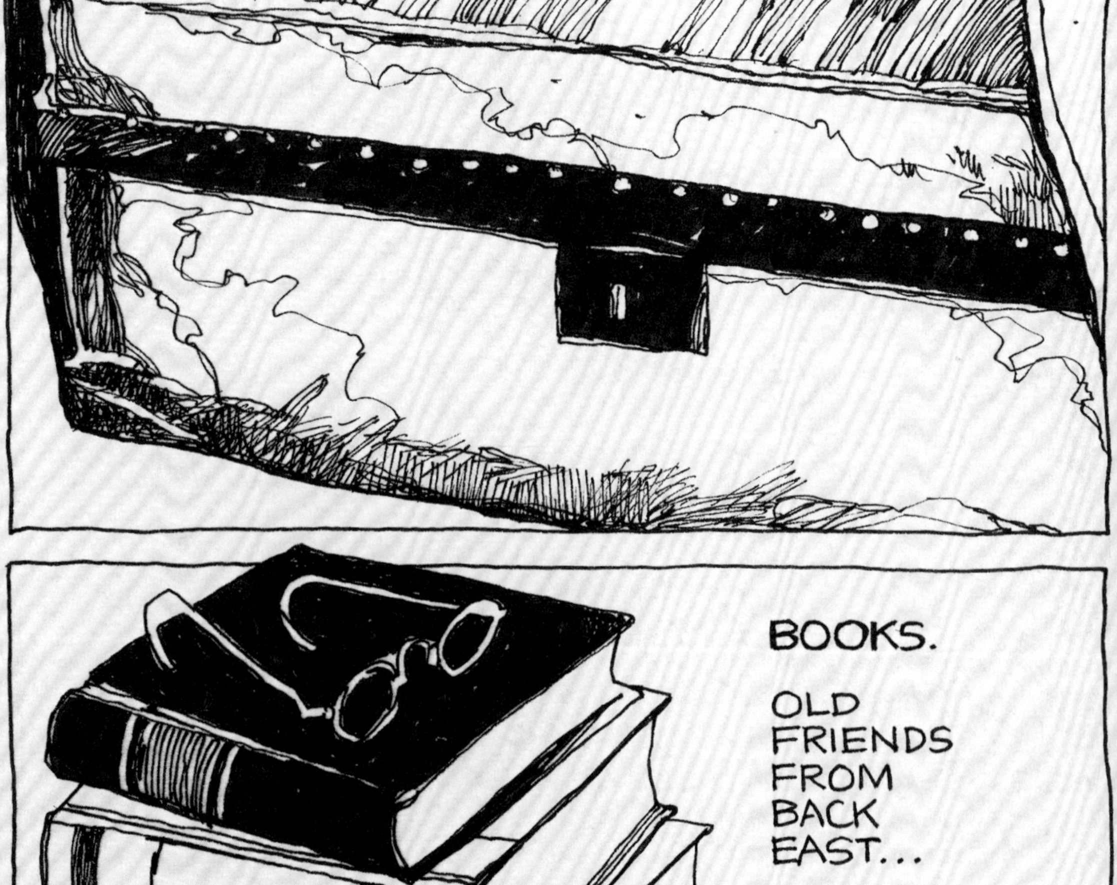
BOOKS.
OLD FRIENDS FROM BACK EAST...

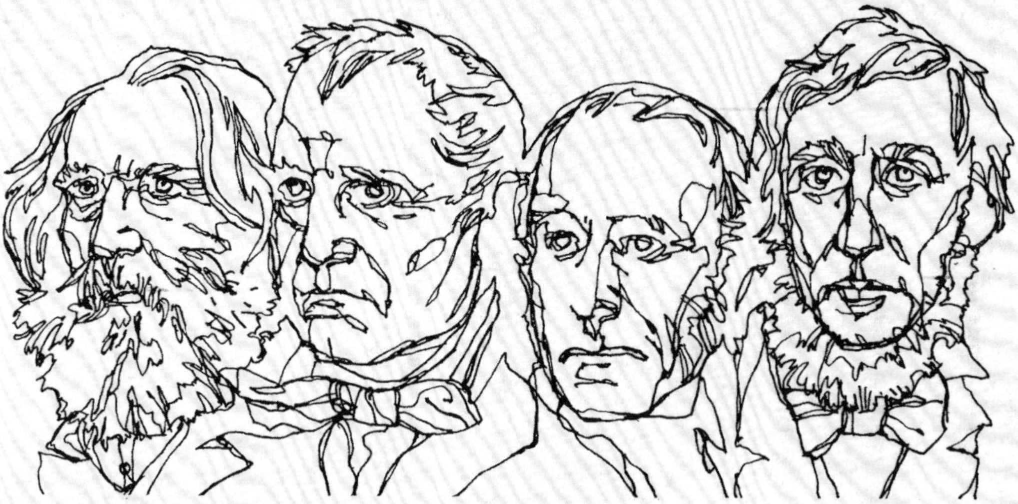

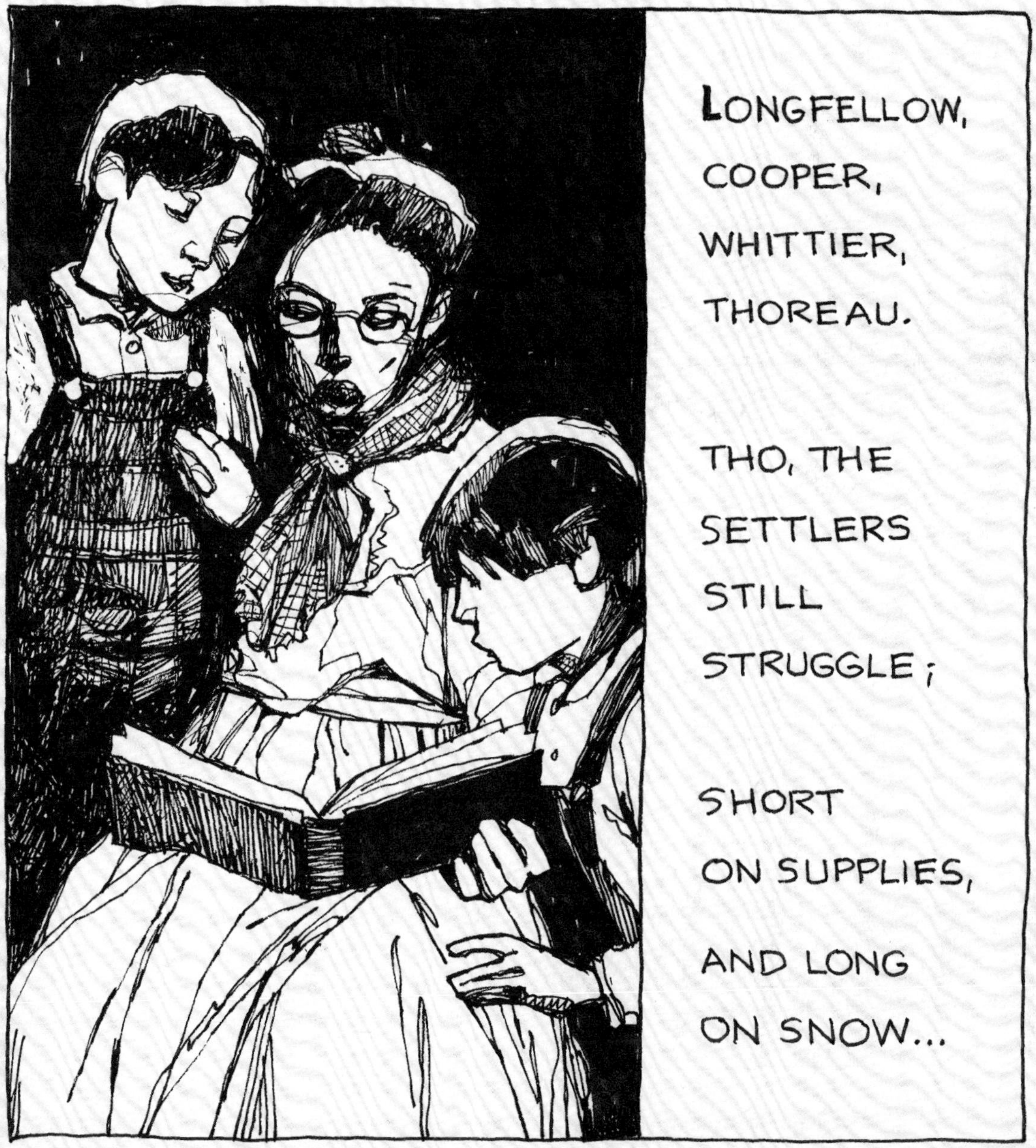
LONGFELLOW,
COOPER,
WHITTIER,
THOREAU.
THO, THE
SETTLERS
STILL
STRUGGLE;
SHORT
ON SUPPLIES,
AND LONG
ON SNOW...

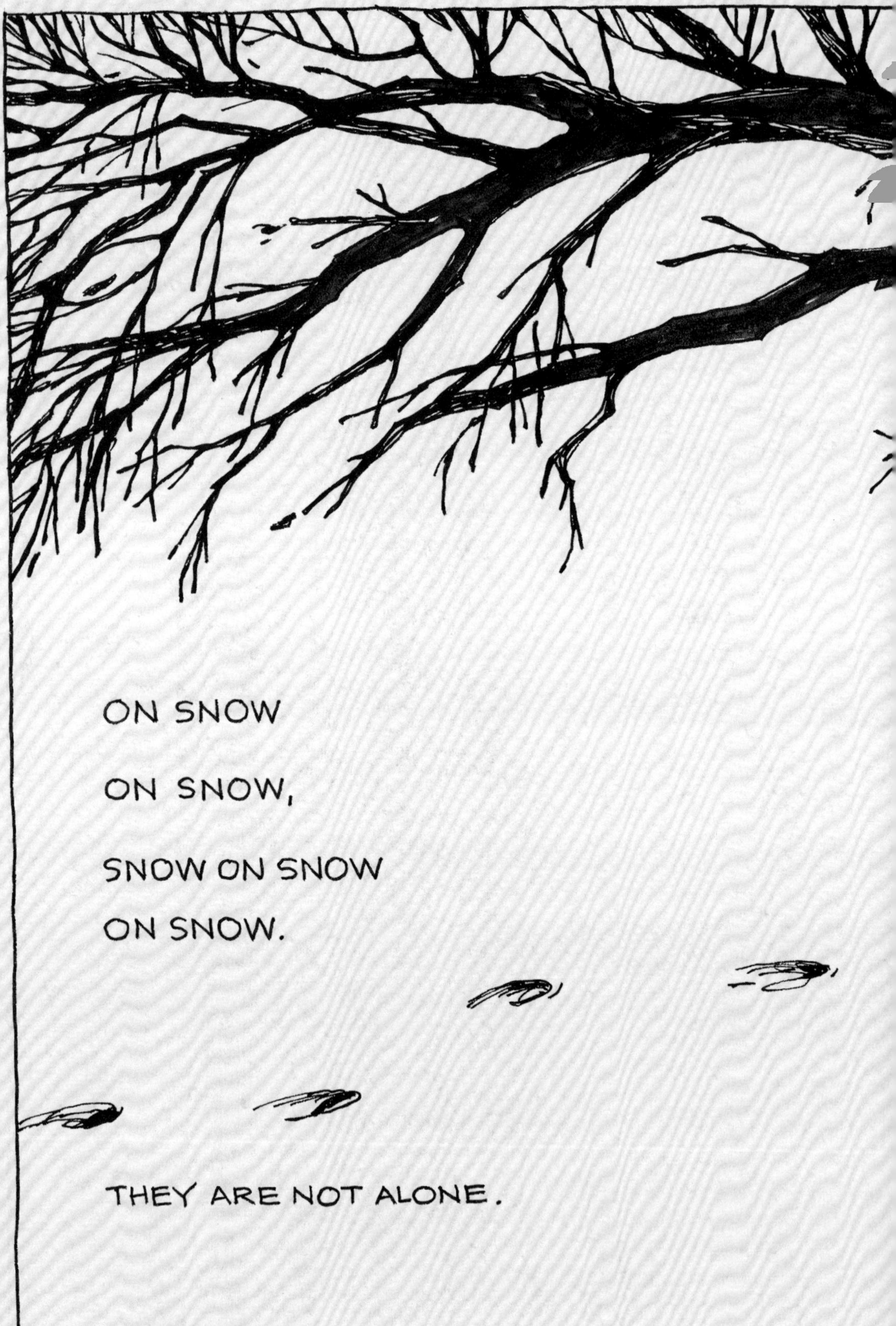
ON SNOW
ON SNOW,
SNOW ON SNOW
ON SNOW.
THEY ARE NOT ALONE.

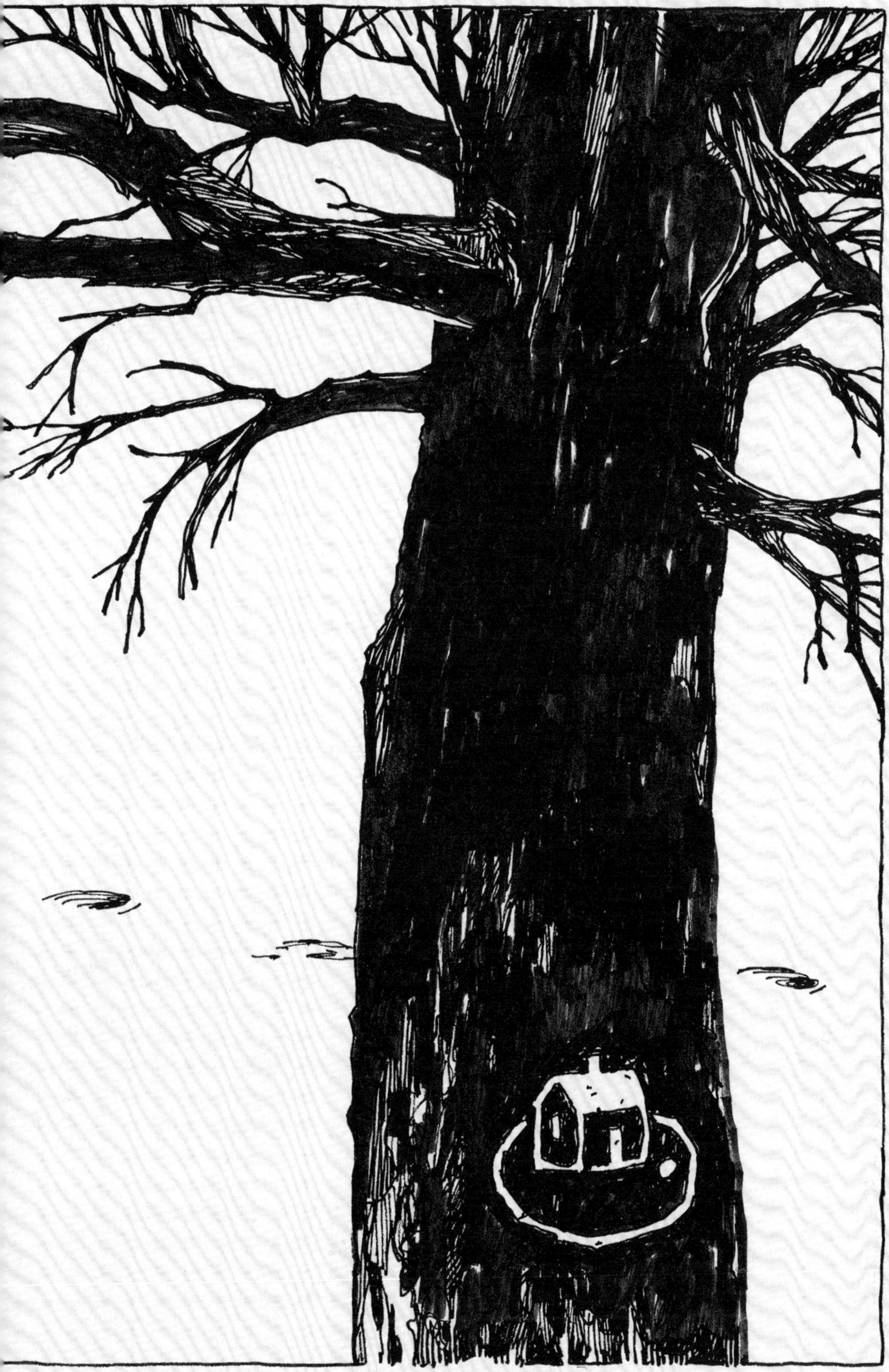

FEBRUARY 1857

THE MOON OF DARK RED CALVES

SMITHLAND, IOWA

ONE HUNDRED MILES SOUTH AND WEST OF THE GARDNER CABIN, THIS TINY HAMLET TUCKED IN THE HILLS ABOVE THE LITTLE SIOUX RIVER ALSO SUFFERS THE CRUEL WINTER.

SINCE DECEMBER, THAT SUFFERING HAS BEEN SHARED WITH A SMALL BAND OF FAMILIAR DAKOTAS CAMPED NEARBY. THEIR LEADER, INKPADUTA, TOLERATES A TESTY RELATIONSHIP WITH THE WHITE MAN...

MEMORIES OF THE HENRY LOTT/SIDOMINDOTA INCIDENT STILL FESTER IN THE BACK OF HIS MIND, WHILE THE LITTLE SIOUX VALLEY OCCUPIES A VERY SPECIAL PLACE IN HIS HEART... THE ANCESTRAL WINTER HUNTING GROUND OF HIS PEOPLE, ONCE TEEMING WITH DEER, ELK AND SMALL GAME.

BUT NOT THIS YEAR.

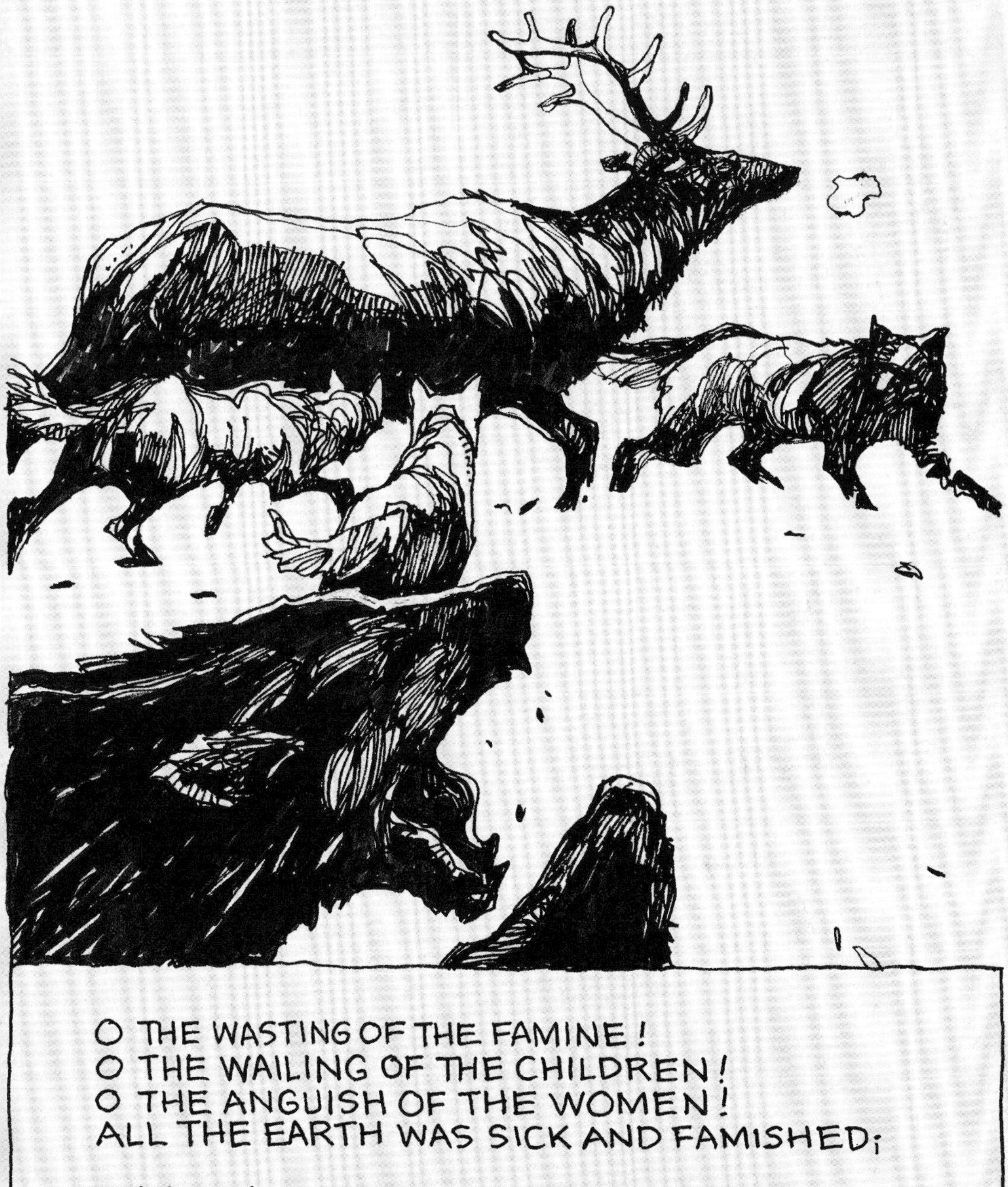

O THE WASTING OF THE FAMINE!
O THE WAILING OF THE CHILDREN!
O THE ANGUISH OF THE WOMEN!
ALL THE EARTH WAS SICK AND FAMISHED;

HUNGRY WAS THE AIR AROUND THEM,
HUNGRY WAS THE SKY ABOVE THEM,
AND THE HUNGRY STARS IN HEAVEN,
LIKE THE EYES OF WOLVES, GLARED AT THEM.

— *HENRY WADSWORTH LONGFELLOW*
THE SONG OF HIAWATHA

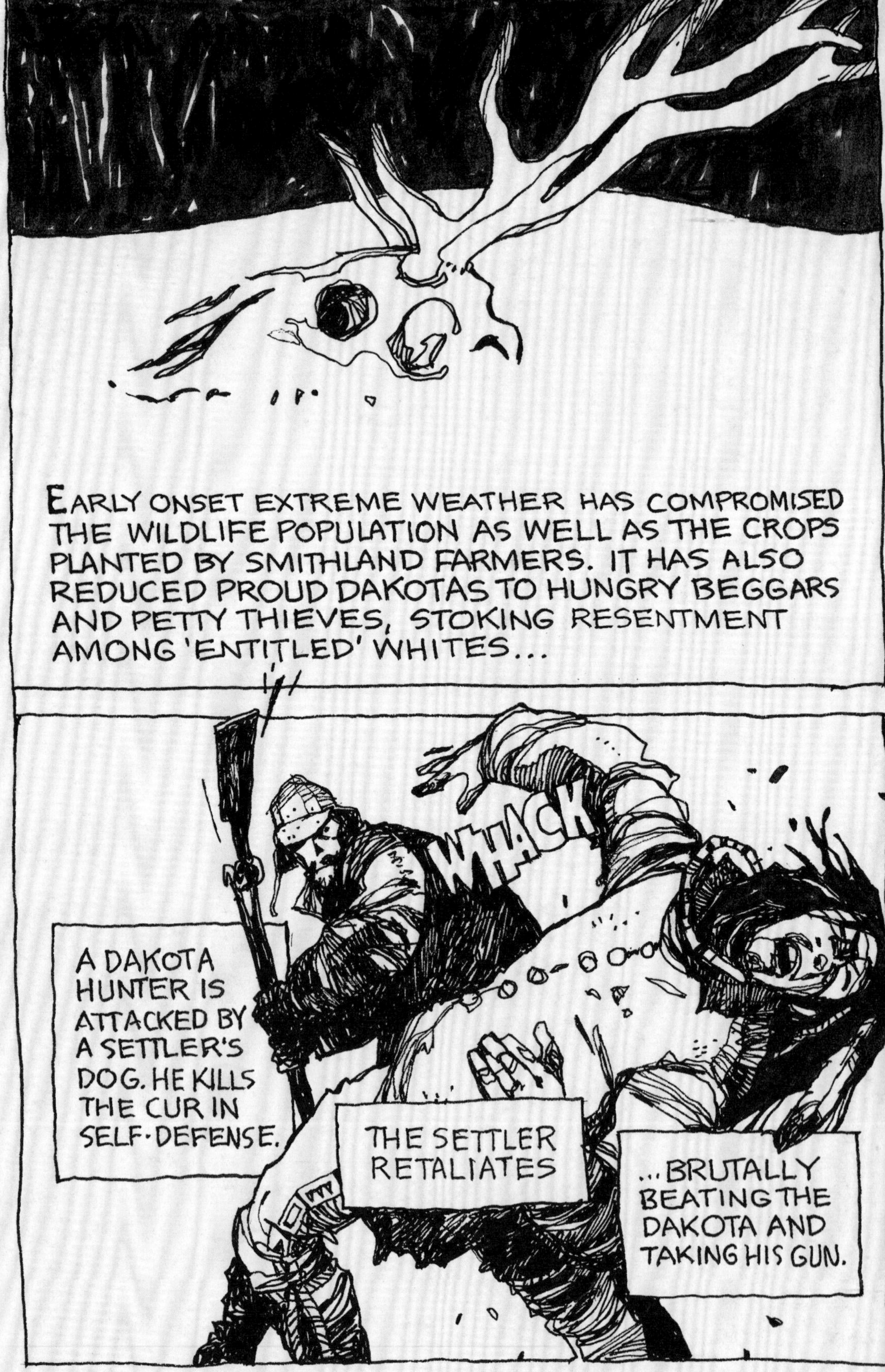
EARLY ONSET EXTREME WEATHER HAS COMPROMISED THE WILDLIFE POPULATION AS WELL AS THE CROPS PLANTED BY SMITHLAND FARMERS. IT HAS ALSO REDUCED PROUD DAKOTAS TO HUNGRY BEGGARS AND PETTY THIEVES, STOKING RESENTMENT AMONG 'ENTITLED' WHITES...
WHACK
A DAKOTA HUNTER IS ATTACKED BY A SETTLER'S DOG. HE KILLS THE CUR IN SELF-DEFENSE.
THE SETTLER RETALIATES
...BRUTALLY BEATING THE DAKOTA AND TAKING HIS GUN.

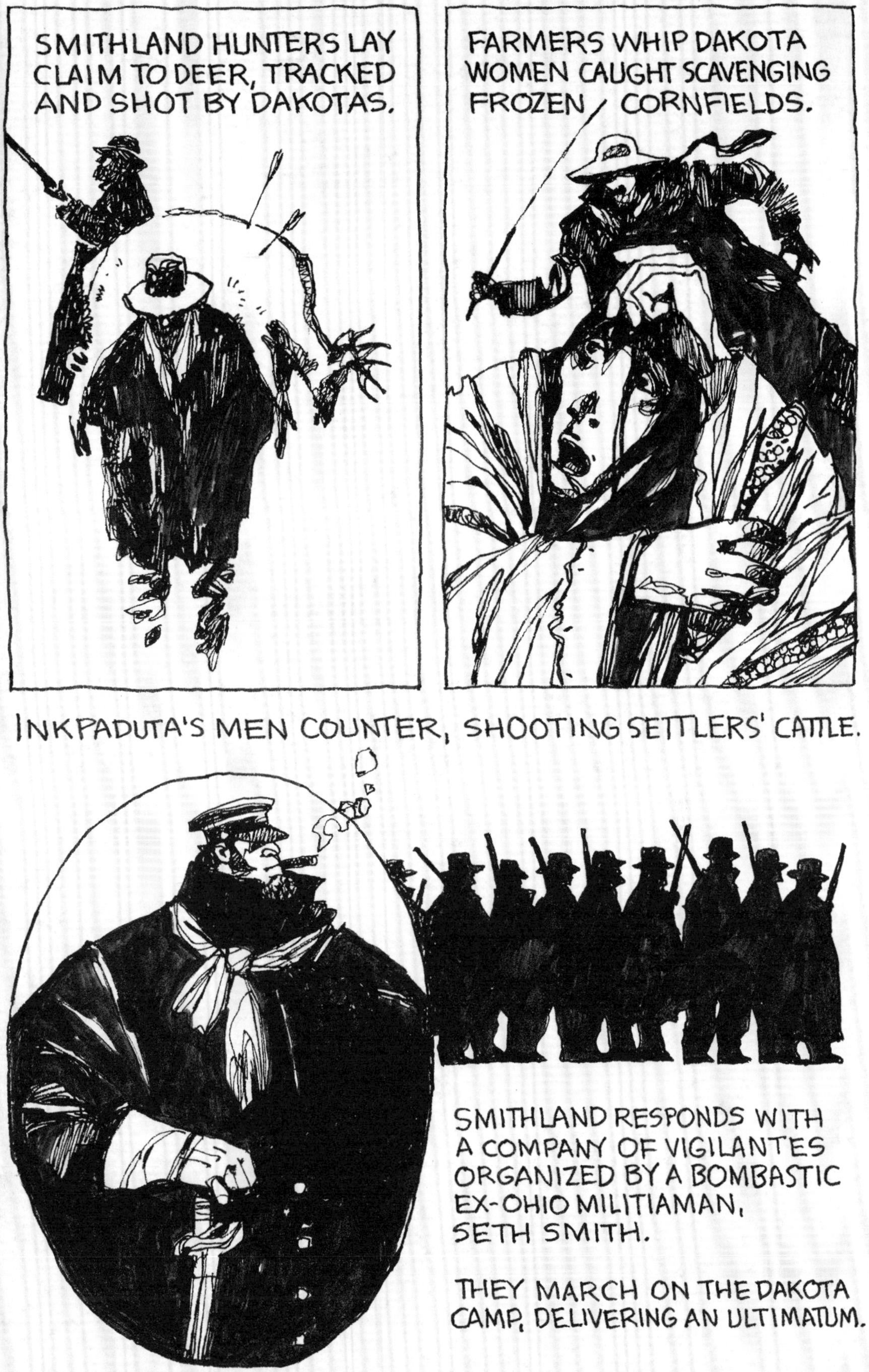
SMITHLAND HUNTERS LAY CLAIM TO DEER, TRACKED AND SHOT BY DAKOTAS.
FARMERS WHIP DAKOTA WOMEN CAUGHT SCAVENGING FROZEN CORNFIELDS.
INKPADUTA'S MEN COUNTER, SHOOTING SETTLERS' CATTLE.
SMITHLAND RESPONDS WITH A COMPANY OF VIGILANTES ORGANIZED BY A BOMBASTIC EX-OHIO MILITIAMAN, SETH SMITH.
THEY MARCH ON THE DAKOTA CAMP, DELIVERING AN ULTIMATUM.

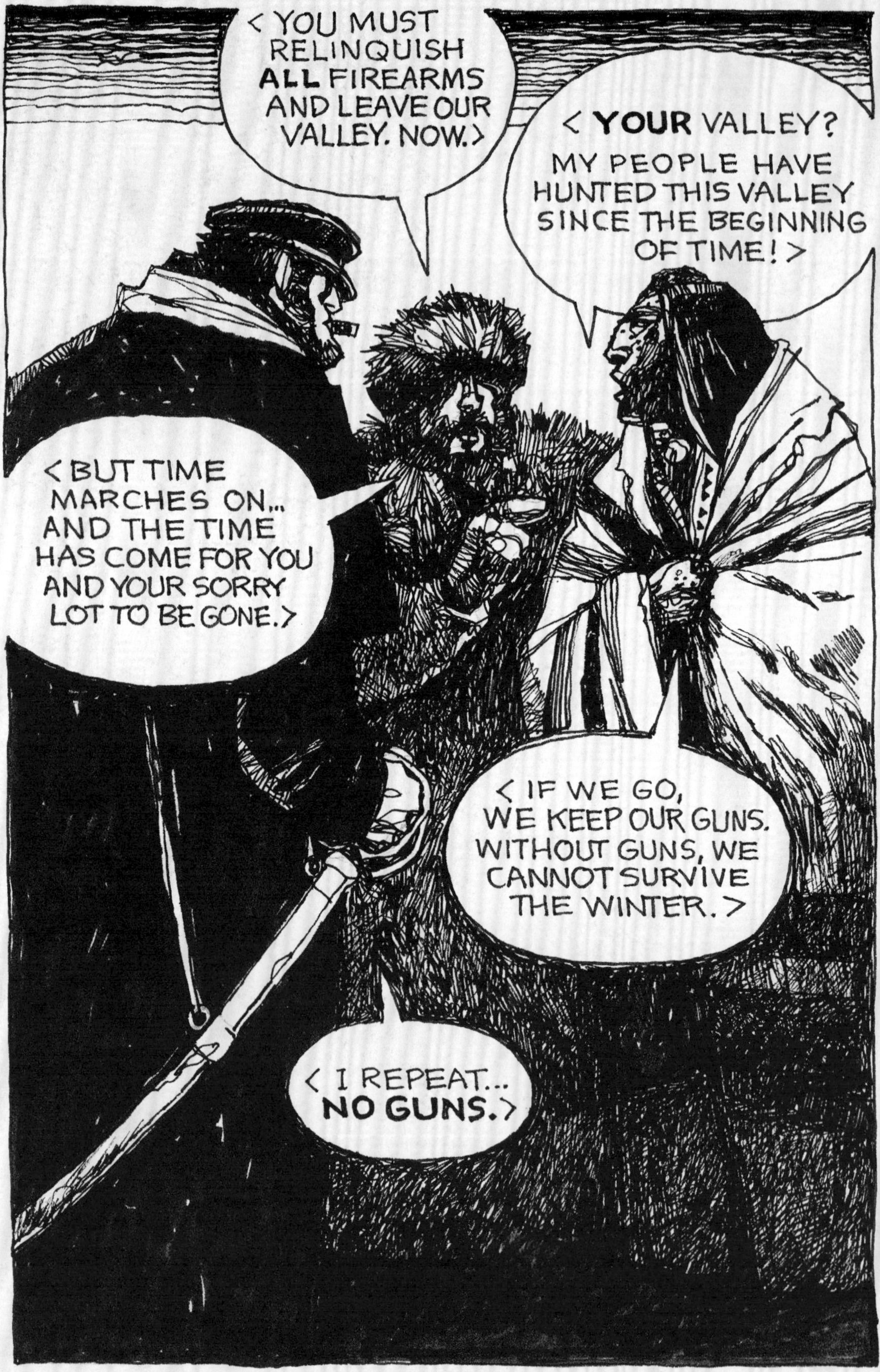

< YOU MUST RELINQUISH **ALL** FIREARMS AND LEAVE OUR VALLEY. NOW. >
< **YOUR** VALLEY? MY PEOPLE HAVE HUNTED THIS VALLEY SINCE THE BEGINNING OF TIME! >
< BUT TIME MARCHES ON... AND THE TIME HAS COME FOR YOU AND YOUR SORRY LOT TO BE GONE. >
< IF WE GO, WE KEEP OUR GUNS. WITHOUT GUNS, WE CANNOT SURVIVE THE WINTER. >
< I REPEAT... **NO GUNS.** >

A DARK CLOUD SETTLES
OVER INKPADUTA AS HE
WATCHES THE WASICHU
'MILITIA' RANSACK HIS
DEFENSELESS VILLAGE,
CONFISCATING FIREARMS.

ANGRY DAKOTAS COLLECT
THE SCATTERED REMAINS
OF THEIR CAMPSITE AND
A FEW GUNS QUIETLY
PROCURED FROM LOCAL
SYMPATHIZERS... AND
HEAD NORTHWARD, UP
THE LITTLE SIOUX VALLEY.

TOWARD THE OKOBOJIS
AND SPIRIT LAKE.

MARCH 1857

THE MOON OF THE SNOWBLIND

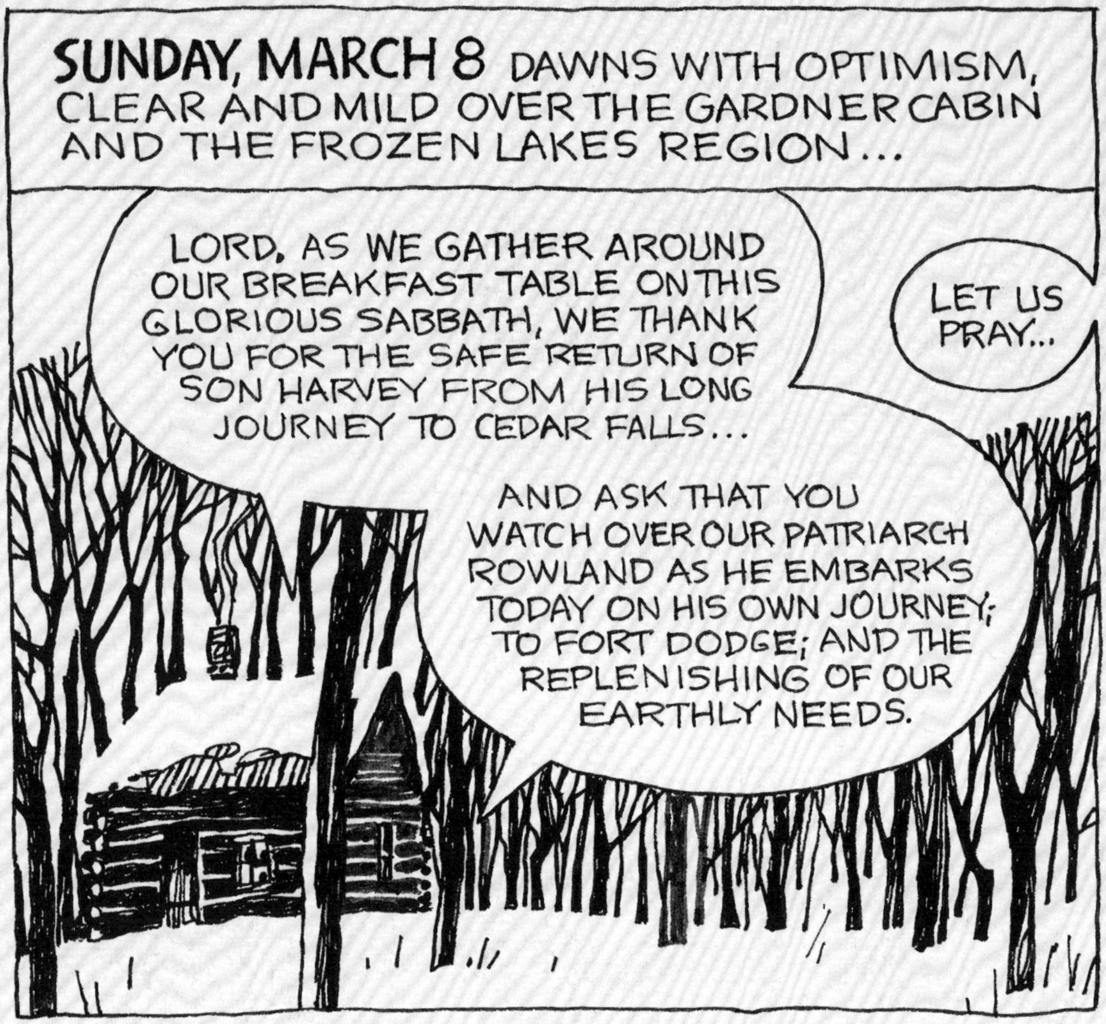
SUNDAY, MARCH 8 DAWNS WITH OPTIMISM, CLEAR AND MILD OVER THE GARDNER CABIN AND THE FROZEN LAKES REGION...
LET US PRAY...
LORD, AS WE GATHER AROUND OUR BREAKFAST TABLE ON THIS GLORIOUS SABBATH, WE THANK YOU FOR THE SAFE RETURN OF SON HARVEY FROM HIS LONG JOURNEY TO CEDAR FALLS...
AND ASK THAT YOU WATCH OVER OUR PATRIARCH ROWLAND AS HE EMBARKS TODAY ON HIS OWN JOURNEY; TO FORT DODGE; AND THE REPLENISHING OF OUR EARTHLY NEEDS.

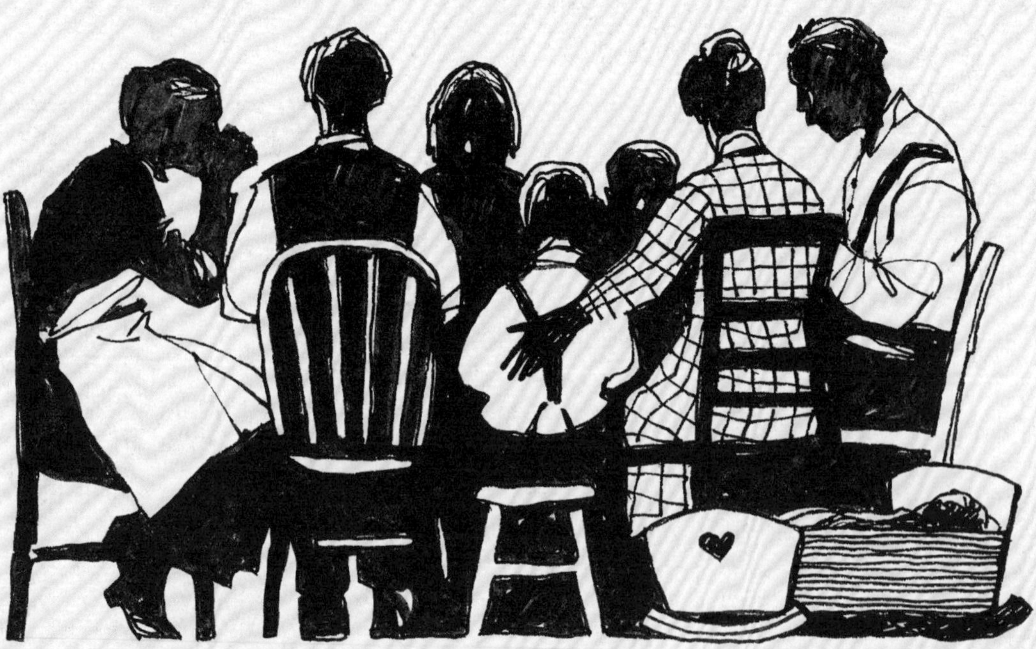

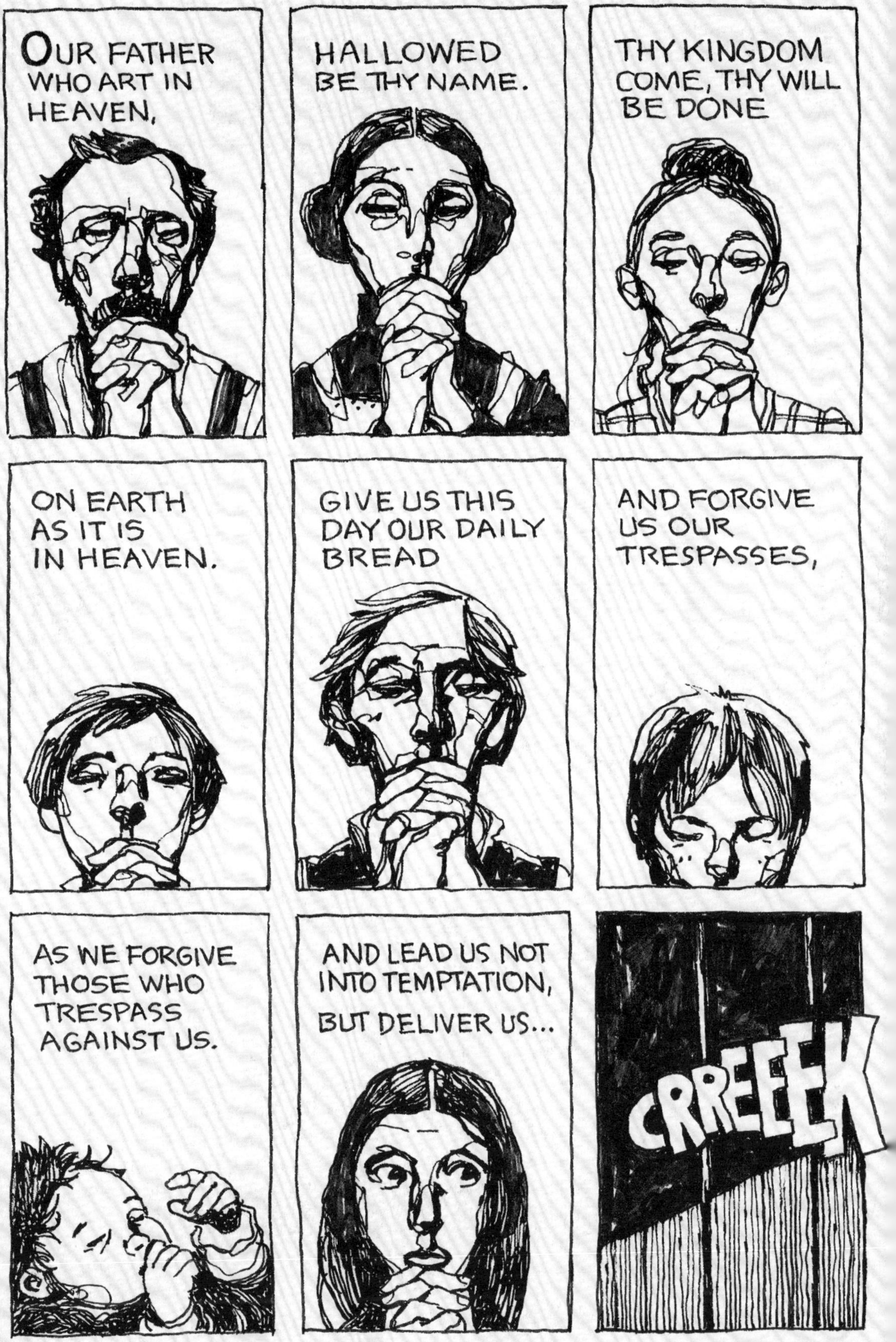

OUR FATHER WHO ART IN HEAVEN,
HALLOWED BE THY NAME.
THY KINGDOM COME, THY WILL BE DONE
ON EARTH AS IT IS IN HEAVEN.
GIVE US THIS DAY OUR DAILY BREAD
AND FORGIVE US OUR TRESPASSES,
AS WE FORGIVE THOSE WHO TRESPASS AGAINST US.
AND LEAD US NOT INTO TEMPTATION,
BUT DELIVER US...
CREEEK

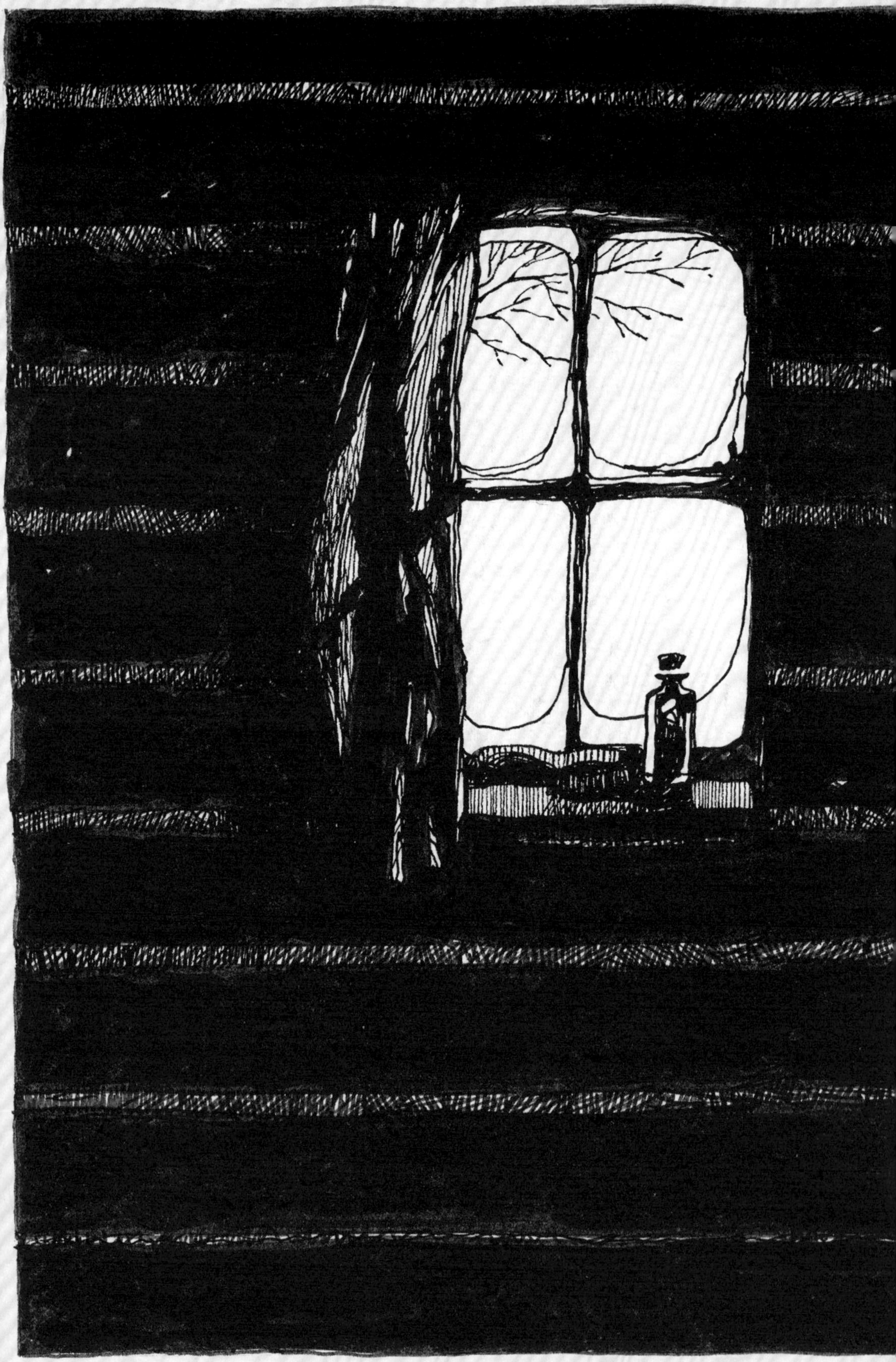

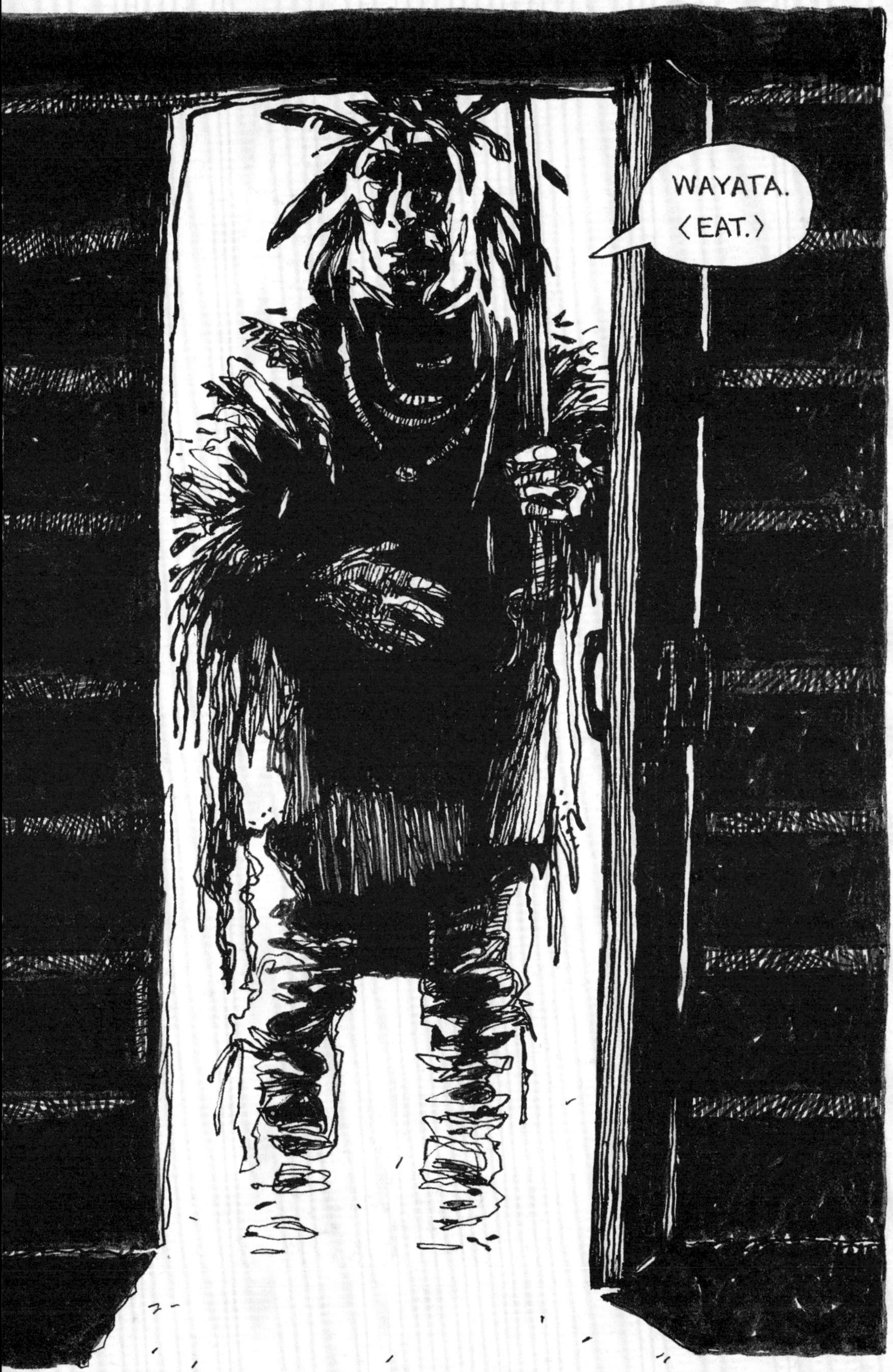
WAYATA.
<EAT.>

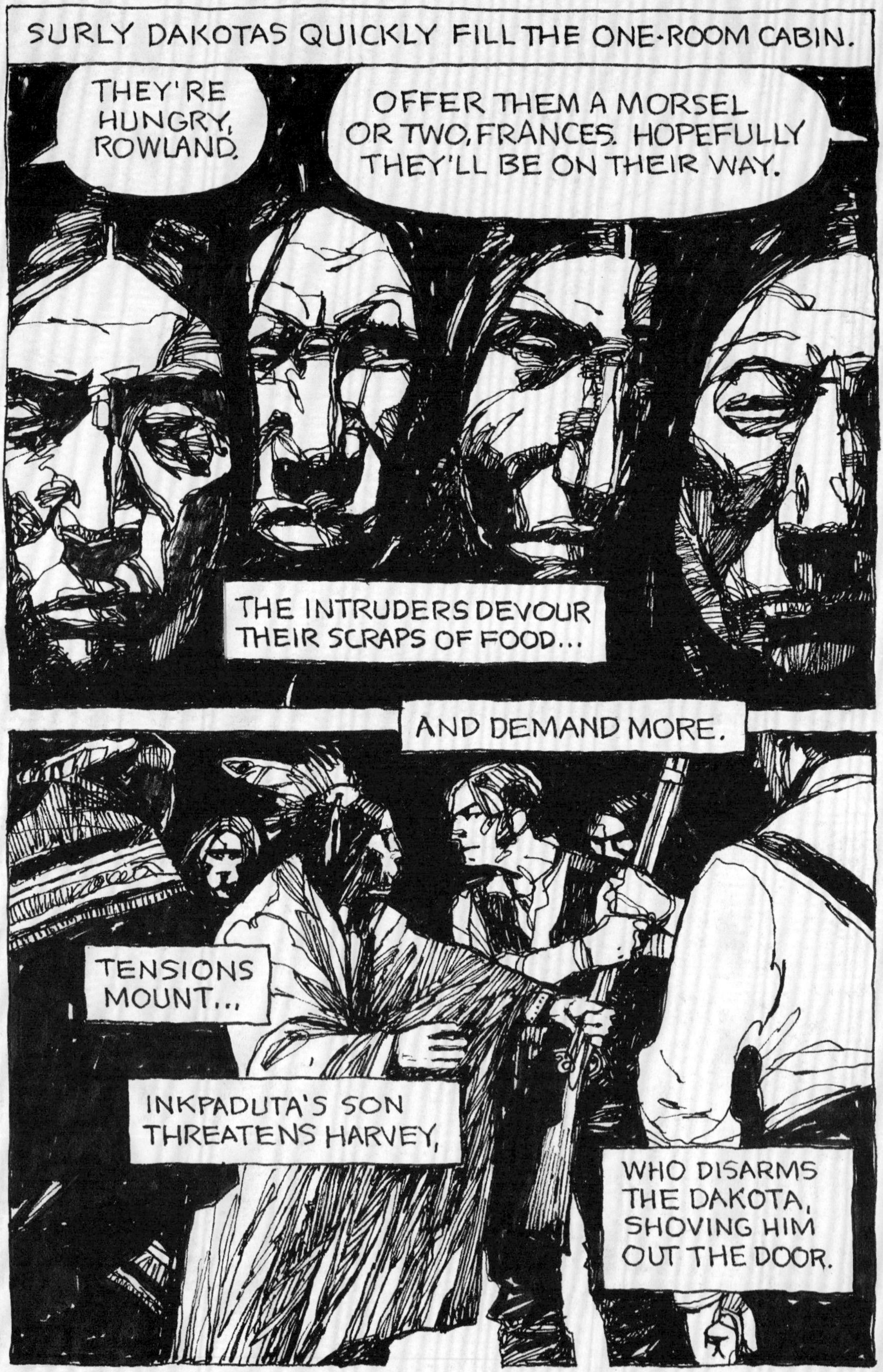
SURLY DAKOTAS QUICKLY FILL THE ONE-ROOM CABIN.
THEY'RE HUNGRY, ROWLAND.
OFFER THEM A MORSEL OR TWO, FRANCES. HOPEFULLY THEY'LL BE ON THEIR WAY.
THE INTRUDERS DEVOUR THEIR SCRAPS OF FOOD...
AND DEMAND MORE.
TENSIONS MOUNT...
INKPADUTA'S SON THREATENS HARVEY,
WHO DISARMS THE DAKOTA, SHOVING HIM OUT THE DOOR.

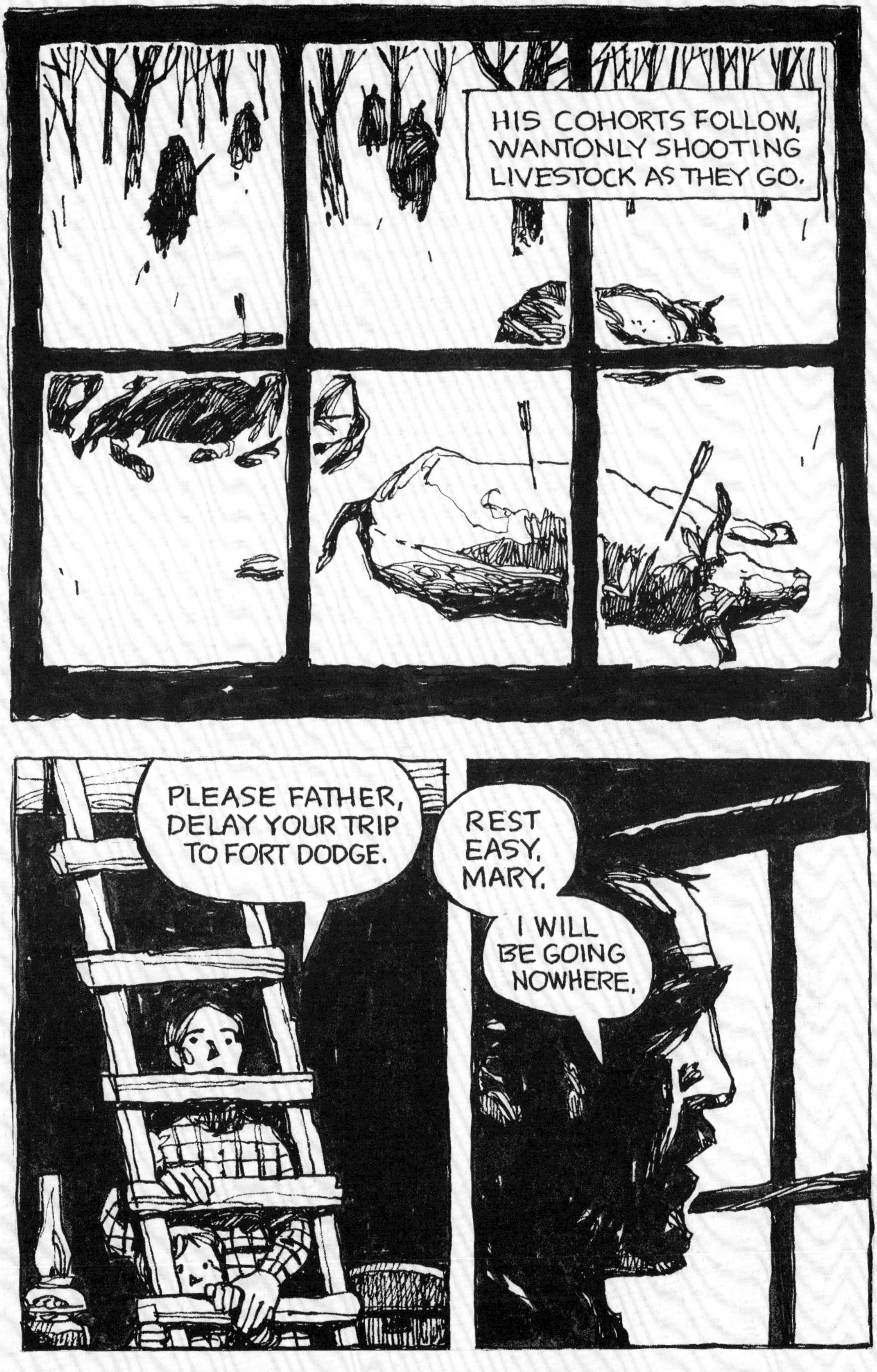
HIS COHORTS FOLLOW, WANTONLY SHOOTING LIVESTOCK AS THEY GO.
PLEASE FATHER, DELAY YOUR TRIP TO FORT DODGE.
REST EASY, MARY.
I WILL BE GOING NOWHERE.

THE DESPERATE BEGGARS HAVE DISAPPEARED AMONG THE TREES, LEAVING THE GARDNER CLAN ON EDGE. MORNING PASSES QUIETLY INTO EARLY AFTERNOON. HARVEY AND A VISITOR, ROBERT CLARK, HAVE DECIDED TO WARN THE GRANGER-MATTOCK CABINS OF THE 'RED MENACE!'

STAY SAFE, HARVEY. I WOULD BE LOST WITHOUT YOU.

MY DEAR, I PROMISE WE SHALL RETURN BEFORE DARK.

MID-AFTERNOON, THEN...   QUIET.

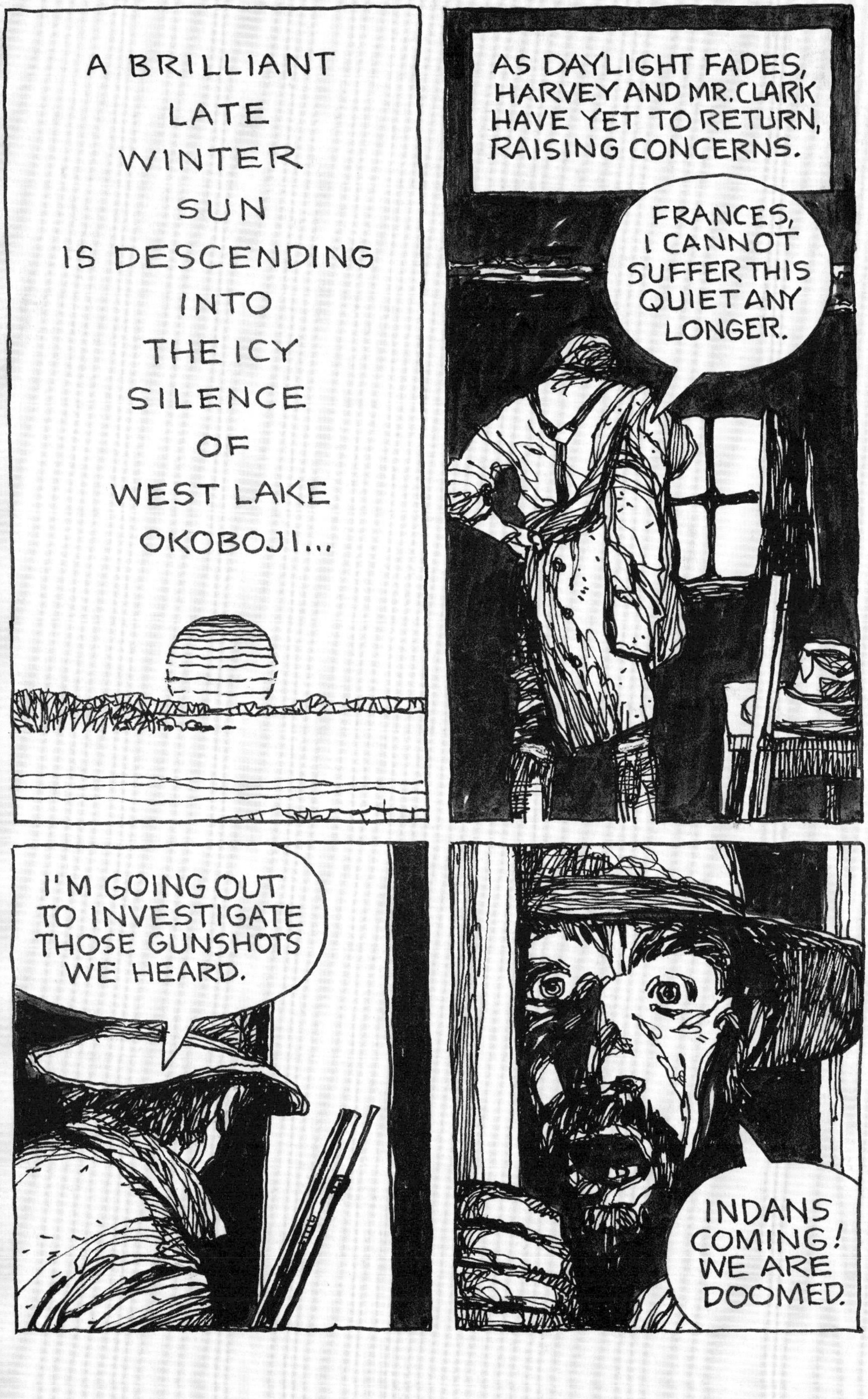
A BRILLIANT LATE WINTER SUN IS DESCENDING INTO THE ICY SILENCE OF WEST LAKE OKOBOJI...
AS DAYLIGHT FADES, HARVEY AND MR. CLARK HAVE YET TO RETURN, RAISING CONCERNS.
FRANCES, I CANNOT SUFFER THIS QUIET ANY LONGER.
I'M GOING OUT TO INVESTIGATE THOSE GUNSHOTS WE HEARD.
INDANS COMING! WE ARE DOOMED.

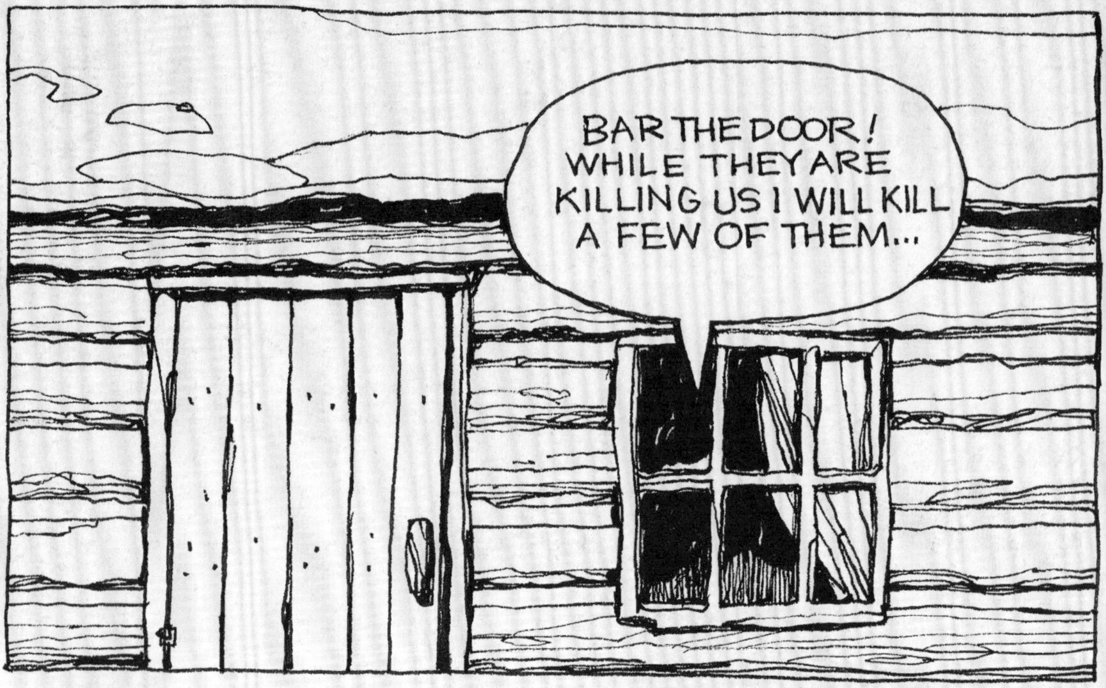
BAR THE DOOR! WHILE THEY ARE KILLING US I WILL KILL A FEW OF THEM...

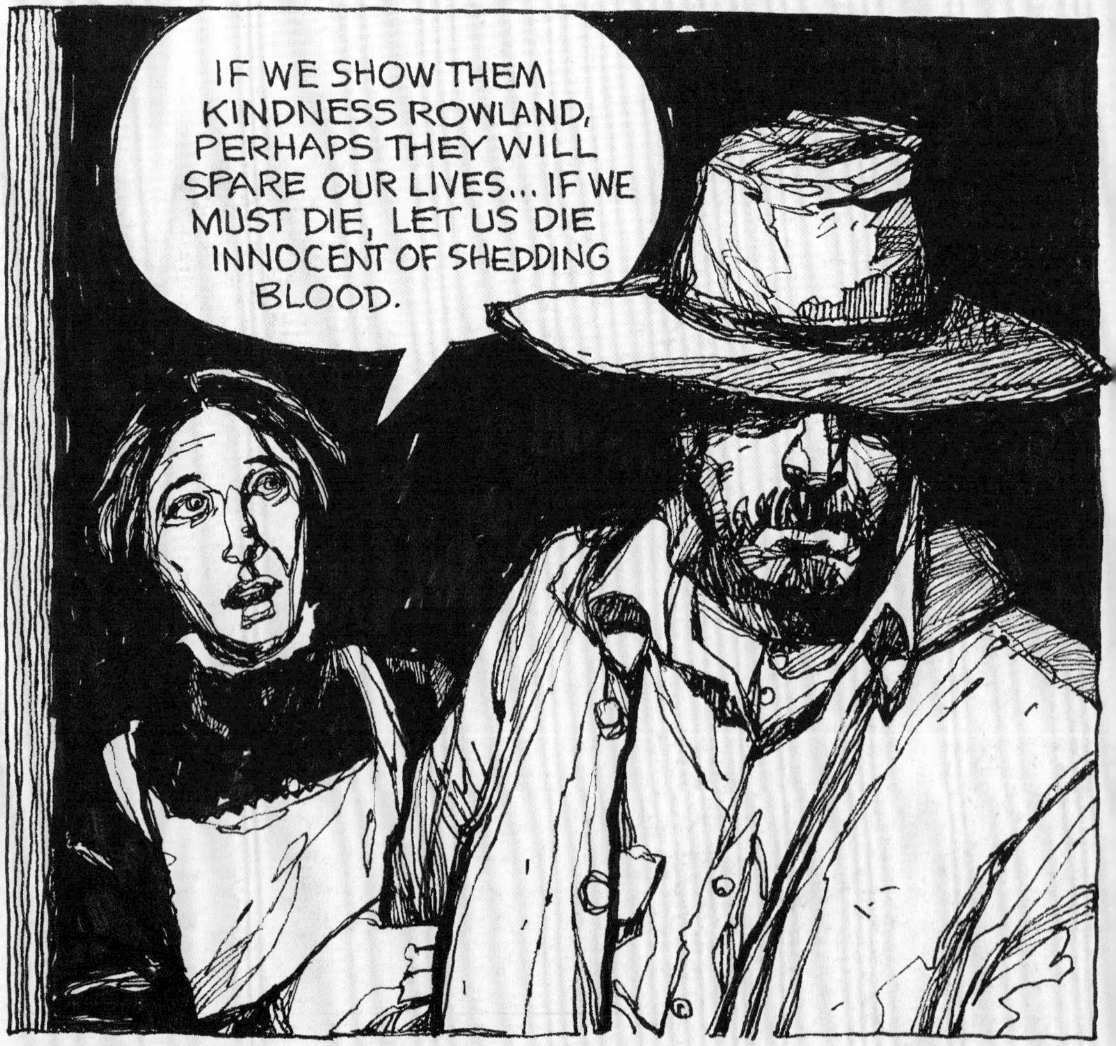
IF WE SHOW THEM KINDNESS ROWLAND, PERHAPS THEY WILL SPARE OUR LIVES... IF WE MUST DIE, LET US DIE INNOCENT OF SHEDDING BLOOD.

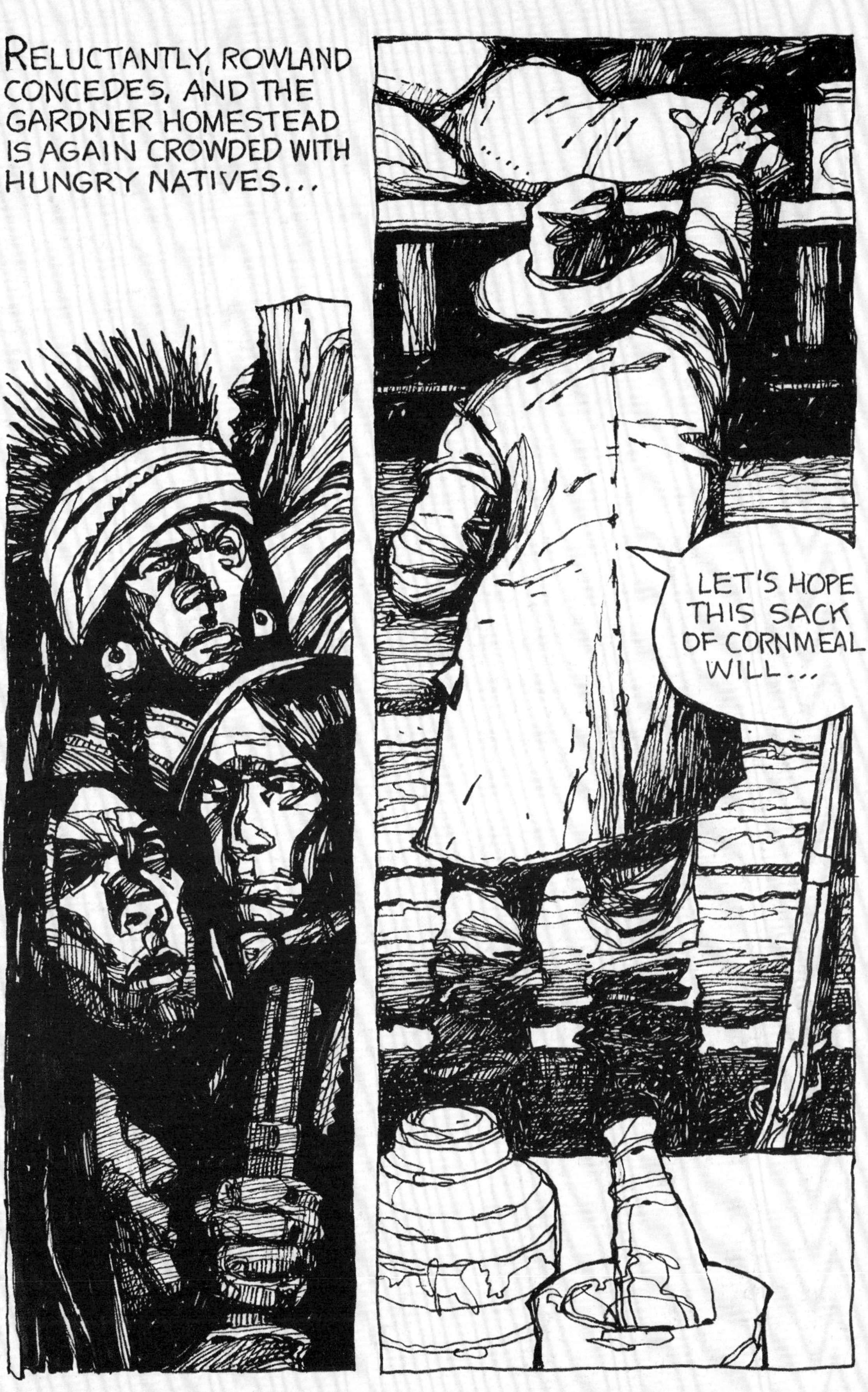
RELUCTANTLY, ROWLAND CONCEDES, AND THE GARDNER HOMESTEAD IS AGAIN CROWDED WITH HUNGRY NATIVES...
LET'S HOPE THIS SACK OF CORNMEAL WILL...

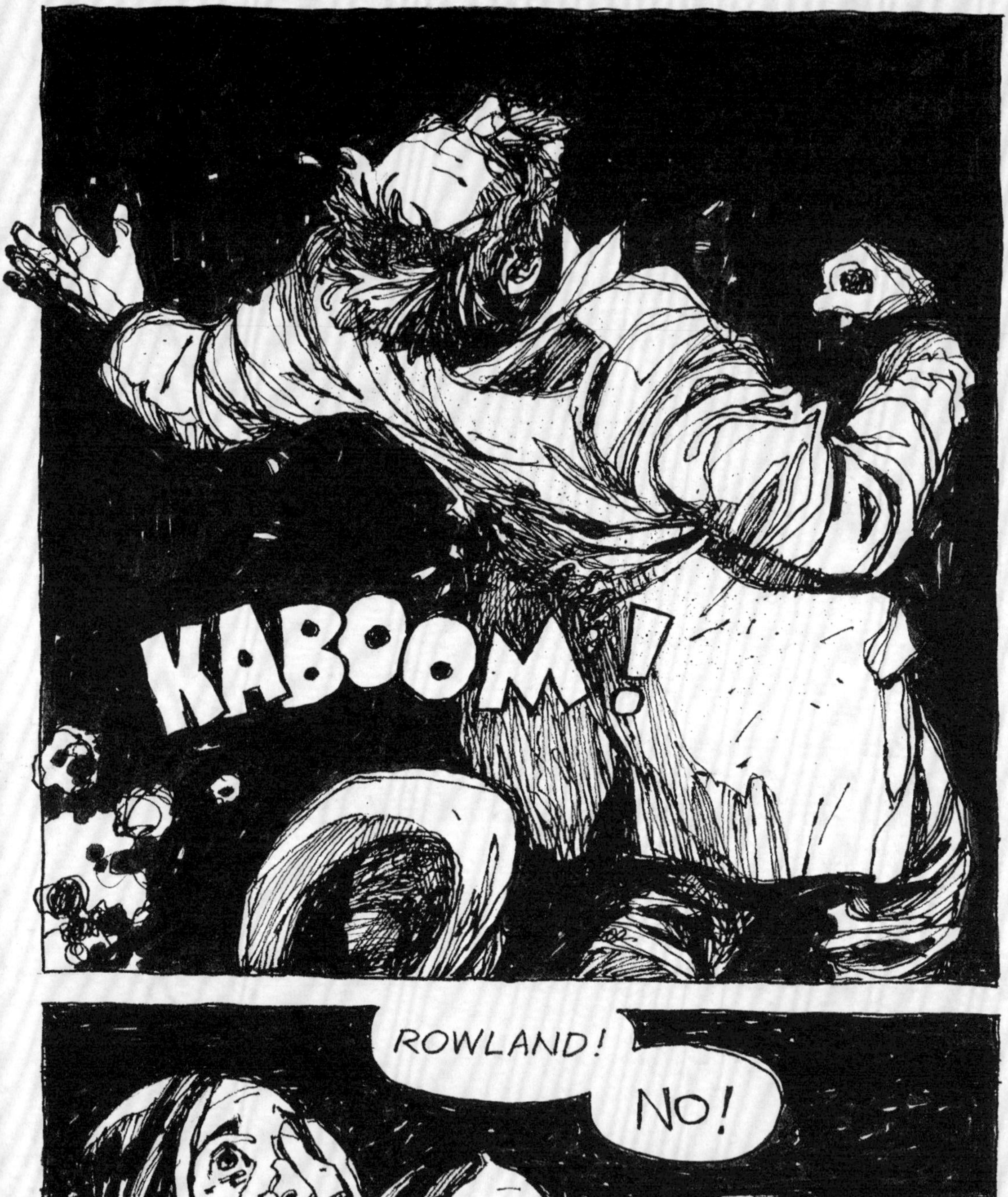
KABOOM!

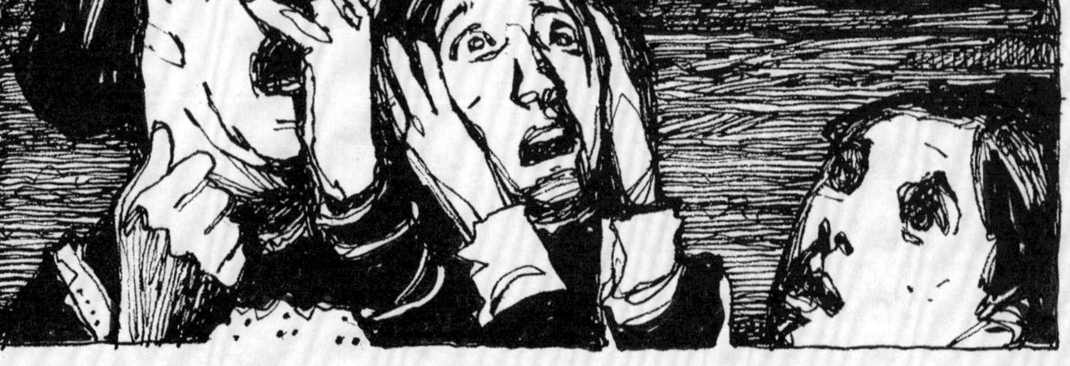
ROWLAND!
NO!

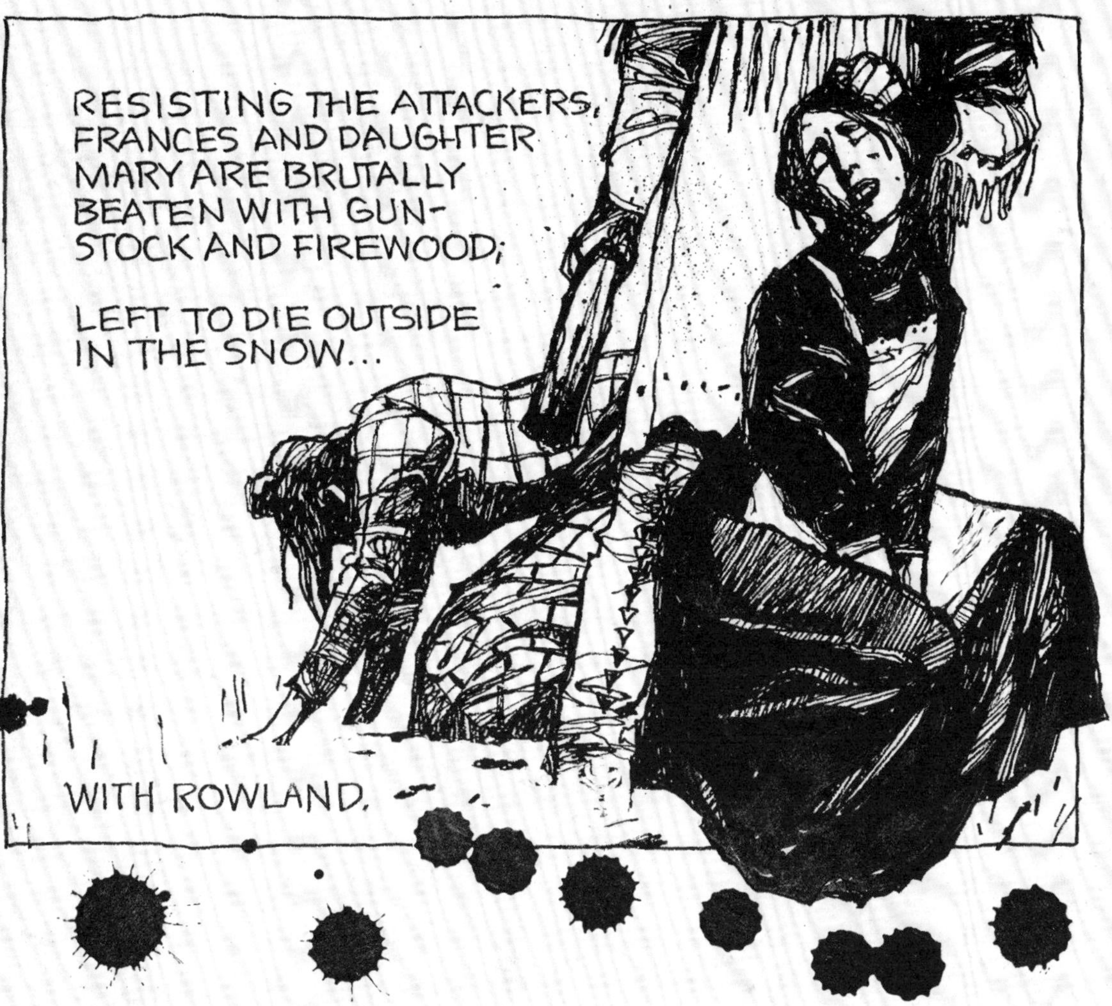
RESISTING THE ATTACKERS, FRANCES AND DAUGHTER MARY ARE BRUTALLY BEATEN WITH GUN-STOCK AND FIREWOOD;
LEFT TO DIE OUTSIDE IN THE SNOW...
WITH ROWLAND.

MEANWHILE, ABBIE IS GATHERING THE TRAUMATIZED CHILDREN TOGETHER IN A DARK CORNER OF THEIR RANSACKED CABIN.

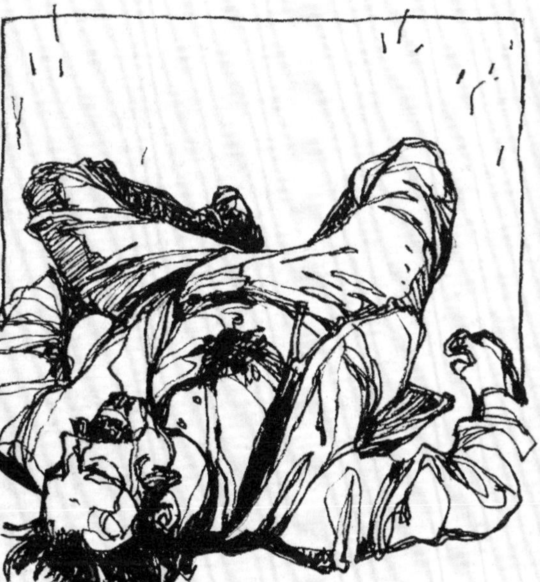

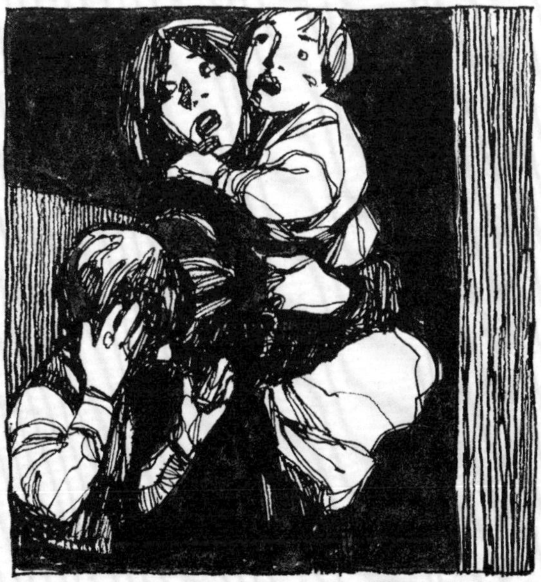

THE DAKOTAS TURN THEIR ATTENTION TO THE FOUR REMAINING SURVIVORS HUDDLED IN THE SHADOWS. THE CHILDREN ARE RIPPED FROM ABBIE'S ARMS AND TAKEN OUTSIDE, TO SUFFER THE SAME FATE AS THEIR MOTHERS.

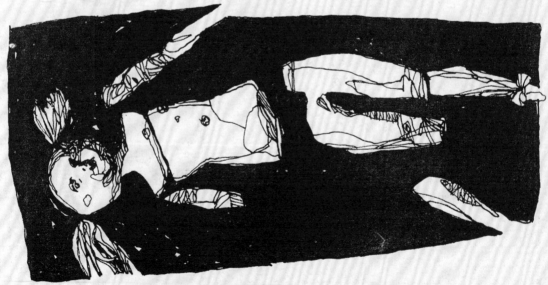

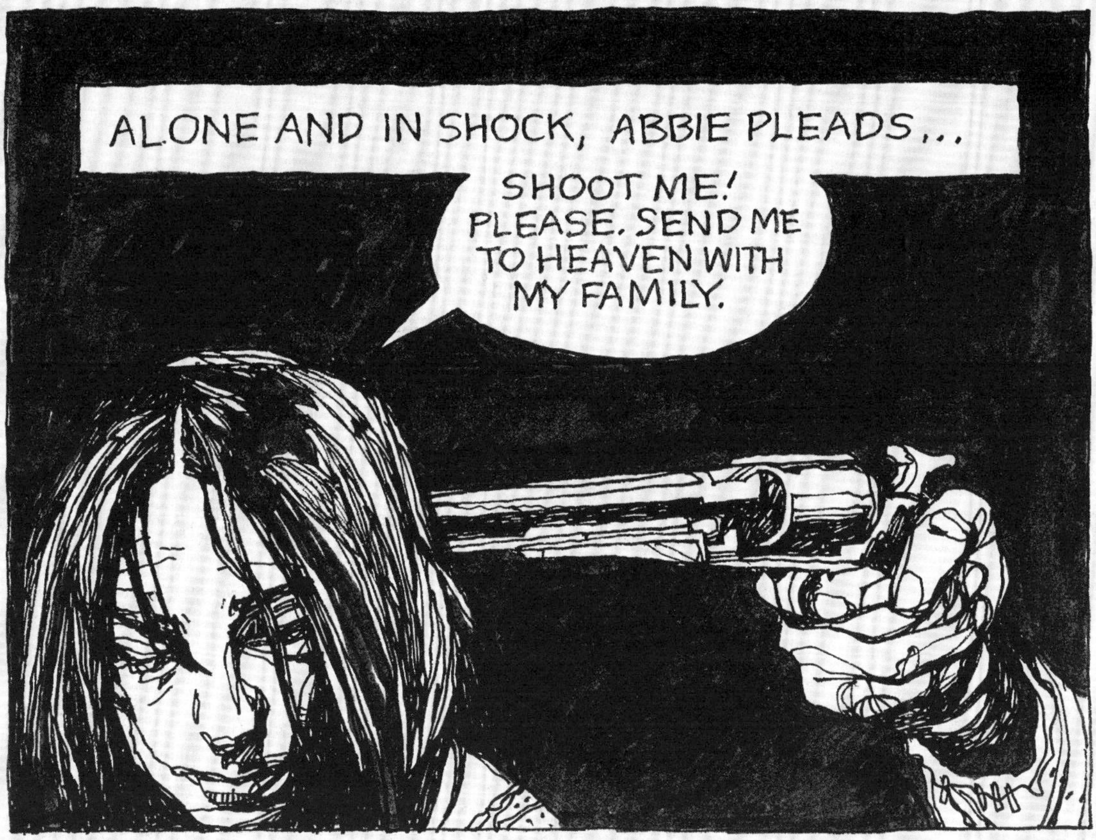
ALONE AND IN SHOCK, ABBIE PLEADS...
SHOOT ME! PLEASE. SEND ME TO HEAVEN WITH MY FAMILY.

BUT NO. SHE IS DRAGGED OUT THE DOOR AND INTO THE NIGHT. PAST THE CORPSES OF HER NIECE AMANDA AND NEPHEW ALBERT, HER SISTER MARY AND BROTHER ROWLAND JR. PAST HER FATHER ROWLAND, AND PAST A BATTERED ANGEL IN THE SNOW... HER DEAR MOTHER, FRANCES.

IN ABBIE'S WORDS, THE VICTIM OF "A SAVAGE MONSTER IN HUMAN FORM, FITTED FOR THE DARKEST CORNER OF HELL."

INKPADUTA...

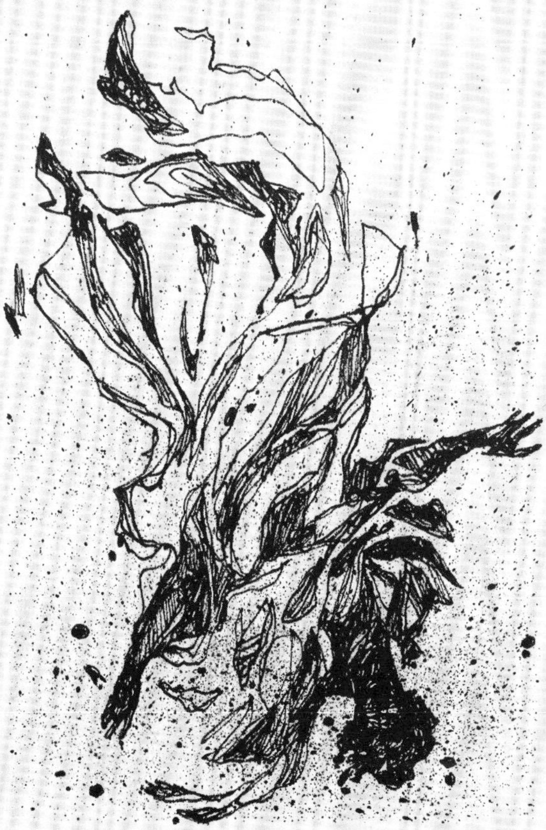

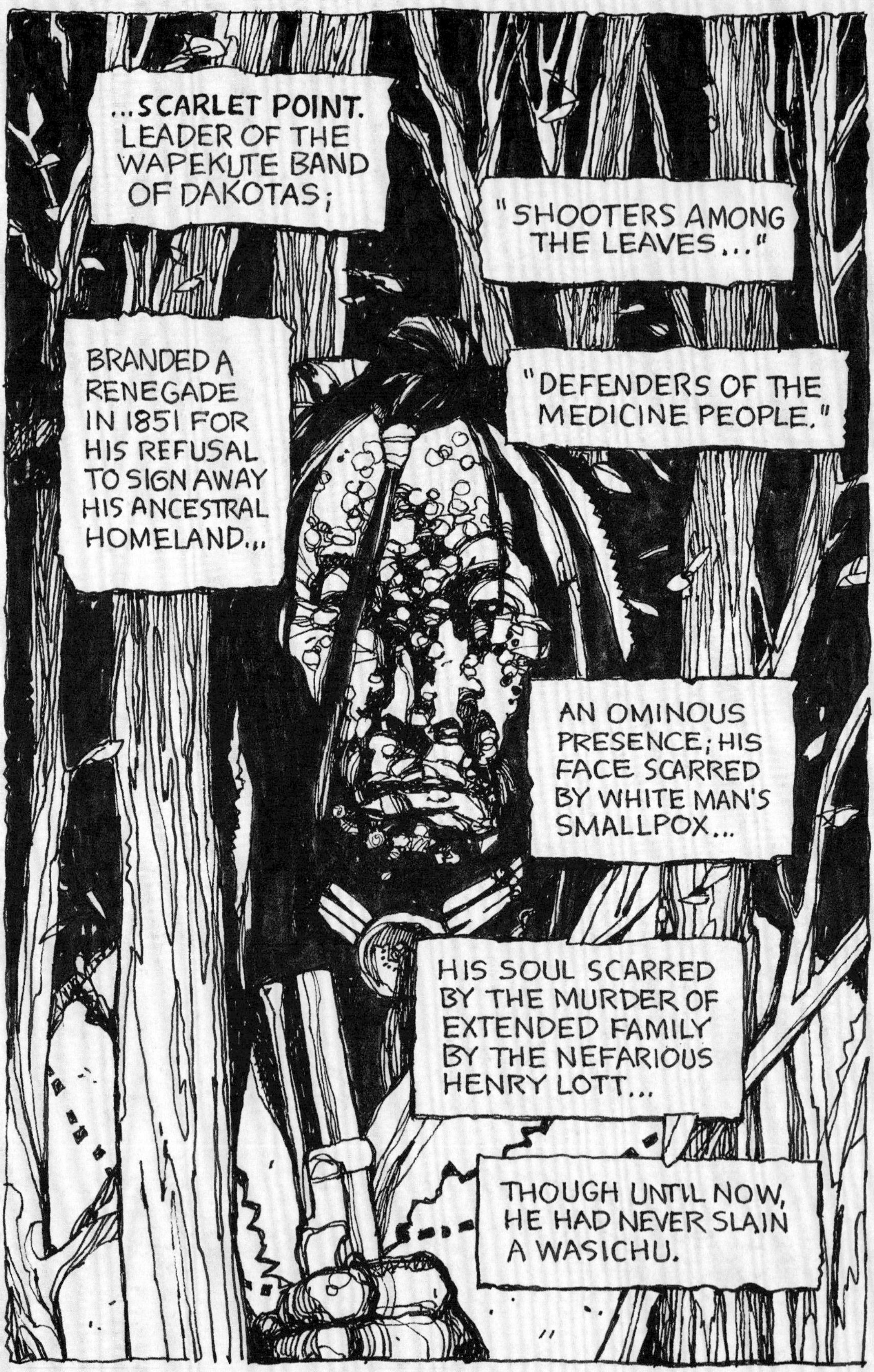
...SCARLET POINT. LEADER OF THE WAPEKUTE BAND OF DAKOTAS;
"SHOOTERS AMONG THE LEAVES..."
BRANDED A RENEGADE IN 1851 FOR HIS REFUSAL TO SIGN AWAY HIS ANCESTRAL HOMELAND...
"DEFENDERS OF THE MEDICINE PEOPLE."
AN OMINOUS PRESENCE; HIS FACE SCARRED BY WHITE MAN'S SMALLPOX...
HIS SOUL SCARRED BY THE MURDER OF EXTENDED FAMILY BY THE NEFARIOUS HENRY LOTT...
THOUGH UNTIL NOW, HE HAD NEVER SLAIN A WASICHU.

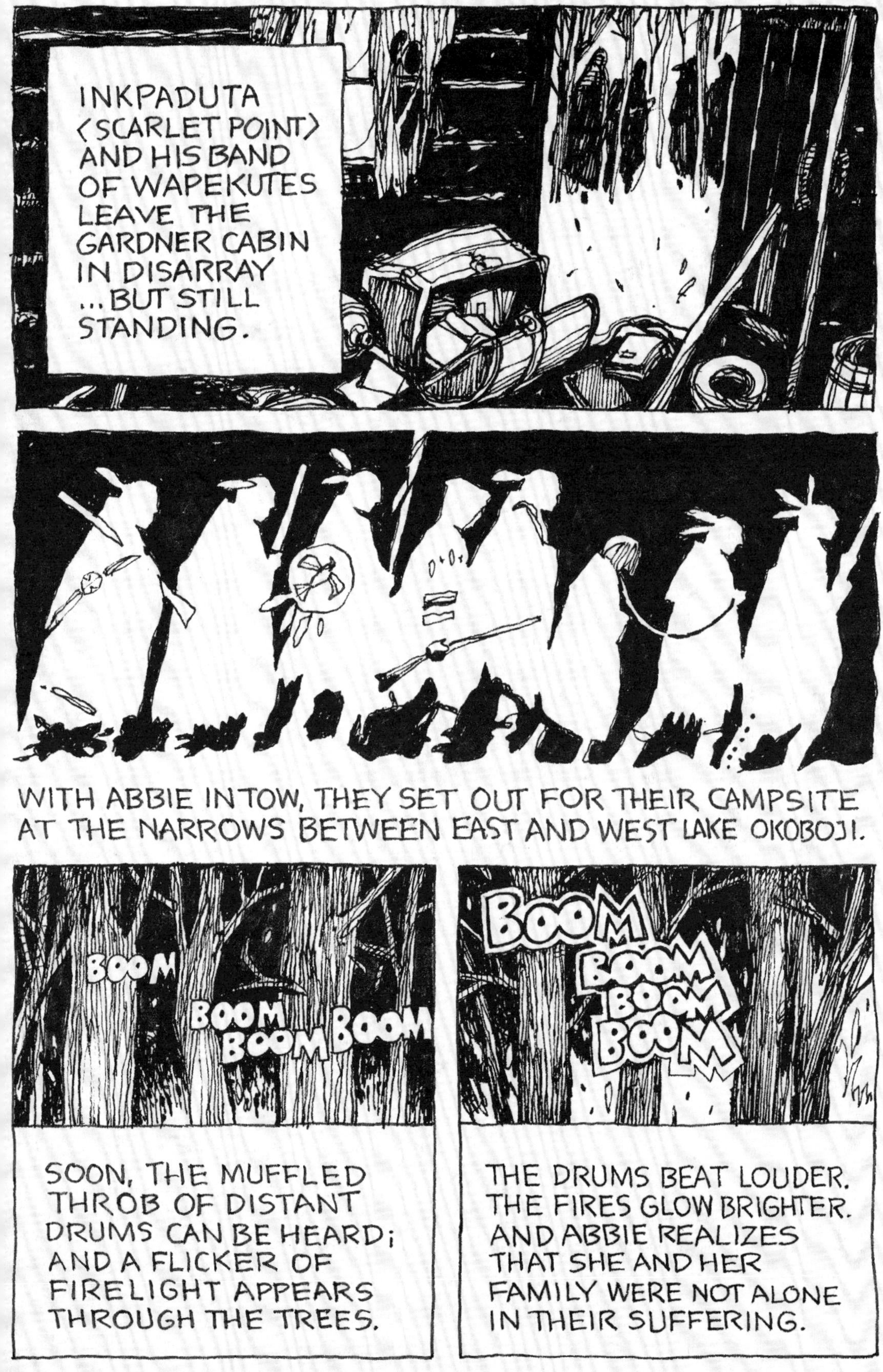
INKPADUTA (SCARLET POINT) AND HIS BAND OF WAPEKUTES LEAVE THE GARDNER CABIN IN DISARRAY ...BUT STILL STANDING.
WITH ABBIE IN TOW, THEY SET OUT FOR THEIR CAMPSITE AT THE NARROWS BETWEEN EAST AND WEST LAKE OKOBOJI.
BOOM
BOOM
BOOM
BOOM
SOON, THE MUFFLED THROB OF DISTANT DRUMS CAN BE HEARD; AND A FLICKER OF FIRELIGHT APPEARS THROUGH THE TREES.
BOOM
BOOM
BOOM
BOOM
THE DRUMS BEAT LOUDER. THE FIRES GLOW BRIGHTER. AND ABBIE REALIZES THAT SHE AND HER FAMILY WERE NOT ALONE IN THEIR SUFFERING.

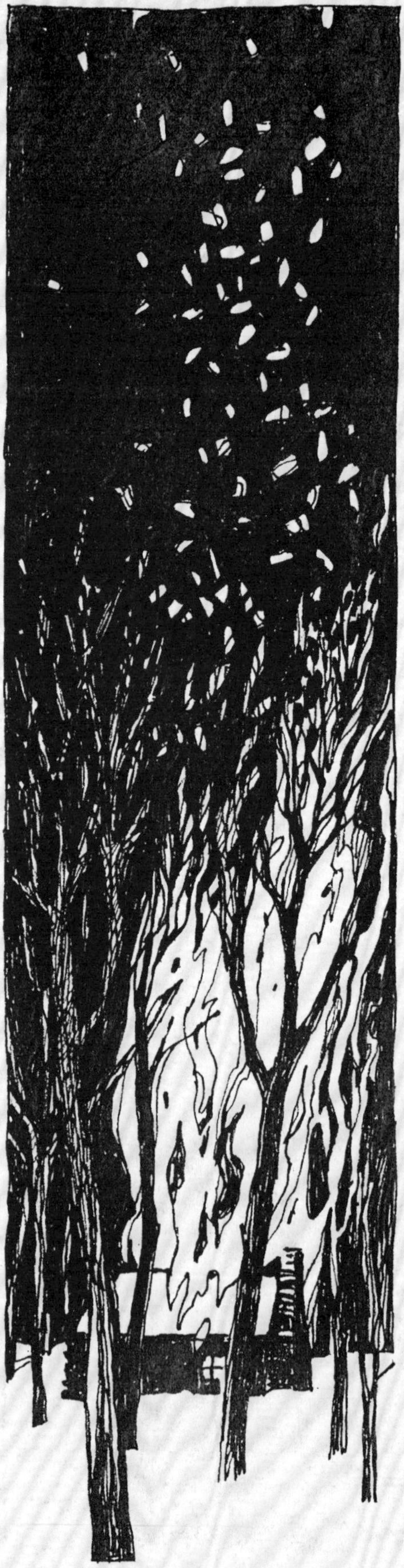

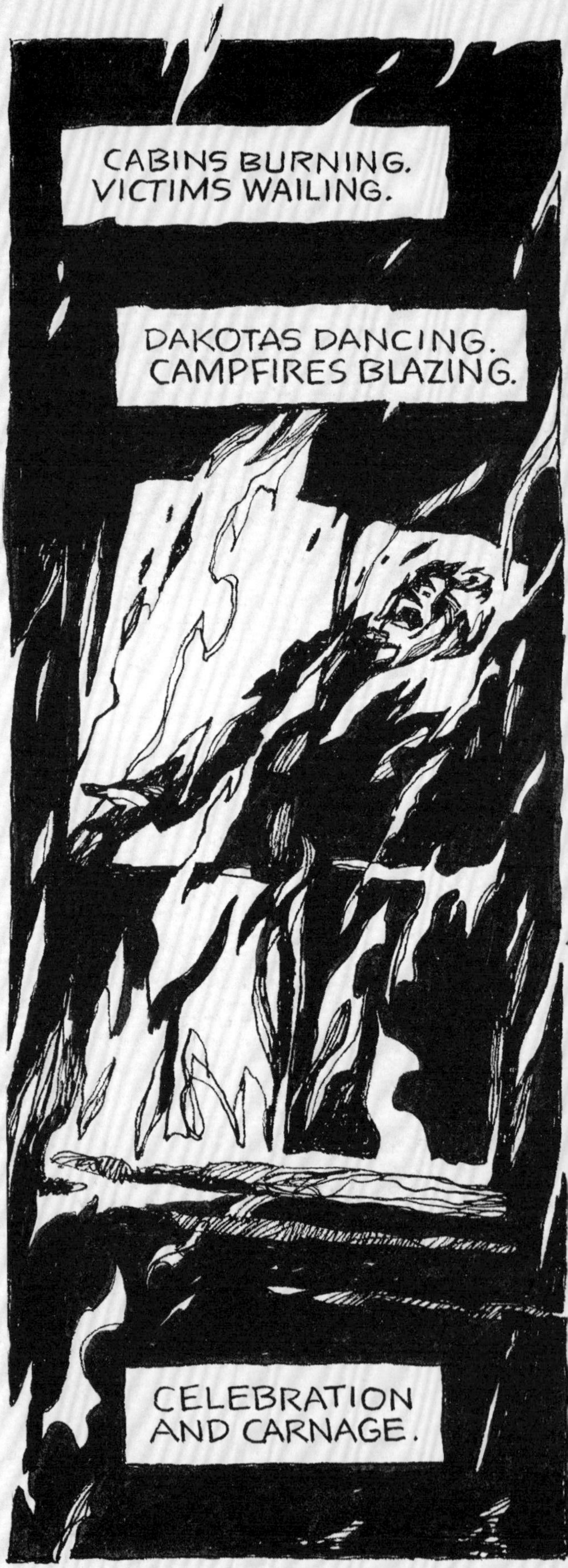
CABINS BURNING.
VICTIMS WAILING.
DAKOTAS DANCING.
CAMPFIRES BLAZING.
CELEBRATION
AND CARNAGE.

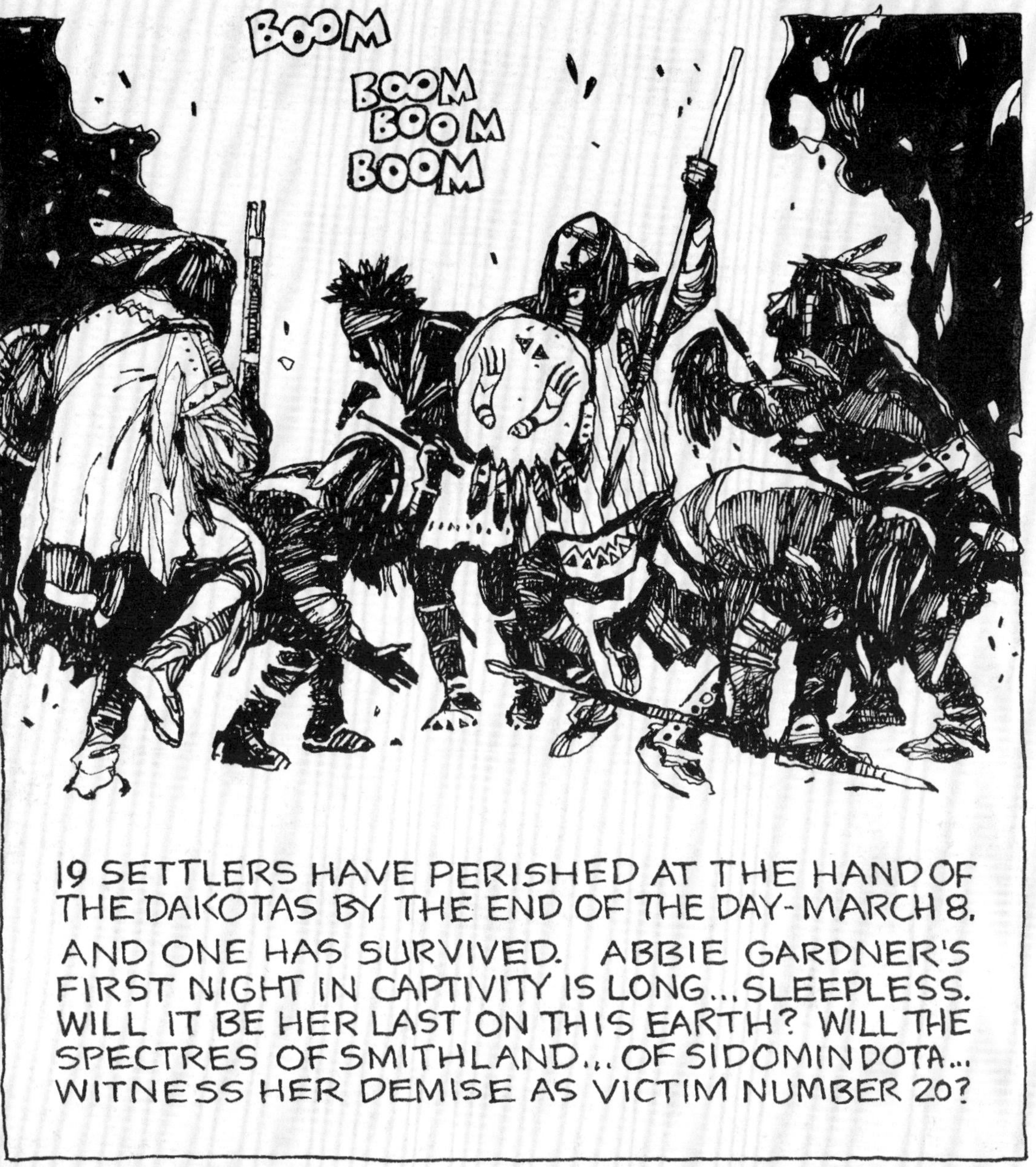
BOOM
BOOM
BOOM
BOOM
19 SETTLERS HAVE PERISHED AT THE HAND OF THE DAKOTAS BY THE END OF THE DAY - MARCH 8.
AND ONE HAS SURVIVED. ABBIE GARDNER'S FIRST NIGHT IN CAPTIVITY IS LONG... SLEEPLESS. WILL IT BE HER LAST ON THIS EARTH? WILL THE SPECTRES OF SMITHLAND... OF SIDOMINDOTA... WITNESS HER DEMISE AS VICTIM NUMBER 20?

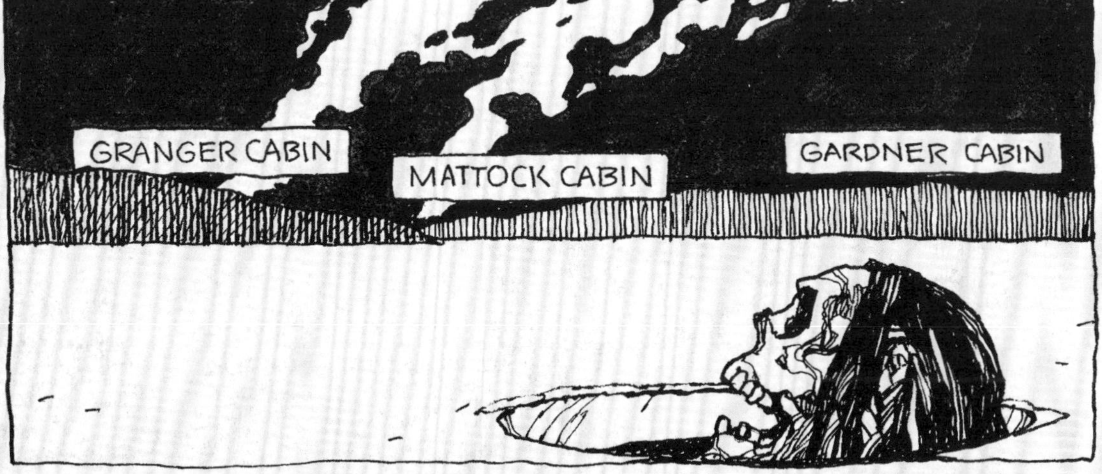
GRANGER CABIN
MATTOCK CABIN
GARDNER CABIN

DESPITE A GRIM NIGHT OF GLOOM, OF DOOM, THE SUN STILL RISES COME MORNING, CASTING ITS LIGHT ACROSS THE FROZEN LAKES, THE SMOLDERING REMAINS OF CABINS, AND THEIR ILL-FATED OCCUPANTS.

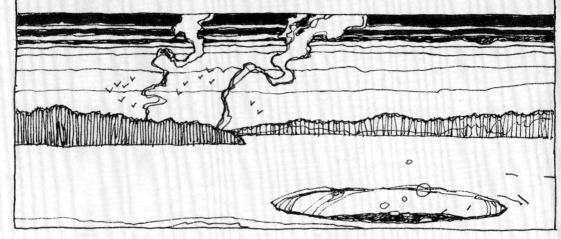

ABBIE WATCHES WARRIORS PAINTED BLACK DEPART INKPADUTA'S CAMP FOR THE OPPOSITE SHORE OF EAST OKOBOJI...THE HOMESTEADS OF THE HOWE AND THATCHER FAMILIES.

THEY ENCOUNTER JOEL HOWE ON HIS WAY TO GRANGER'S CABIN, UNAWARE OF THE MASSACRE. HE'S SHOT DEAD IN HIS TRACKS,...

HIS CORPSE MUTILATED.

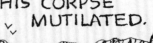

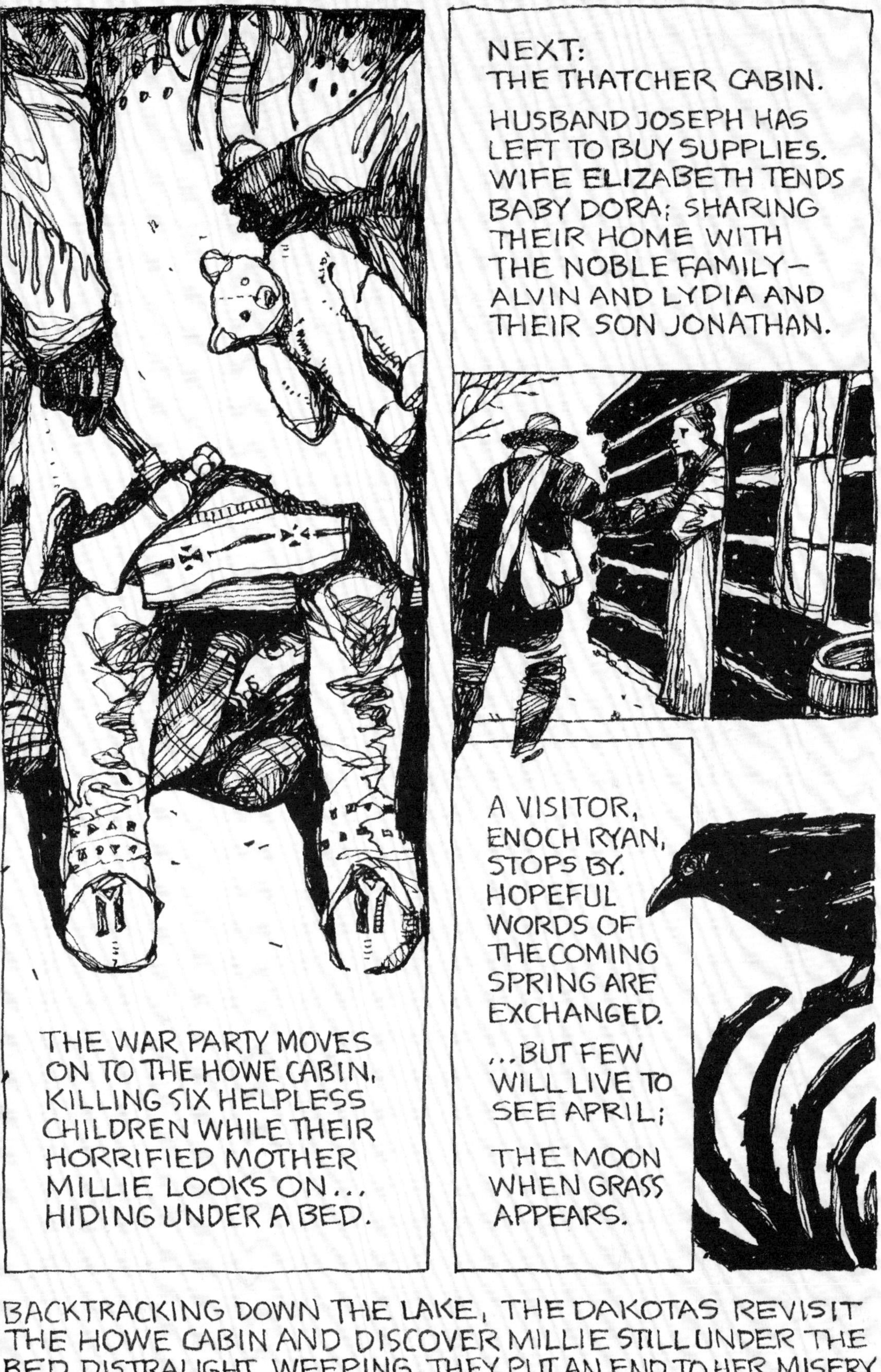
THE WAR PARTY MOVES ON TO THE HOWE CABIN, KILLING SIX HELPLESS CHILDREN WHILE THEIR HORRIFIED MOTHER MILLIE LOOKS ON... HIDING UNDER A BED.
NEXT: THE THATCHER CABIN.
HUSBAND JOSEPH HAS LEFT TO BUY SUPPLIES. WIFE ELIZABETH TENDS BABY DORA; SHARING THEIR HOME WITH THE NOBLE FAMILY— ALVIN AND LYDIA AND THEIR SON JONATHAN.
A VISITOR, ENOCH RYAN, STOPS BY. HOPEFUL WORDS OF THE COMING SPRING ARE EXCHANGED.
...BUT FEW WILL LIVE TO SEE APRIL;
THE MOON WHEN GRASS APPEARS.

BACKTRACKING DOWN THE LAKE, THE DAKOTAS REVISIT THE HOWE CABIN AND DISCOVER MILLIE STILL UNDER THE BED, DISTRAUGHT, WEEPING. THEY PUT AN END TO HER MISERY.

DUSK FOLLOWS THE BLACKENED WARRIORS AS THEY RETRACE THE SHORELINE, BACK TO THEIR ENCAMPMENT... WITH THEM, A PAIR OF TRAUMATIZED HOSTAGES; ELIZABETH THATCHER AND LYDIA NOBLE.

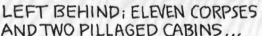

LEFT BEHIND; ELEVEN CORPSES AND TWO PILLAGED CABINS...

UPON ARRIVAL, THE WOMEN ARE JOINED WITH ABBIE. ALL THREE ARE FORCED TO BRAID THEIR HAIR AND PAINT THEIR FACES IN THE DAKOTA WAY...THEN DISPATCHED TO SEPARATE LODGES OVERNIGHT.

<I PRAY, THE MORE DISTANCE WE MAKE BETWEEN THE WASICHU AND THE WAPEKUTE, THE MORE LIKELY ARE WE TO ONCE AGAIN BECOME ONE WITH THE ELK ...WITH THE BISON.>

TUESDAY MORNING, 10 MARCH. INKPADUTA'S PEOPLE HAVE PULLED DOWN THEIR TIPIS, AND WITH THEIR CAPTIVES, SET OUT ACROSS THE FROZEN WEST LAKE OKOBOJI.

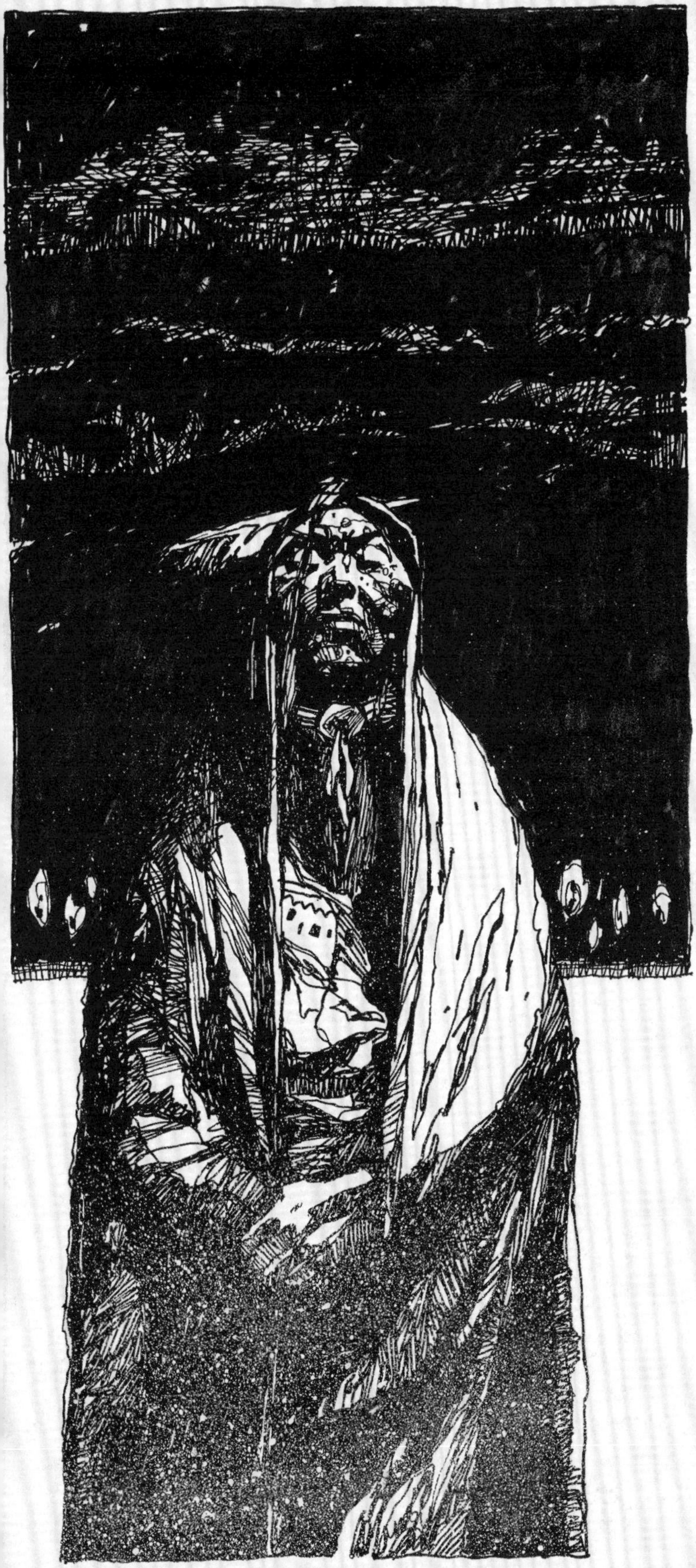

NIGHTFALL.

DAKOTA CAMPFIRES FLICKER AMONG THE TREES ON THE NORTH SHORE.

ALONE ON THE LAKE, INKPADUTA PONDERS THIS ANGRY WINTER... THESE DIFFICULT TIMES.

A FAMILIAR VOICE EMERGES FROM THE ICY FOG. A VISION... WITH AN OMINOUS MESSAGE FROM MNI SOTA MAKOCE... FROM THE PROPHET UNKTEHI.

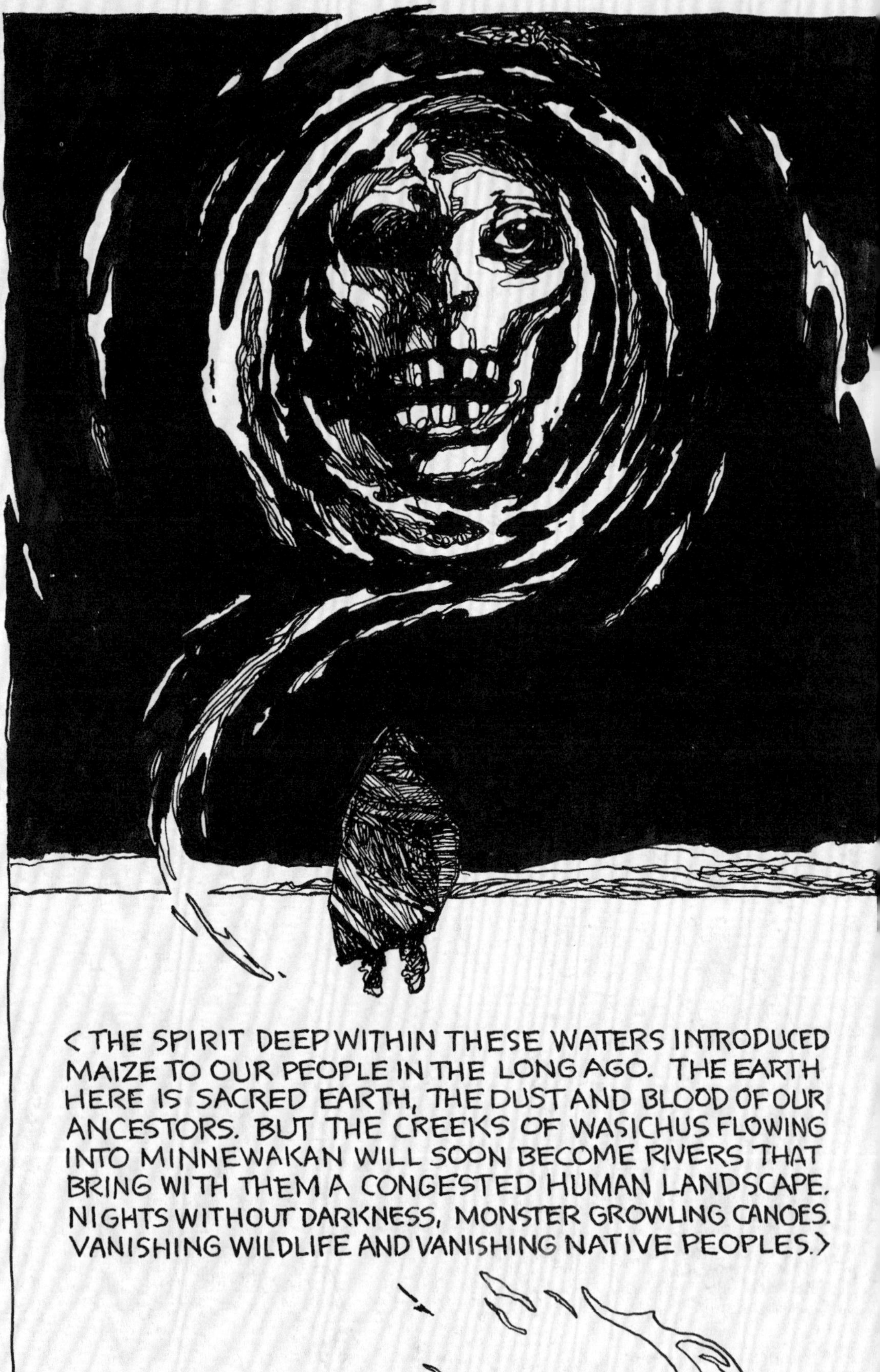
< THE SPIRIT DEEP WITHIN THESE WATERS INTRODUCED MAIZE TO OUR PEOPLE IN THE LONG AGO. THE EARTH HERE IS SACRED EARTH, THE DUST AND BLOOD OF OUR ANCESTORS. BUT THE CREEKS OF WASICHUS FLOWING INTO MINNEWAKAN WILL SOON BECOME RIVERS THAT BRING WITH THEM A CONGESTED HUMAN LANDSCAPE. NIGHTS WITHOUT DARKNESS, MONSTER GROWLING CANOES. VANISHING WILDLIFE AND VANISHING NATIVE PEOPLES.>

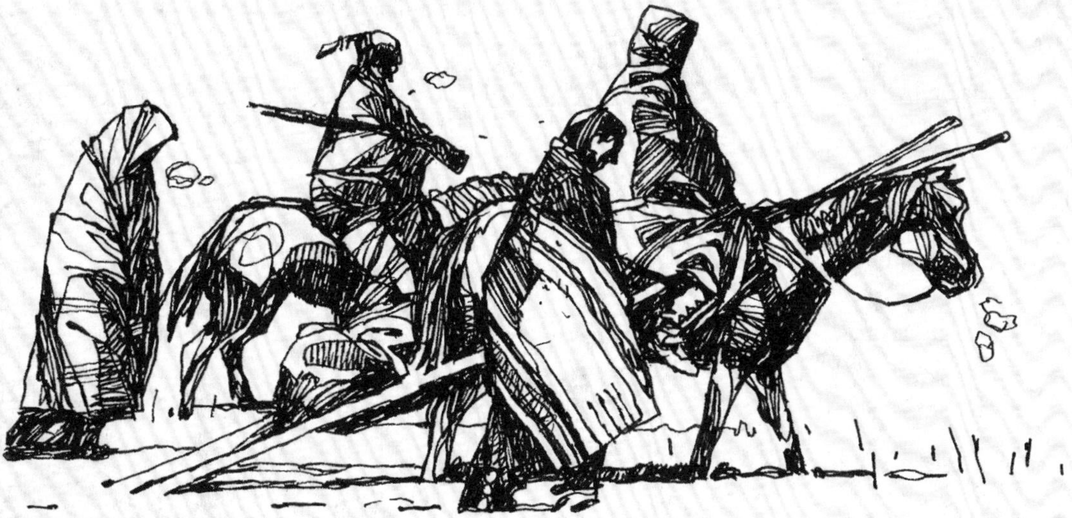

WEDNESDAY, MARCH 11. THE WAPEKUTES ARE AGAIN ON THE MOVE, NORTH TOWARD MINNESOTA. COME LATE AFTERNOON, THEY MAKE CAMP IN A STAND OF TIMBER, JUST TO THE WEST OF SPIRIT LAKE.

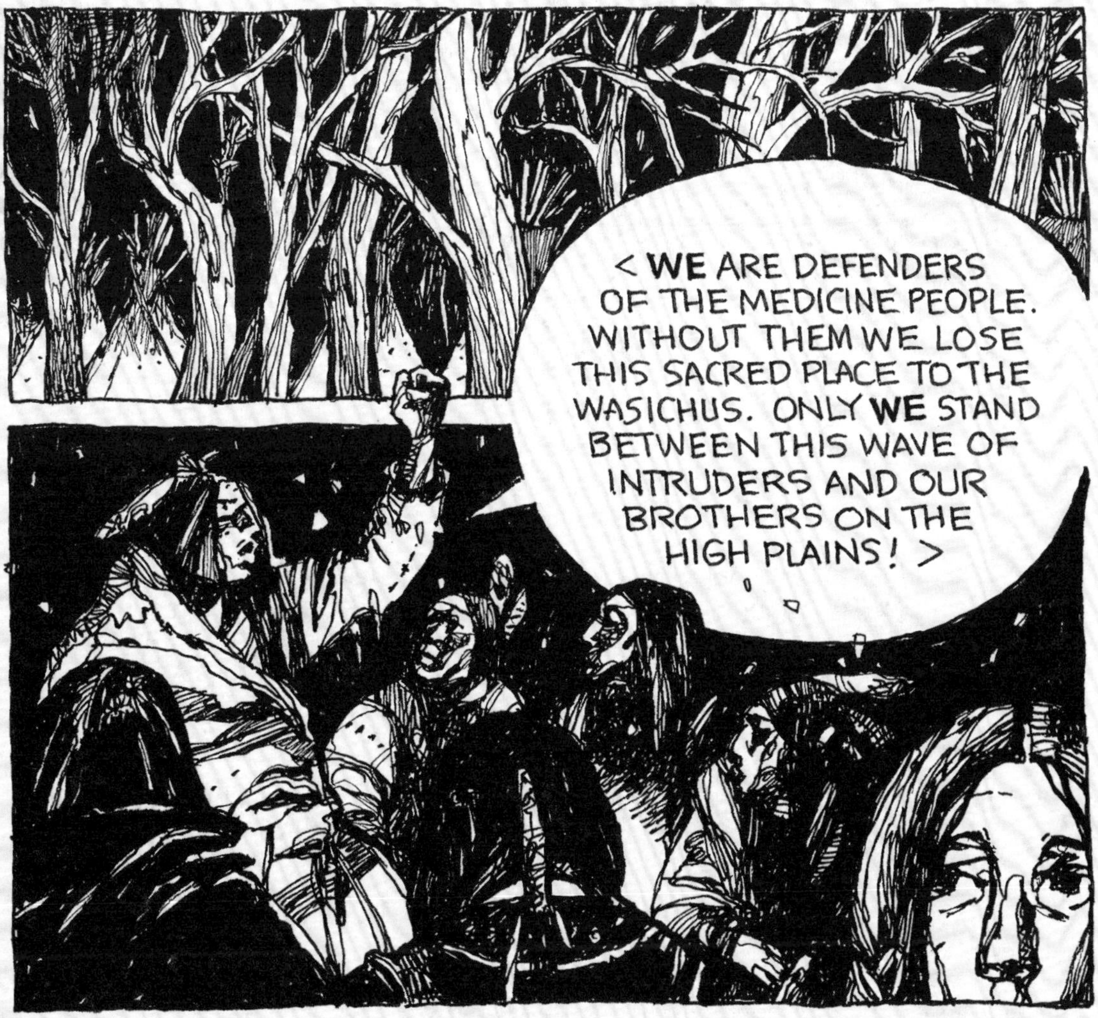
< **WE** ARE DEFENDERS OF THE MEDICINE PEOPLE. WITHOUT THEM WE LOSE THIS SACRED PLACE TO THE WASICHUS. ONLY **WE** STAND BETWEEN THIS WAVE OF INTRUDERS AND OUR BROTHERS ON THE HIGH PLAINS! >

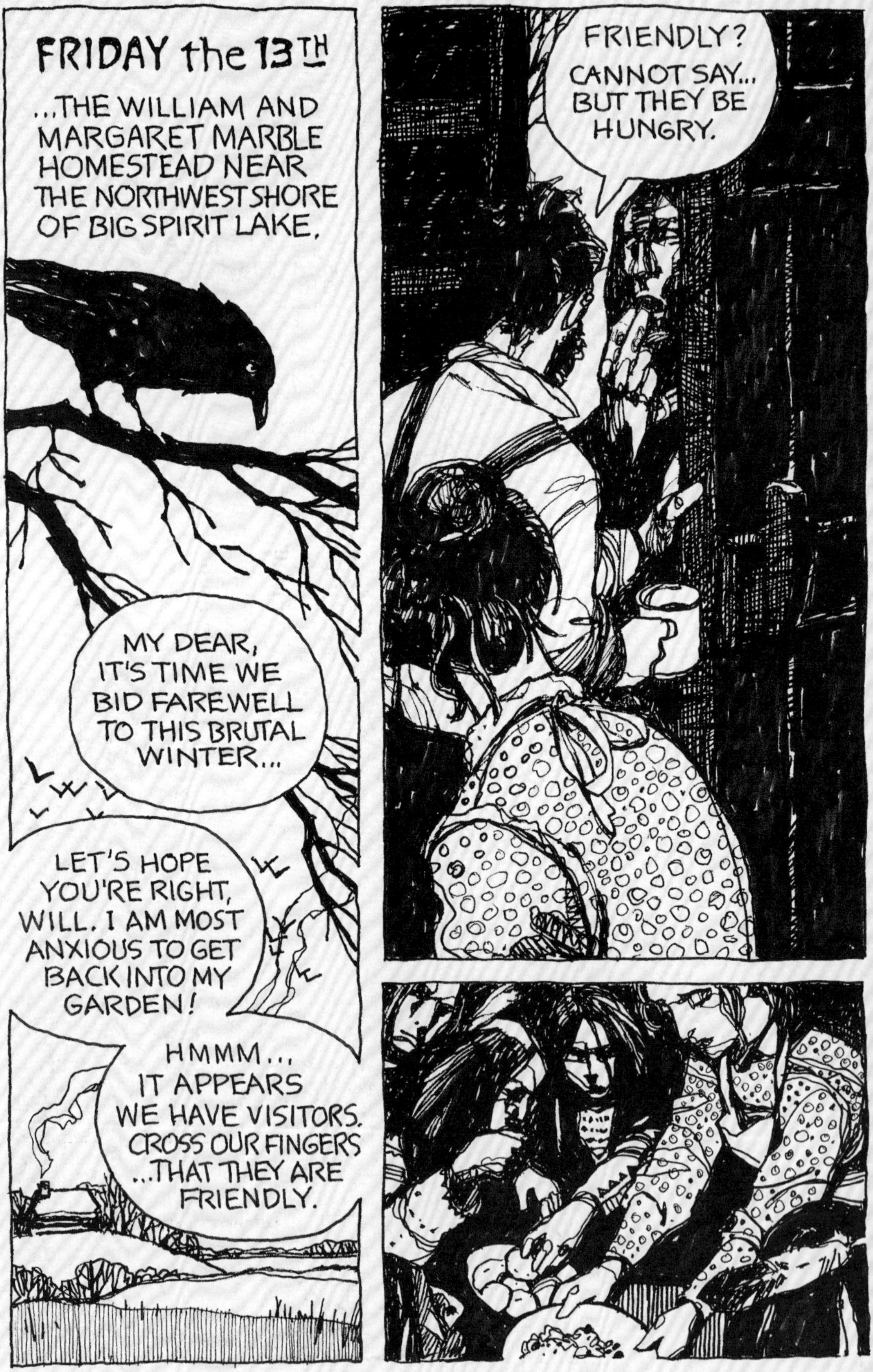
FRIDAY the 13TH
...THE WILLIAM AND MARGARET MARBLE HOMESTEAD NEAR THE NORTHWEST SHORE OF BIG SPIRIT LAKE.
MY DEAR, IT'S TIME WE BID FAREWELL TO THIS BRUTAL WINTER...
LET'S HOPE YOU'RE RIGHT, WILL. I AM MOST ANXIOUS TO GET BACK INTO MY GARDEN!
HMMM..., IT APPEARS WE HAVE VISITORS. CROSS OUR FINGERS ...THAT THEY ARE FRIENDLY.
FRIENDLY? CANNOT SAY... BUT THEY BE HUNGRY.

HAVING SATISFIED THEIR HUNGER, THE VISITORS PROPOSE A SHOOTING CONTEST.

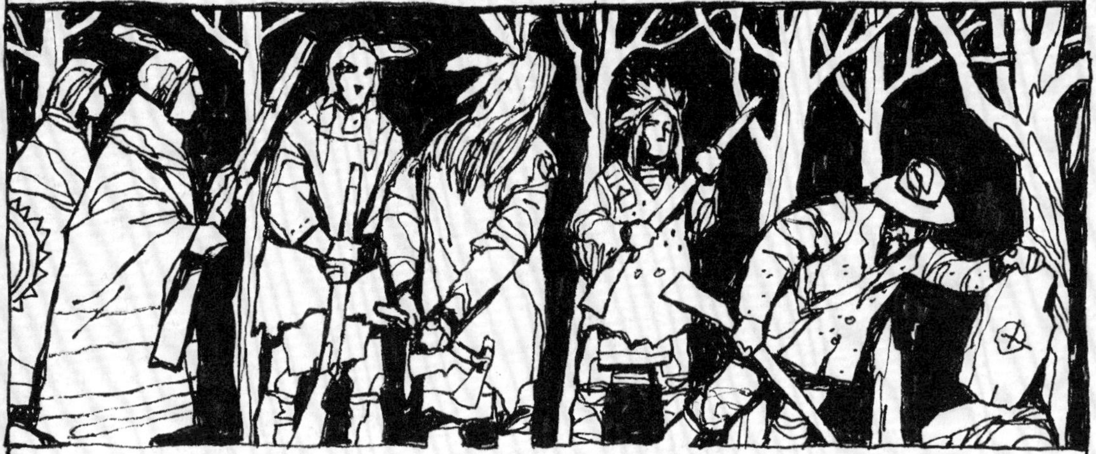

WITH HIS WIFE WATCHING NERVOUSLY FROM THEIR CABIN, WILLIAM IMPROVISES A TARGET.

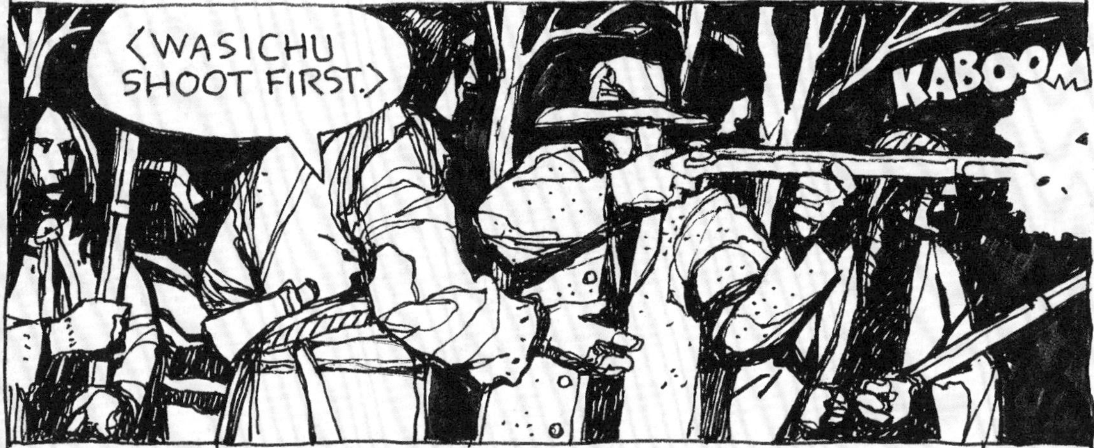
<WASICHU SHOOT FIRST.>
KABOOM

HIS LONG GUN EMPTY AFTER SHOOTING DOWN THE TARGET, HE MOVES TO RESET...

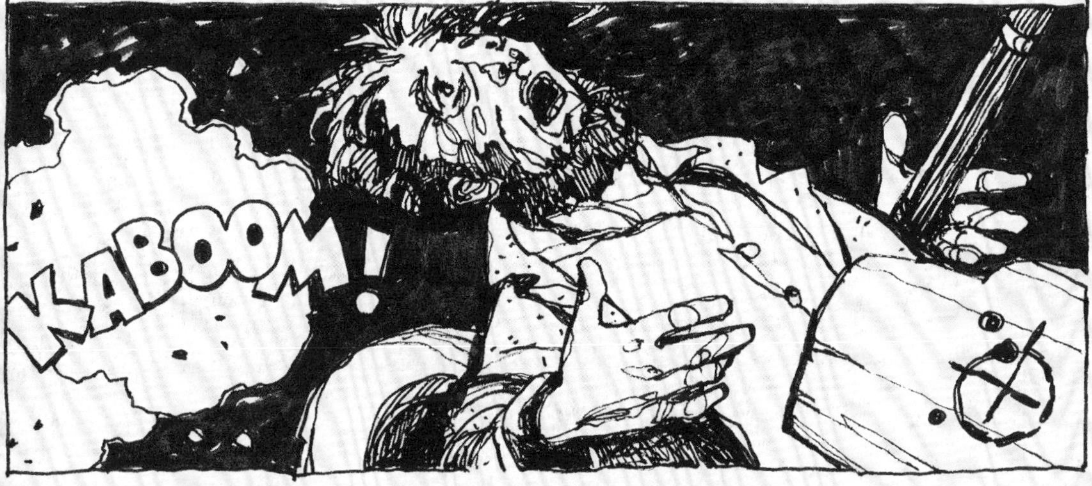
KABOOM!

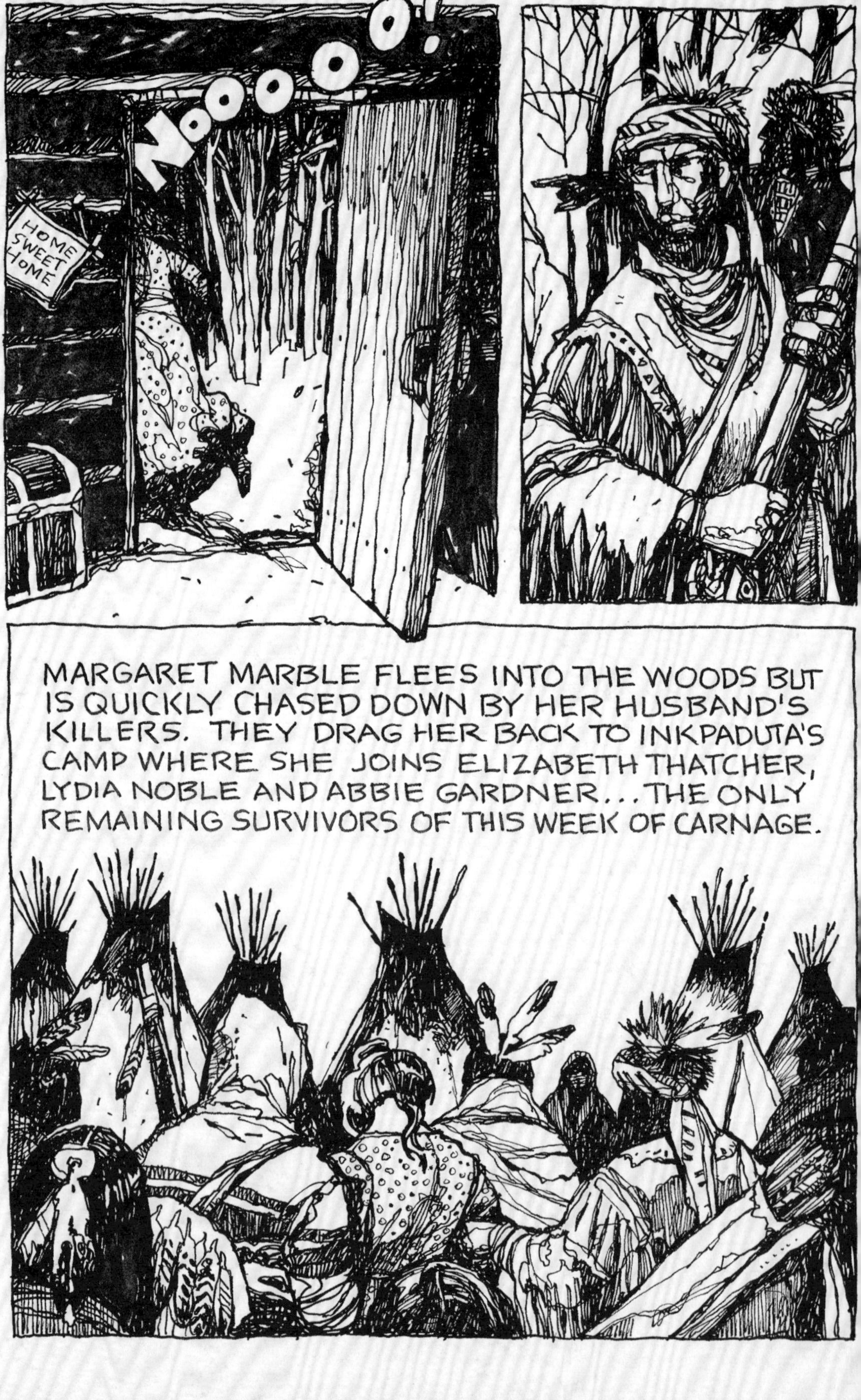
NOOOOOO!
HOME SWEET HOME
MARGARET MARBLE FLEES INTO THE WOODS BUT IS QUICKLY CHASED DOWN BY HER HUSBAND'S KILLERS. THEY DRAG HER BACK TO INKPADUTA'S CAMP WHERE SHE JOINS ELIZABETH THATCHER, LYDIA NOBLE AND ABBIE GARDNER... THE ONLY REMAINING SURVIVORS OF THIS WEEK OF CARNAGE.

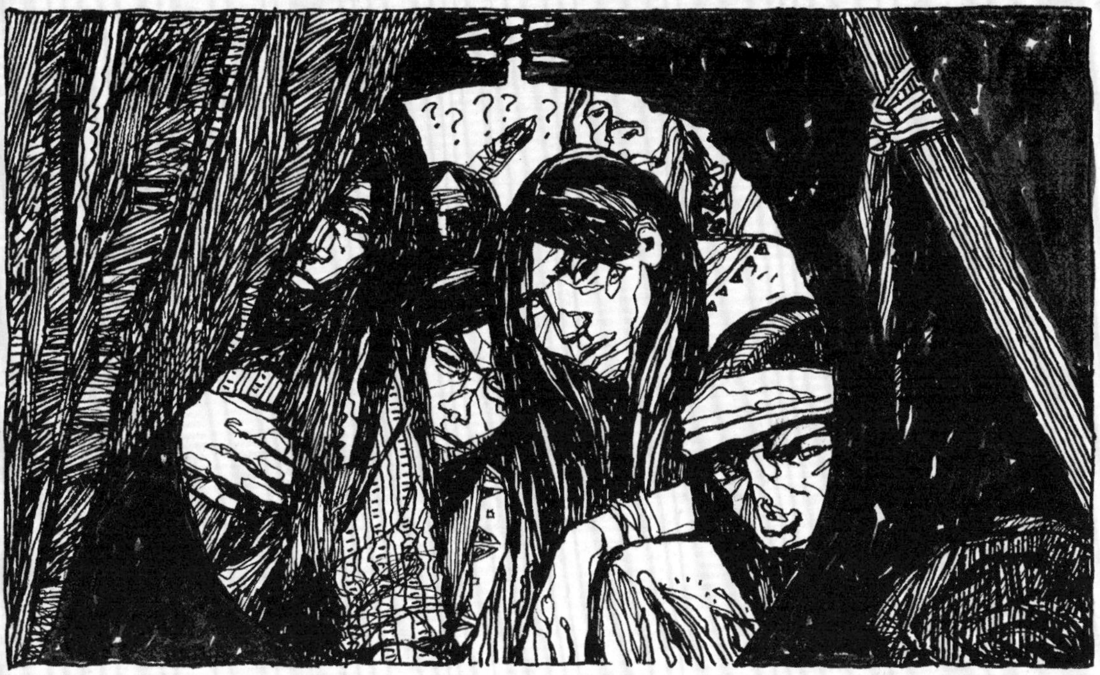
?????

HUDDLED TOGETHER IN A TIPI, THE PALE-FACED WOMEN ARE A CURIOSITY TO THEIR CAPTORS.

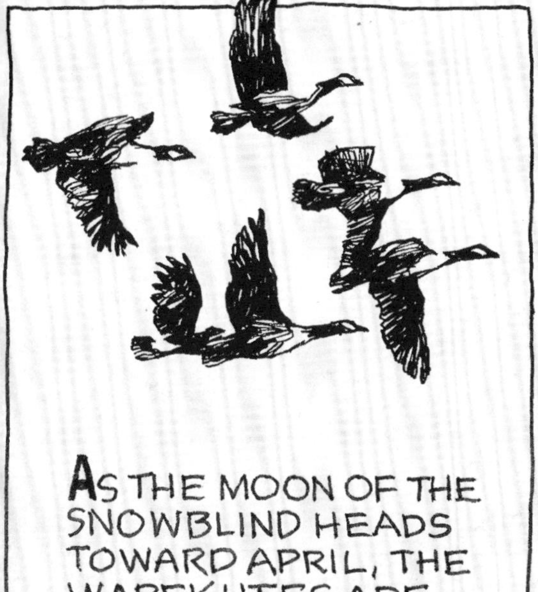
AS THE MOON OF THE SNOWBLIND HEADS TOWARD APRIL, THE WAPEKUTES ARE HEADING NORTH, TO MINNESOTA; WHILE 'REPORTS' FOLLOWING THE MASSACRE HAVE THE ENTIRE REGION ON EDGE...

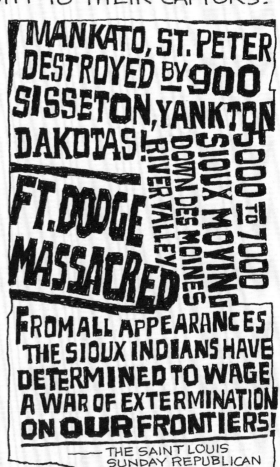

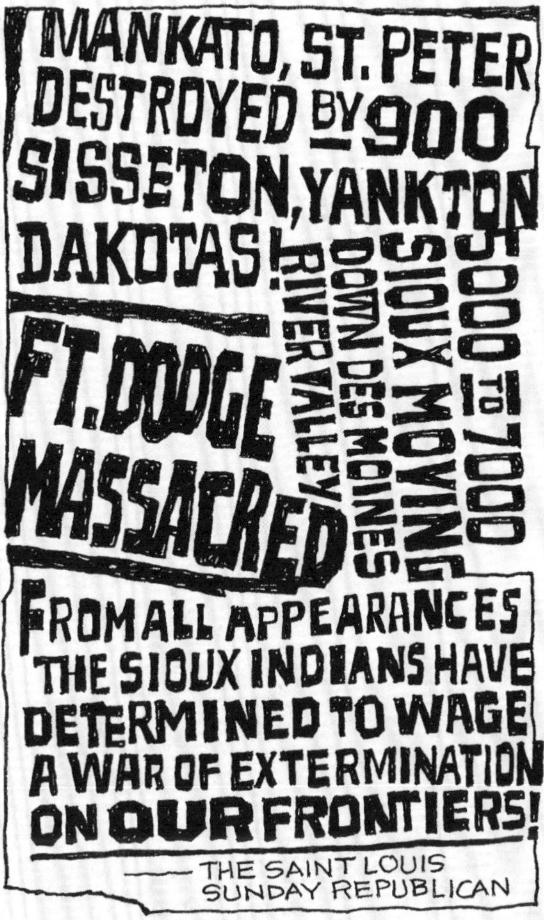
MANKATO, ST. PETER DESTROYED BY 900 SISSETON, YANKTON DAKOTAS!
5000 TO 7000 SIOUX MOVING DOWN DES MOINES RIVER VALLEY
FT. DODGE MASSACRED
FROM ALL APPEARANCES THE SIOUX INDIANS HAVE DETERMINED TO WAGE A WAR OF EXTERMINATION ON OUR FRONTIERS!
— THE SAINT LOUIS SUNDAY REPUBLICAN

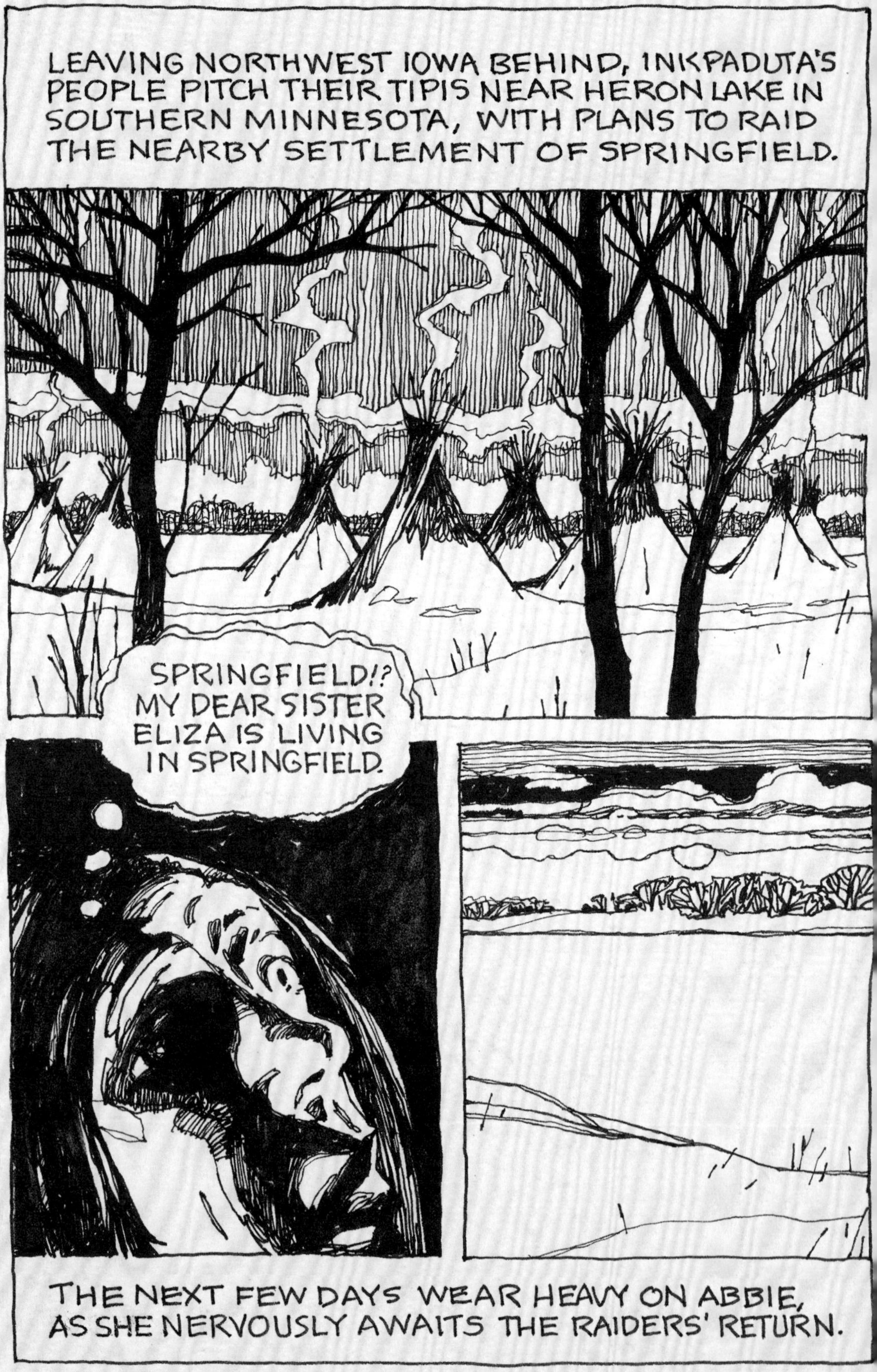
LEAVING NORTHWEST IOWA BEHIND, INKPADUTA'S PEOPLE PITCH THEIR TIPIS NEAR HERON LAKE IN SOUTHERN MINNESOTA, WITH PLANS TO RAID THE NEARBY SETTLEMENT OF SPRINGFIELD.
SPRINGFIELD!? MY DEAR SISTER ELIZA IS LIVING IN SPRINGFIELD.
THE NEXT FEW DAYS WEAR HEAVY ON ABBIE, AS SHE NERVOUSLY AWAITS THE RAIDERS' RETURN.

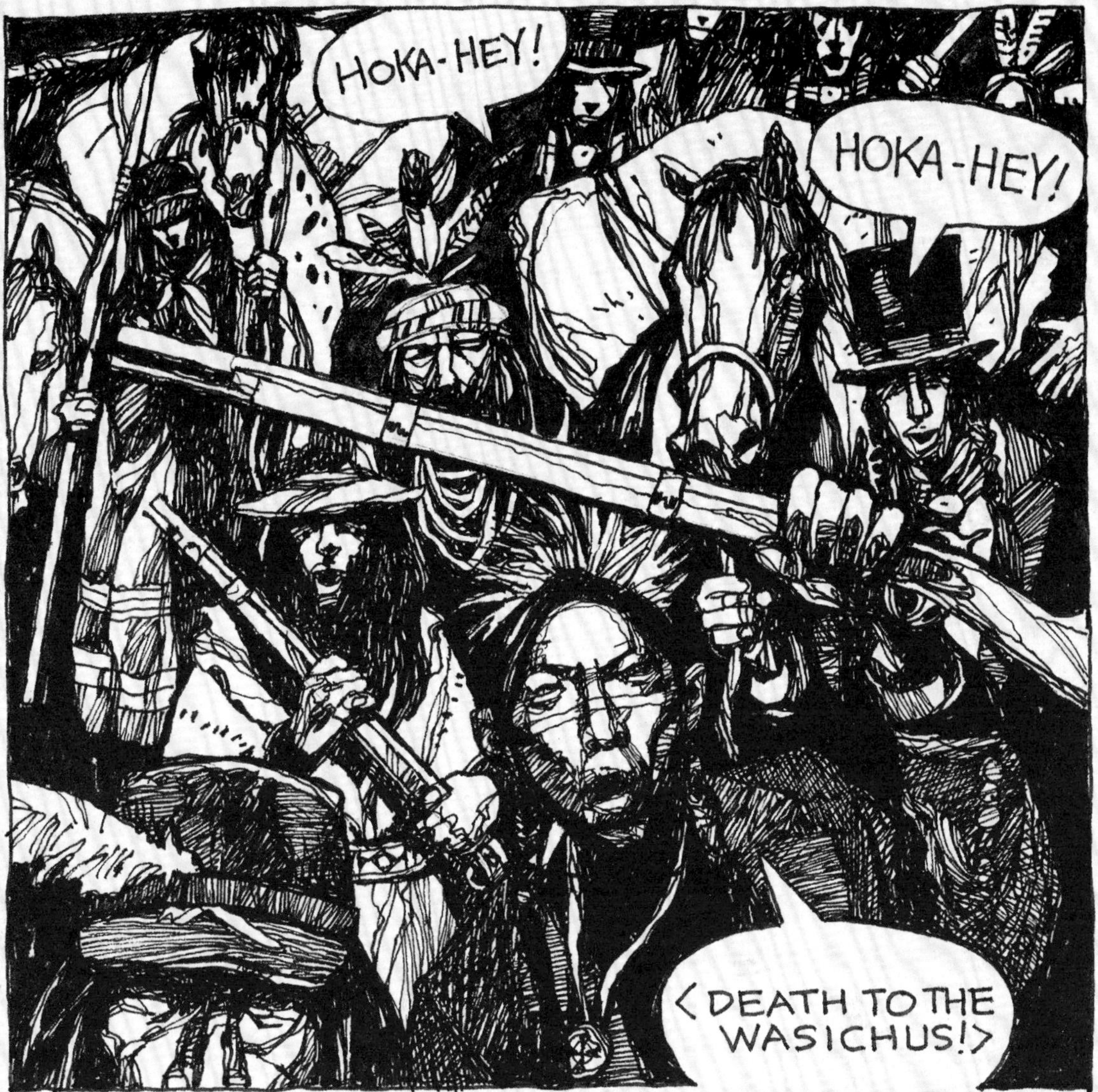
HOKA-HEY!
HOKA-HEY!
<DEATH TO THE WASICHUS!>

EVENTUALLY THEY APPEAR, CELEBRATING THEIR SPOILS AND STORIES, THEIR VICTORIES AND VICTIMS... BUT NO WORD OF ELIZA.

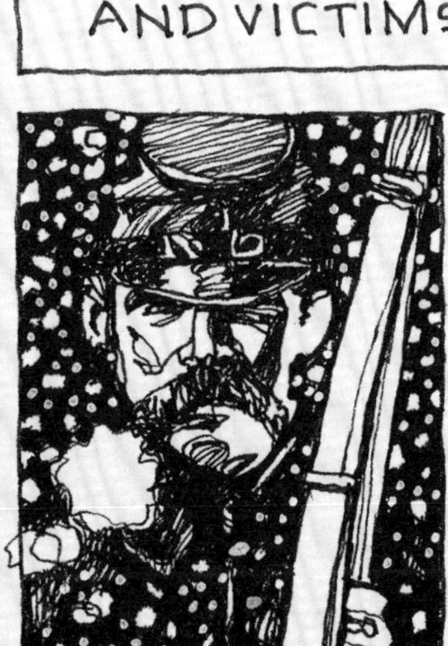

MEANWHILE, THE U.S. MILITARY RESPONSE TO SPIRIT LAKE IS NEUTRALIZED BY HEAVY SNOW IN MINNESOTA AND A MORMON REVOLT IN UTAH.

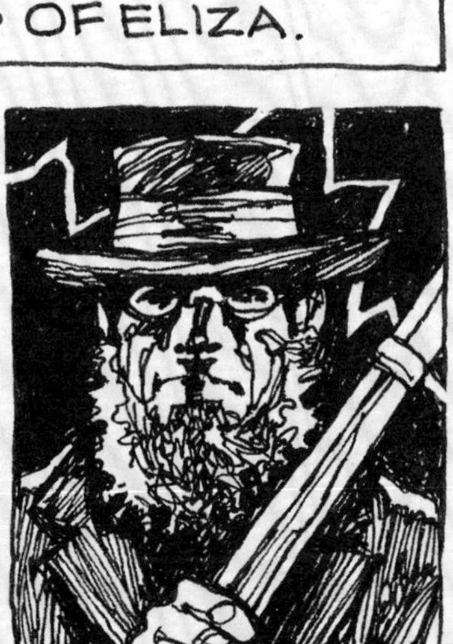

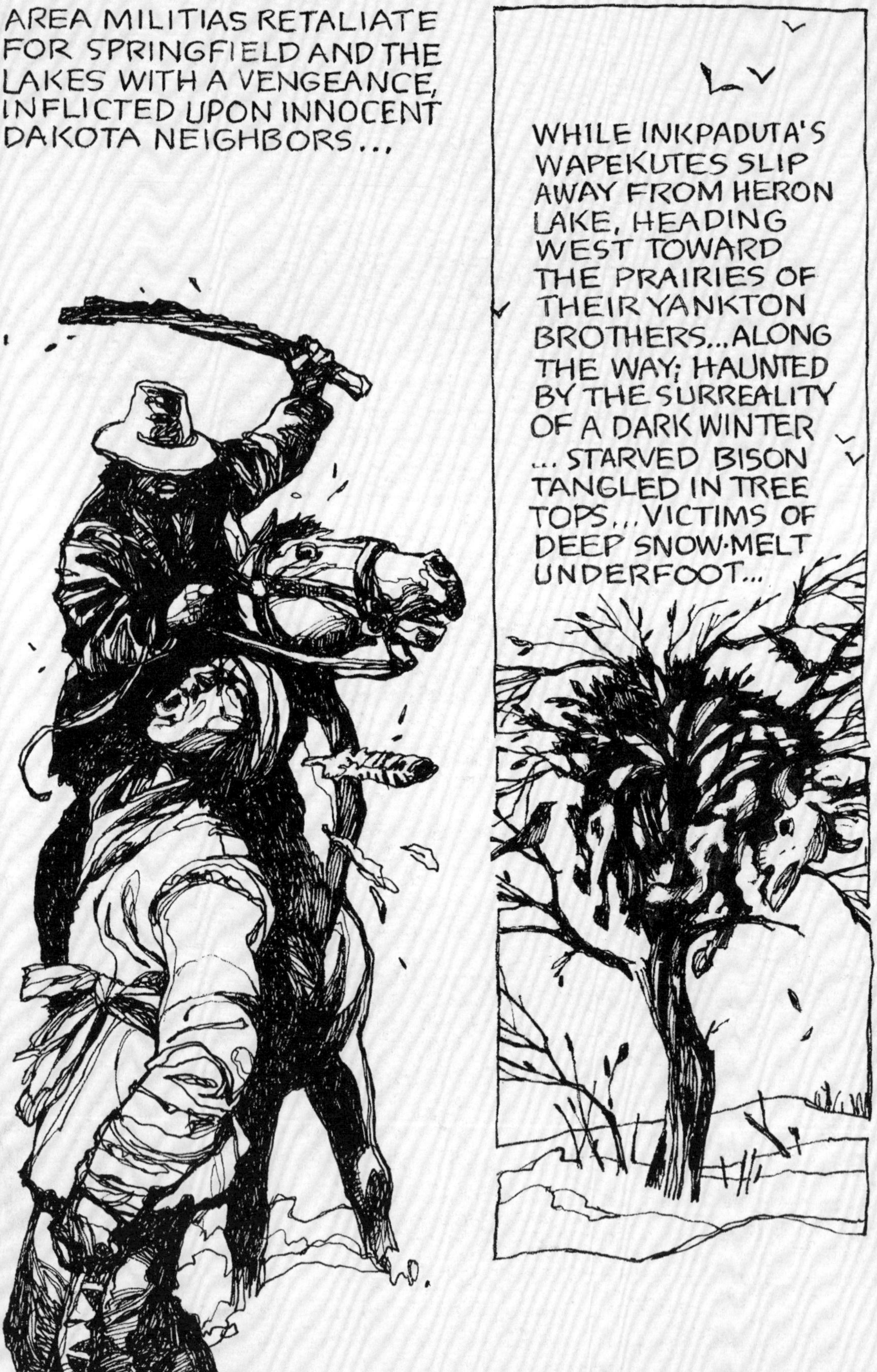
AREA MILITIAS RETALIATE FOR SPRINGFIELD AND THE LAKES WITH A VENGEANCE, INFLICTED UPON INNOCENT DAKOTA NEIGHBORS...
WHILE INKPADUTA'S WAPEKUTES SLIP AWAY FROM HERON LAKE, HEADING WEST TOWARD THE PRAIRIES OF THEIR YANKTON BROTHERS...ALONG THE WAY; HAUNTED BY THE SURREALITY OF A DARK WINTER ... STARVED BISON TANGLED IN TREE TOPS... VICTIMS OF DEEP SNOW·MELT UNDERFOOT...

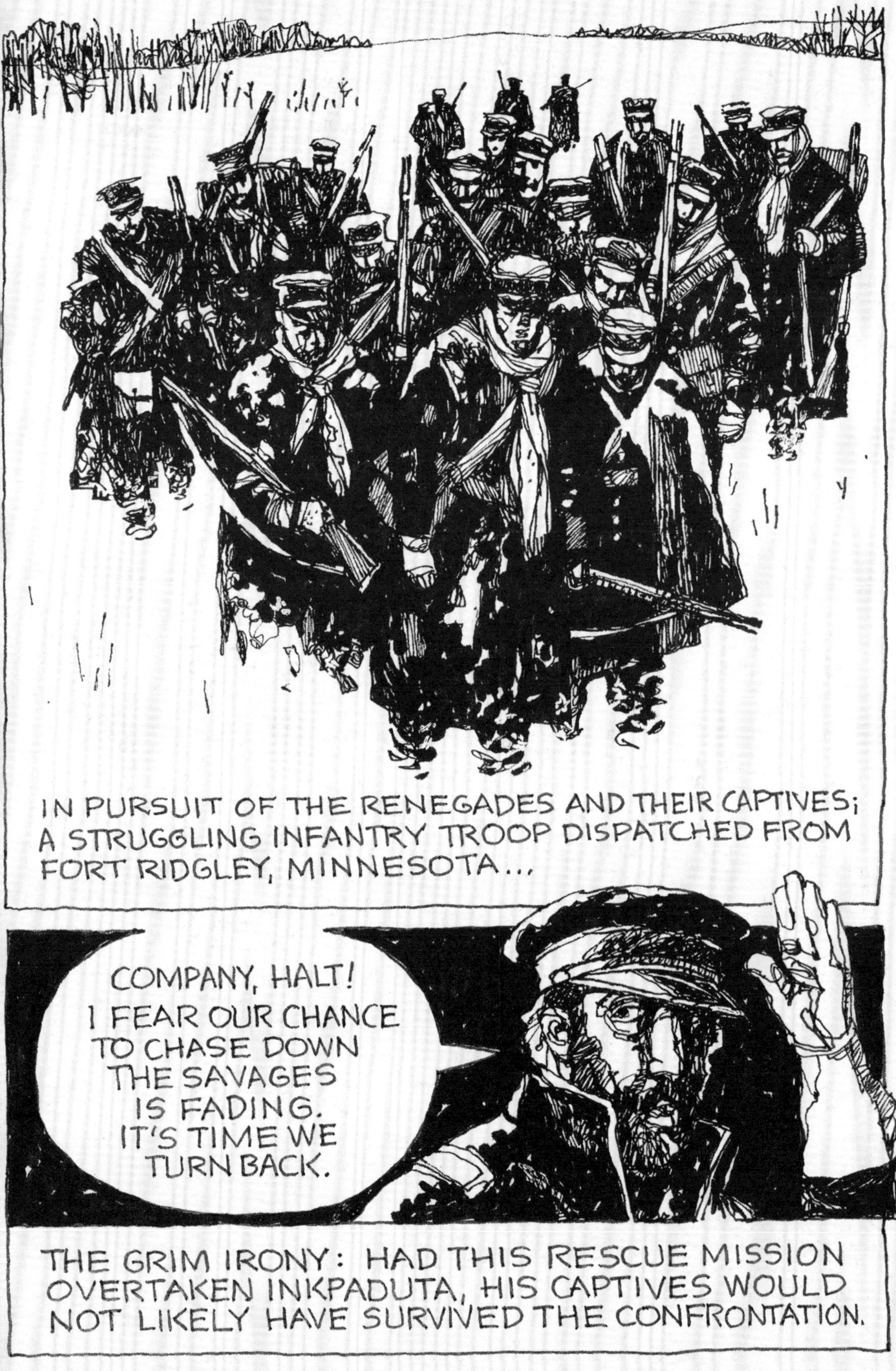
IN PURSUIT OF THE RENEGADES AND THEIR CAPTIVES; A STRUGGLING INFANTRY TROOP DISPATCHED FROM FORT RIDGLEY, MINNESOTA...
COMPANY, HALT! I FEAR OUR CHANCE TO CHASE DOWN THE SAVAGES IS FADING. IT'S TIME WE TURN BACK.
THE GRIM IRONY: HAD THIS RESCUE MISSION OVERTAKEN INKPADUTA, HIS CAPTIVES WOULD NOT LIKELY HAVE SURVIVED THE CONFRONTATION.

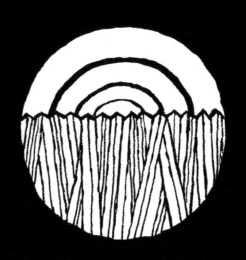

APRIL 1857

THE MOON WHEN GRASS APPEARS

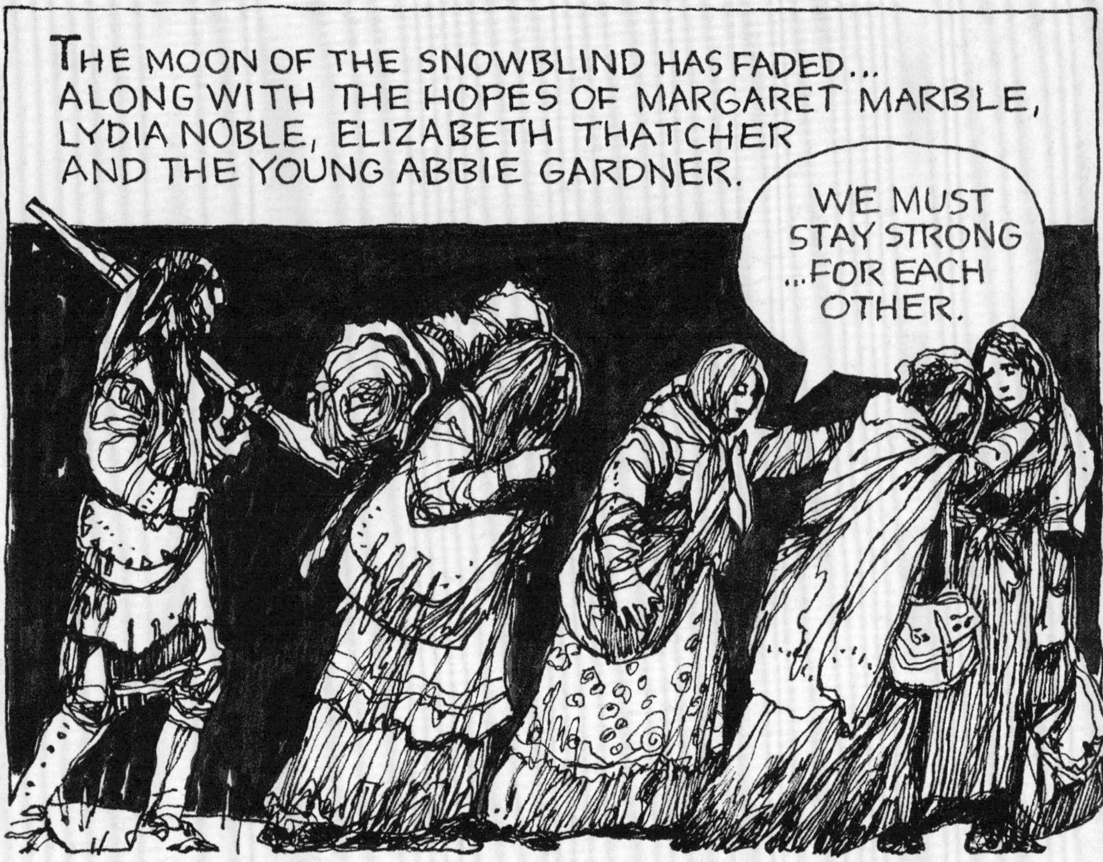
THE MOON OF THE SNOWBLIND HAS FADED...
ALONG WITH THE HOPES OF MARGARET MARBLE, LYDIA NOBLE, ELIZABETH THATCHER AND THE YOUNG ABBIE GARDNER.
WE MUST STAY STRONG ...FOR EACH OTHER.

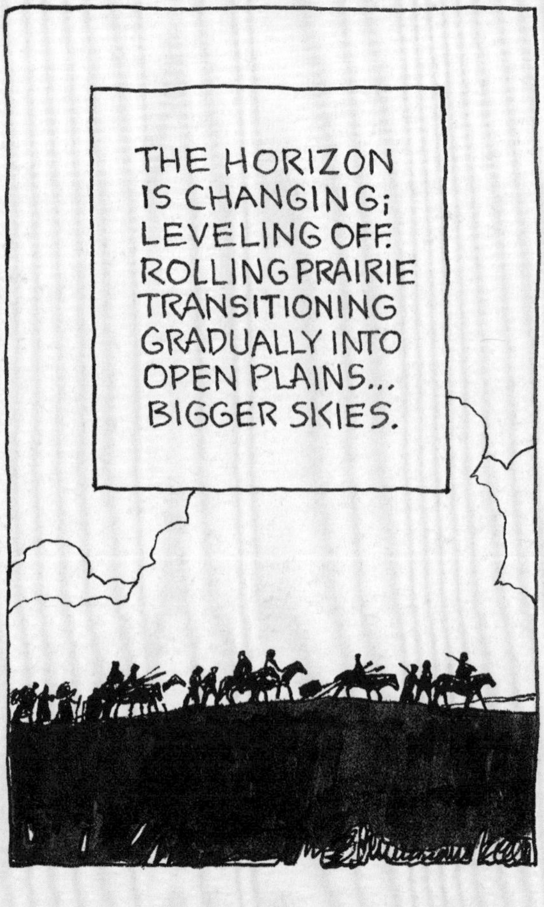
THE HORIZON IS CHANGING; LEVELING OFF. ROLLING PRAIRIE TRANSITIONING GRADUALLY INTO OPEN PLAINS... BIGGER SKIES.

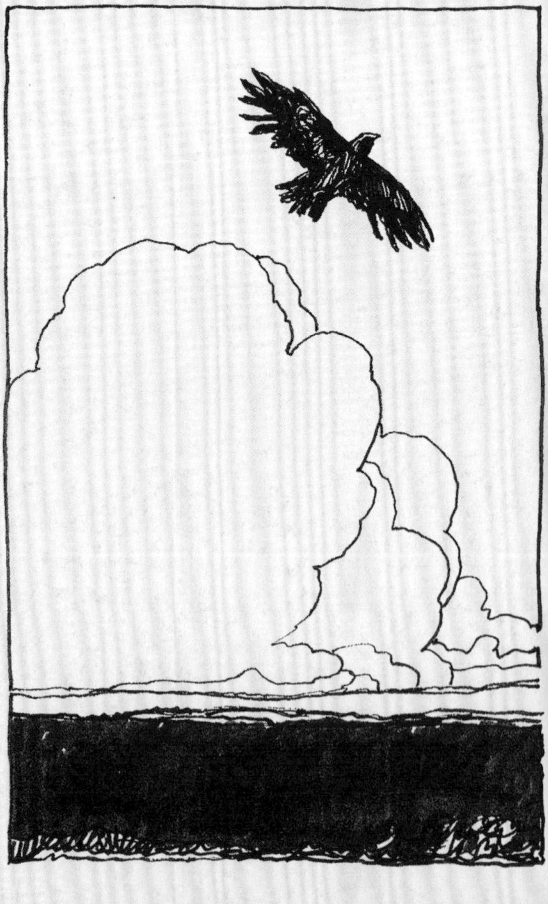

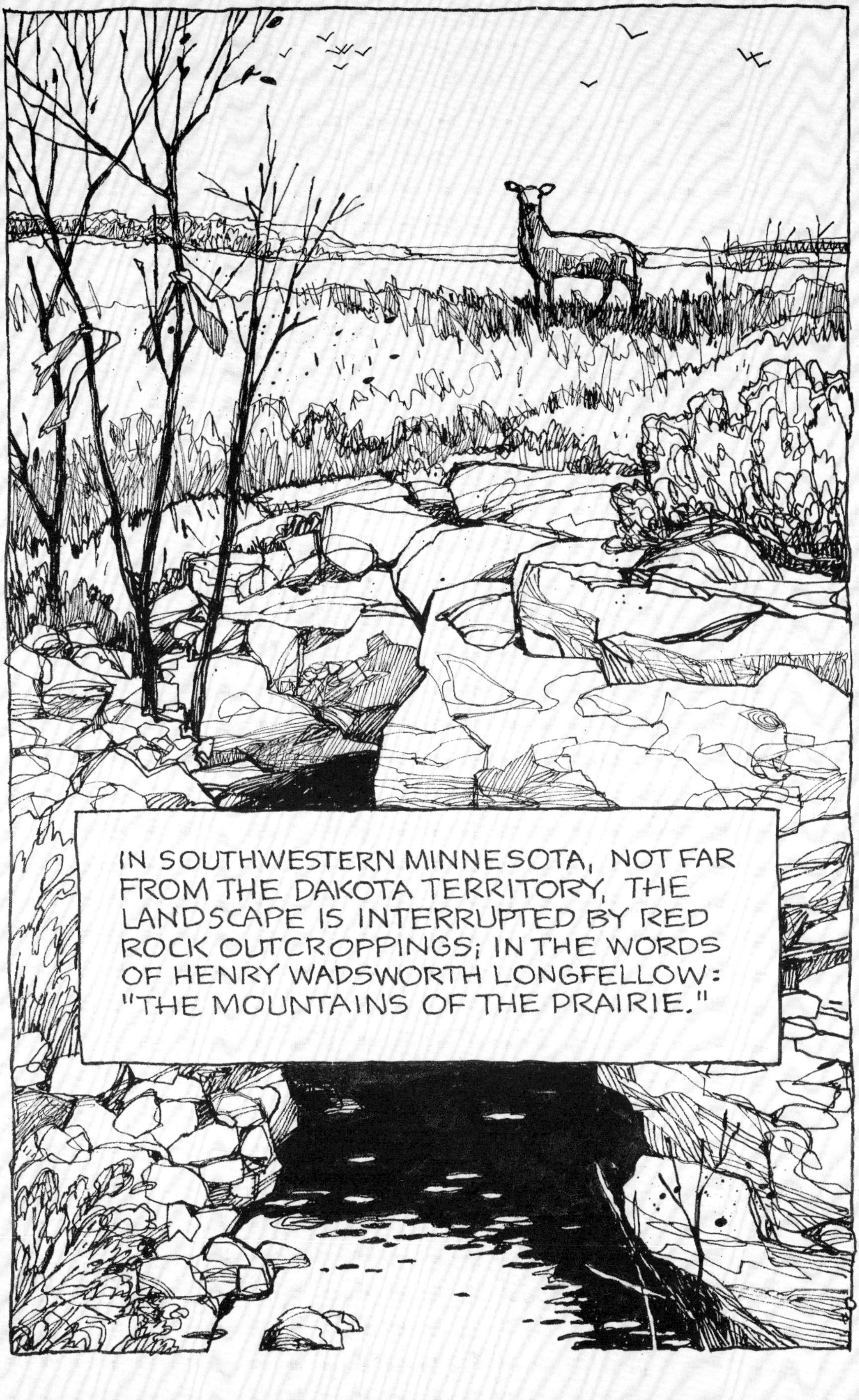
IN SOUTHWESTERN MINNESOTA, NOT FAR FROM THE DAKOTA TERRITORY, THE LANDSCAPE IS INTERRUPTED BY RED ROCK OUTCROPPINGS; IN THE WORDS OF HENRY WADSWORTH LONGFELLOW: "THE MOUNTAINS OF THE PRAIRIE."

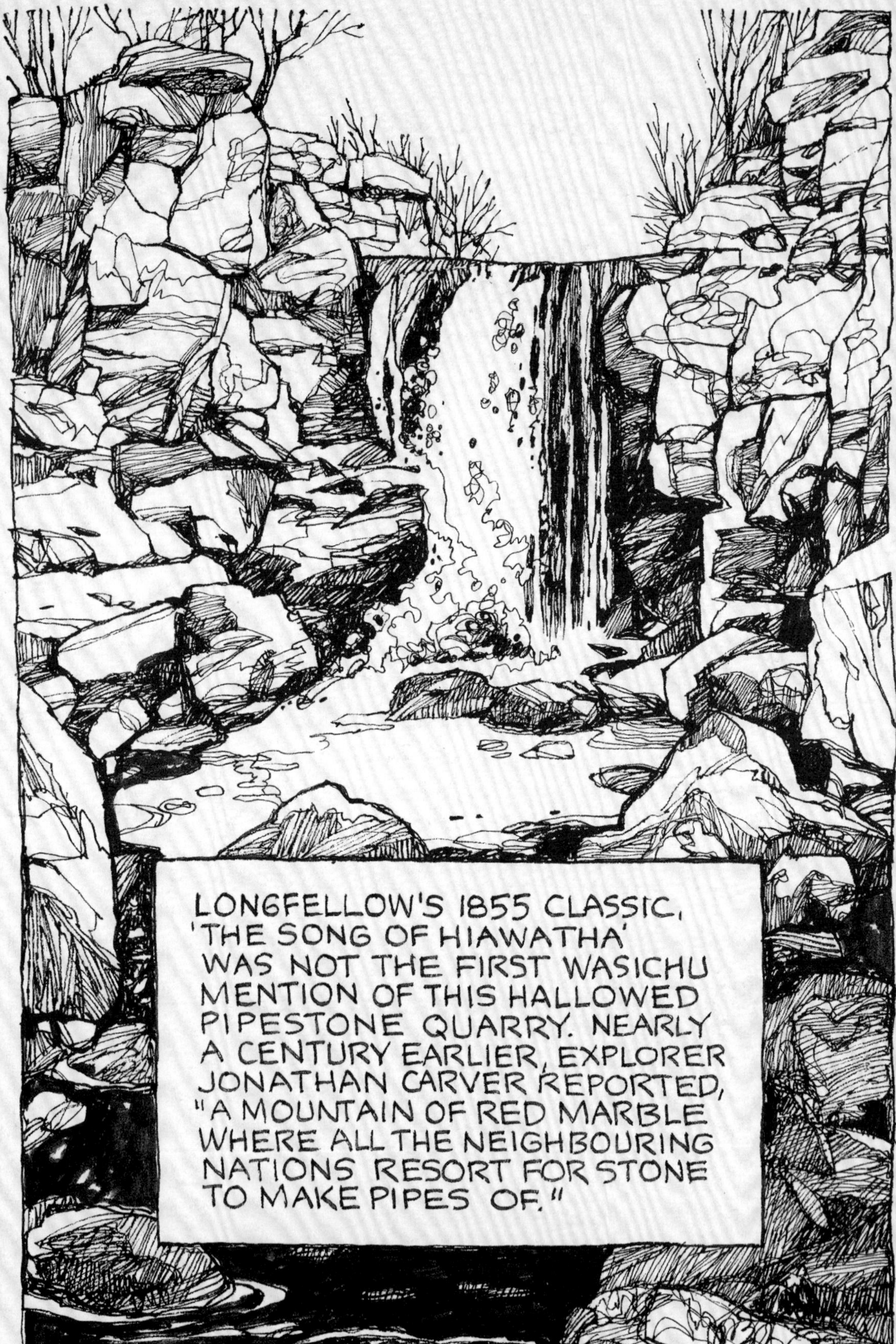
LONGFELLOW'S 1855 CLASSIC, 'THE SONG OF HIAWATHA' WAS NOT THE FIRST WASICHU MENTION OF THIS HALLOWED PIPESTONE QUARRY. NEARLY A CENTURY EARLIER, EXPLORER JONATHAN CARVER REPORTED, "A MOUNTAIN OF RED MARBLE WHERE ALL THE NEIGHBOURING NATIONS RESORT FOR STONE TO MAKE PIPES OF."

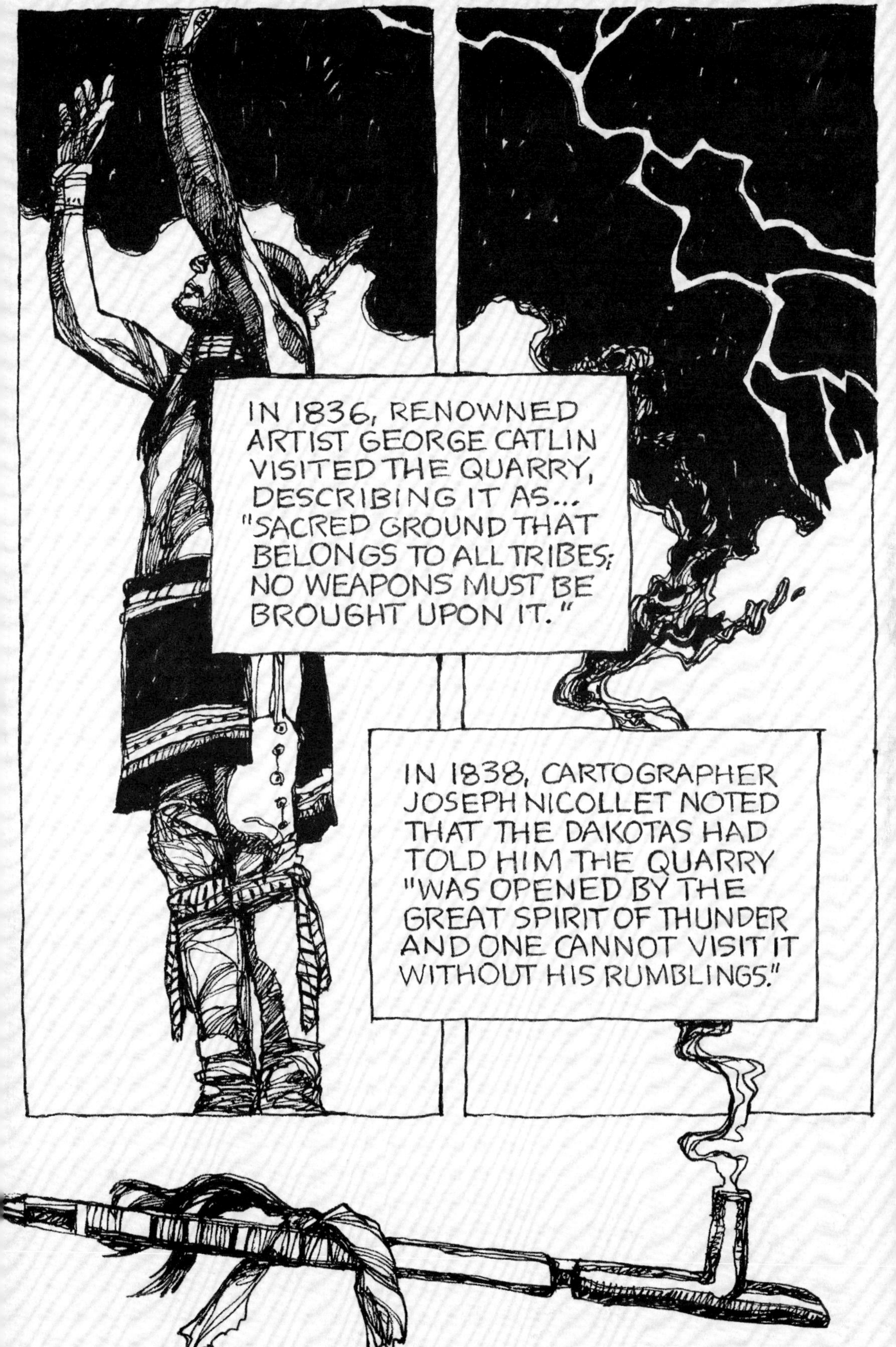
IN 1836, RENOWNED ARTIST GEORGE CATLIN VISITED THE QUARRY, DESCRIBING IT AS... "SACRED GROUND THAT BELONGS TO ALL TRIBES; NO WEAPONS MUST BE BROUGHT UPON IT."
IN 1838, CARTOGRAPHER JOSEPH NICOLLET NOTED THAT THE DAKOTAS HAD TOLD HIM THE QUARRY "WAS OPENED BY THE GREAT SPIRIT OF THUNDER AND ONE CANNOT VISIT IT WITHOUT HIS RUMBLINGS."

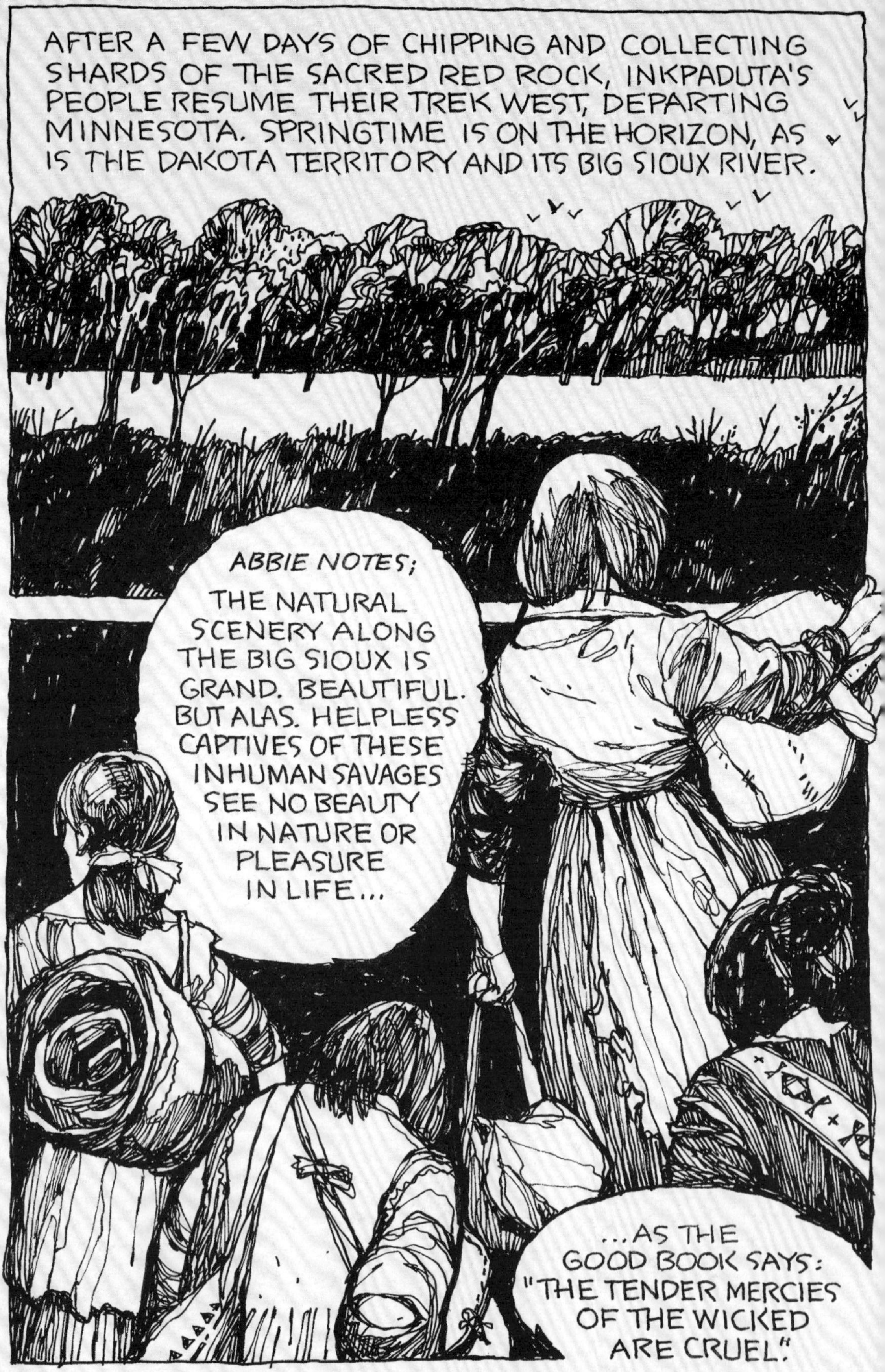
AFTER A FEW DAYS OF CHIPPING AND COLLECTING SHARDS OF THE SACRED RED ROCK, INKPADUTA'S PEOPLE RESUME THEIR TREK WEST, DEPARTING MINNESOTA. SPRINGTIME IS ON THE HORIZON, AS IS THE DAKOTA TERRITORY AND ITS BIG SIOUX RIVER.
ABBIE NOTES; THE NATURAL SCENERY ALONG THE BIG SIOUX IS GRAND. BEAUTIFUL. BUT ALAS. HELPLESS CAPTIVES OF THESE INHUMAN SAVAGES SEE NO BEAUTY IN NATURE OR PLEASURE IN LIFE...
...AS THE GOOD BOOK SAYS: "THE TENDER MERCIES OF THE WICKED ARE CRUEL."

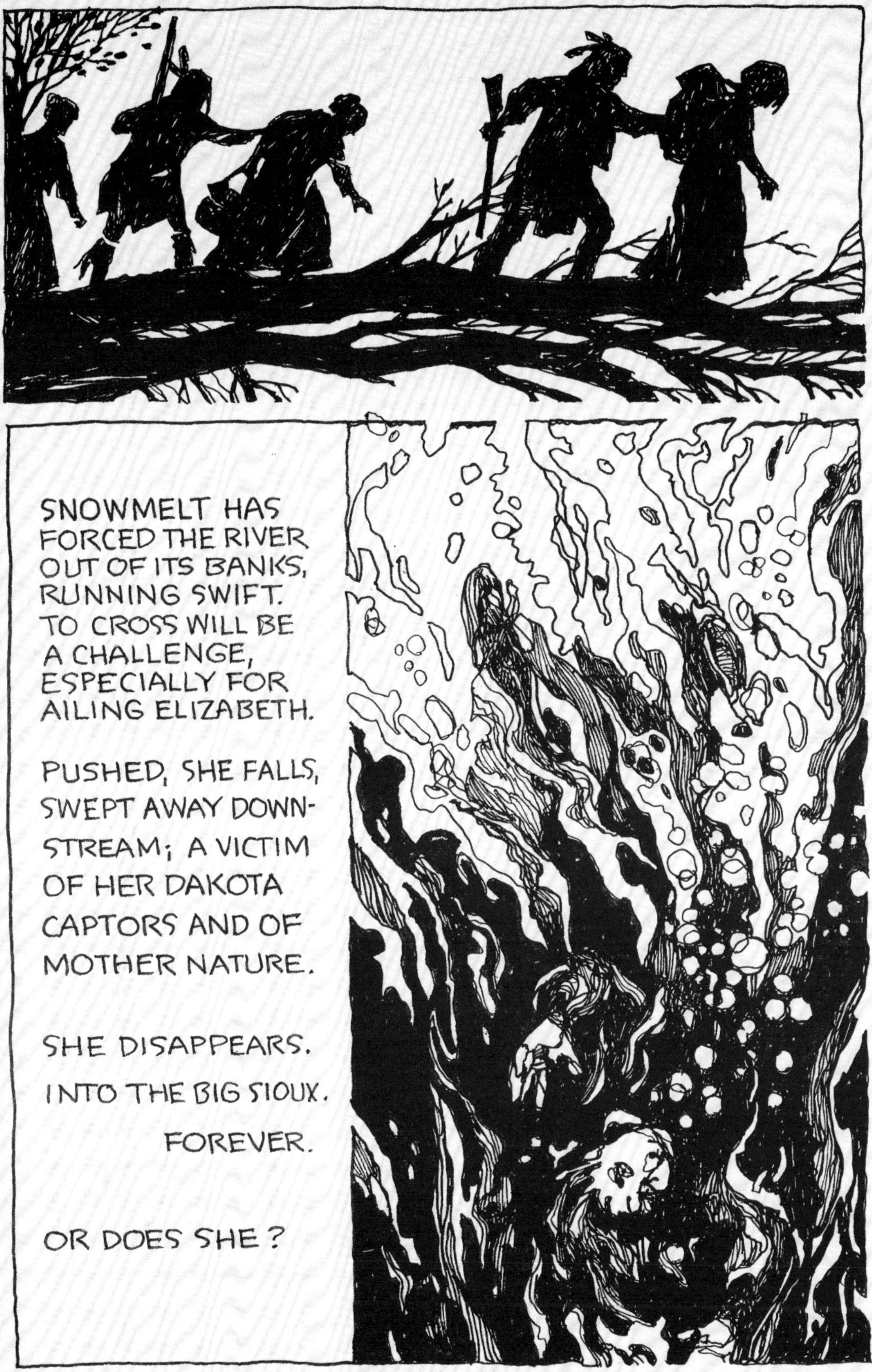
SNOWMELT HAS FORCED THE RIVER OUT OF ITS BANKS, RUNNING SWIFT. TO CROSS WILL BE A CHALLENGE, ESPECIALLY FOR AILING ELIZABETH.
PUSHED, SHE FALLS, SWEPT AWAY DOWN-STREAM; A VICTIM OF HER DAKOTA CAPTORS AND OF MOTHER NATURE.
SHE DISAPPEARS.
INTO THE BIG SIOUX.
FOREVER.
OR DOES SHE?

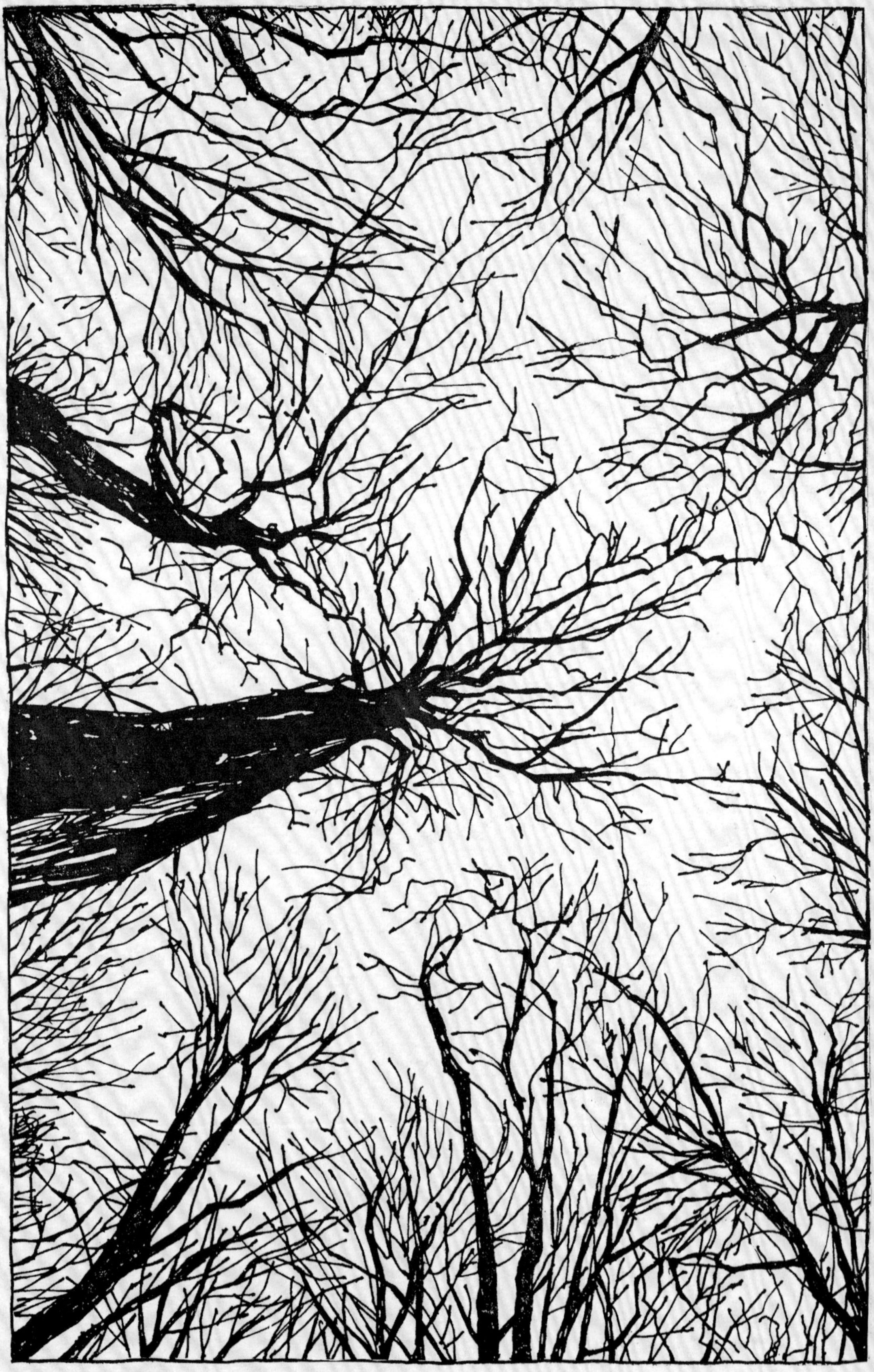

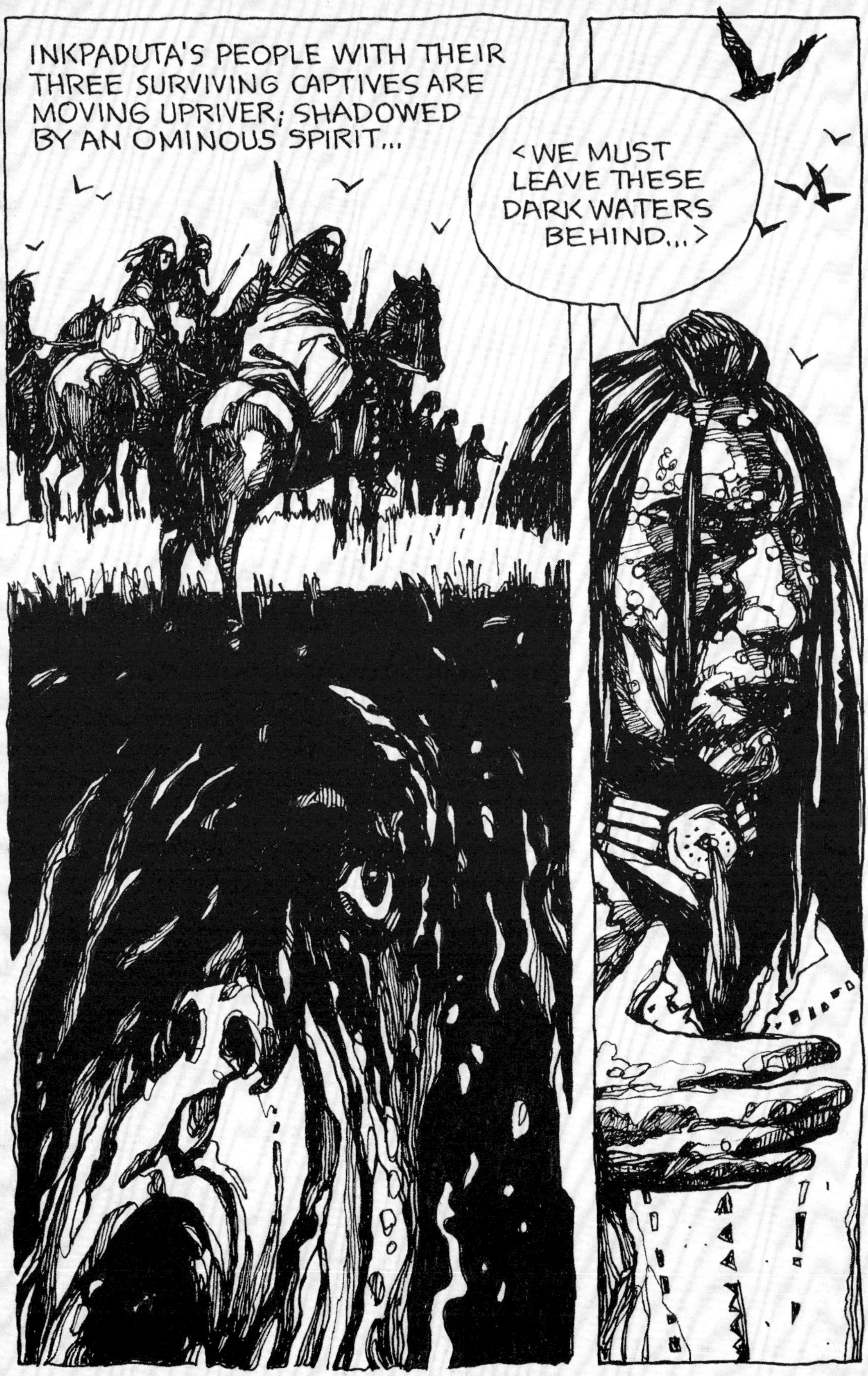
INKPADUTA'S PEOPLE WITH THEIR THREE SURVIVING CAPTIVES ARE MOVING UPRIVER; SHADOWED BY AN OMINOUS SPIRIT...
<WE MUST LEAVE THESE DARK WATERS BEHIND...>

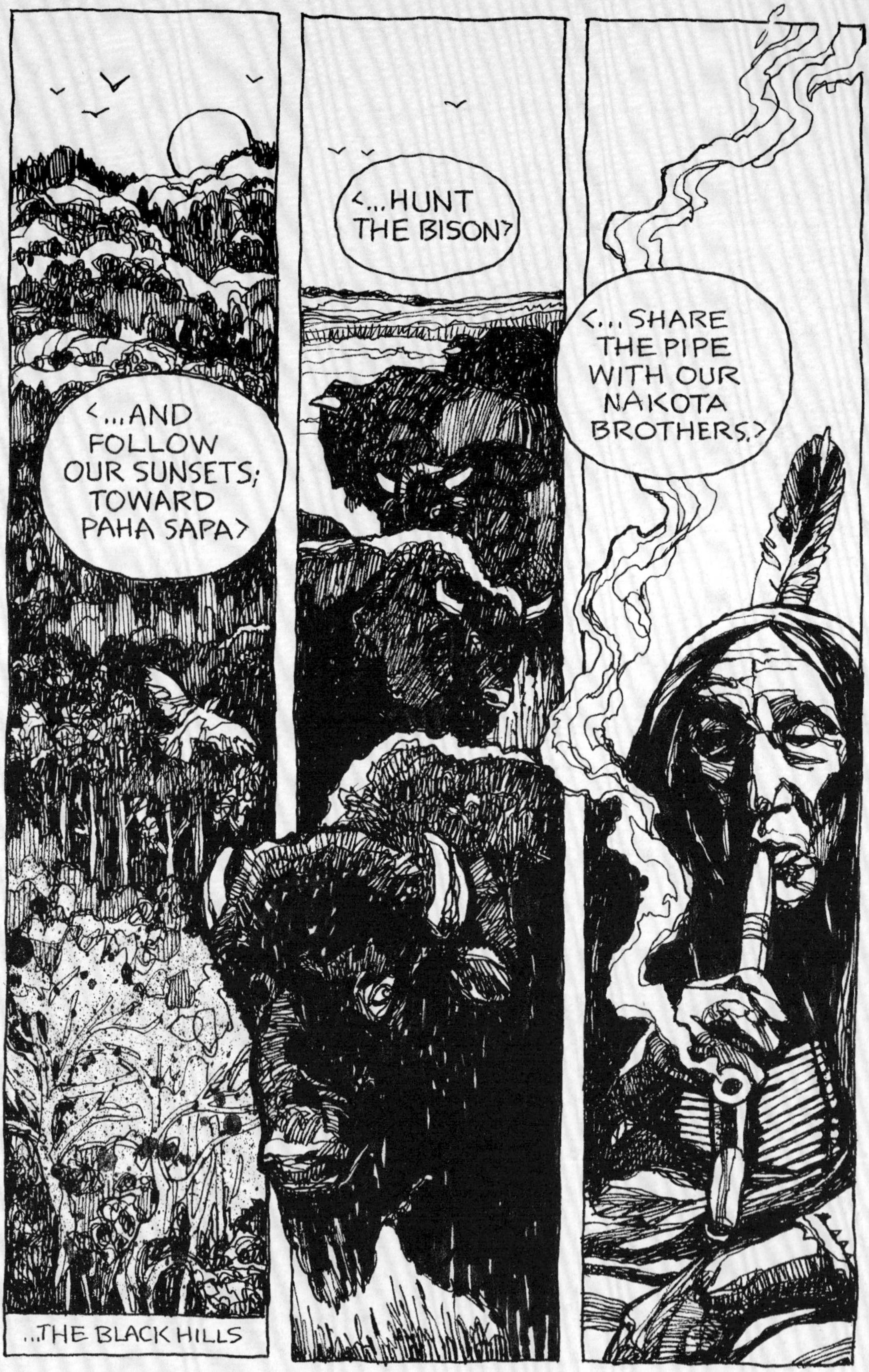

<...AND FOLLOW OUR SUNSETS; TOWARD PAHA SAPA>
...THE BLACK HILLS
<...HUNT THE BISON>
<...SHARE THE PIPE WITH OUR NAKOTA BROTHERS.>

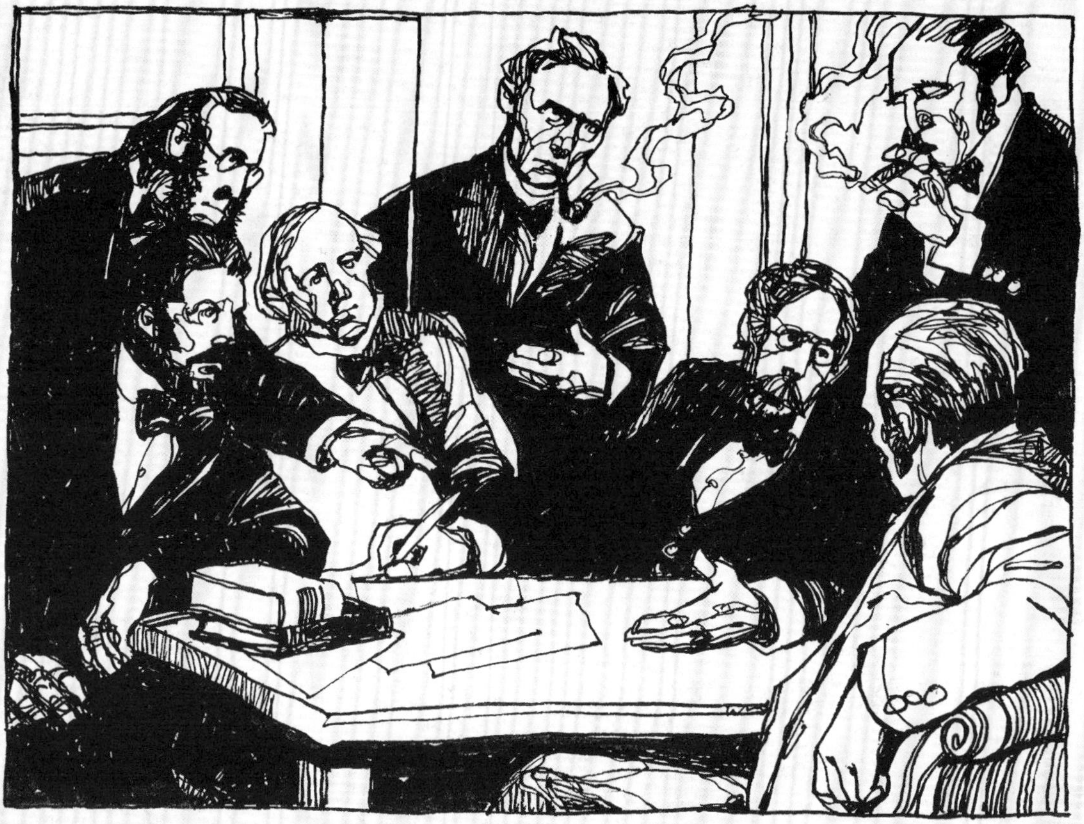

MEANWHILE; TO THE EAST, MINNESOTA'S TERRITORIAL LAWMAKERS ARE APPROVING THE SUM OF $10,000 TO HELP TRACK DOWN AND BUY BACK ANY MASSACRE SURVIVORS HELD BY THE DAKOTAS... ENCOURAGING INDIAN AGENT CHARLES FLANDRAU TO RECRUIT TWO WAHPETON SIOUX CHRISTIAN CONVERTS FOR THE TASK.

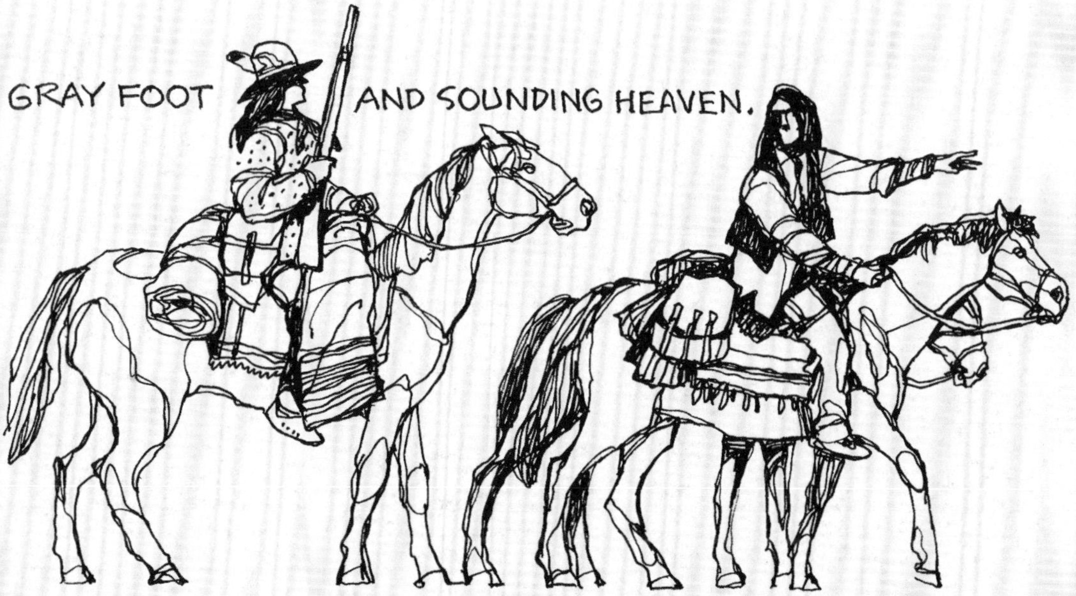
GRAY FOOT
AND SOUNDING HEAVEN.

MAY 1857

THE MOON WHEN PONIES SHED

THE WAPEKUTES CONTINUE TRAVELING WEST, NOW WELL-BEYOND THE BIG SIOUX RIVER...

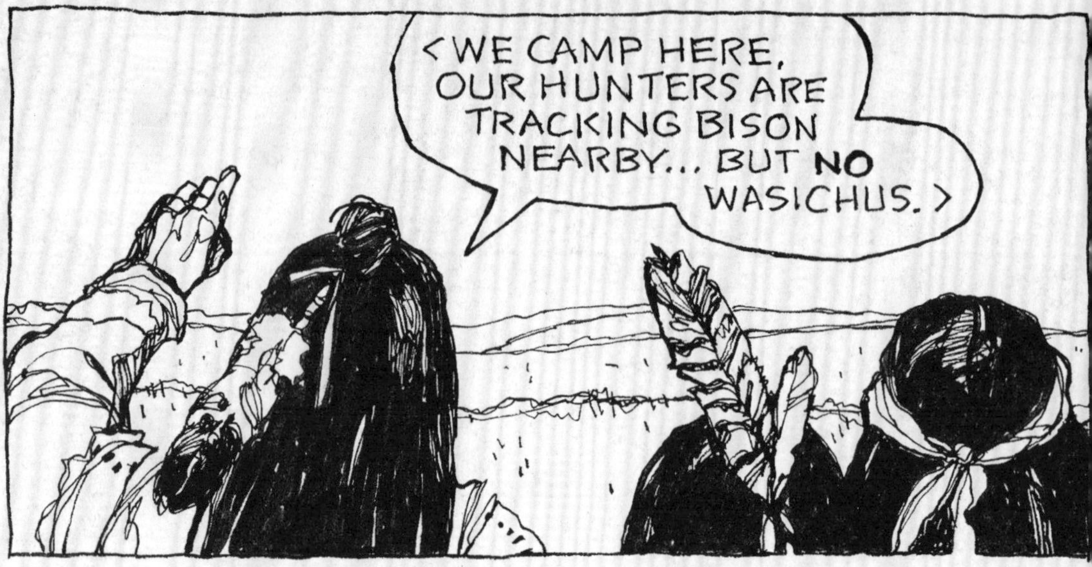
<WE CAMP HERE, OUR HUNTERS ARE TRACKING BISON NEARBY... BUT NO WASICHUS.>

AS DAYLIGHT FADES, FLANDRAU'S DAKOTAS APPEAR... AND ARE PROMPTLY CONFRONTED BY INKPADUTA.

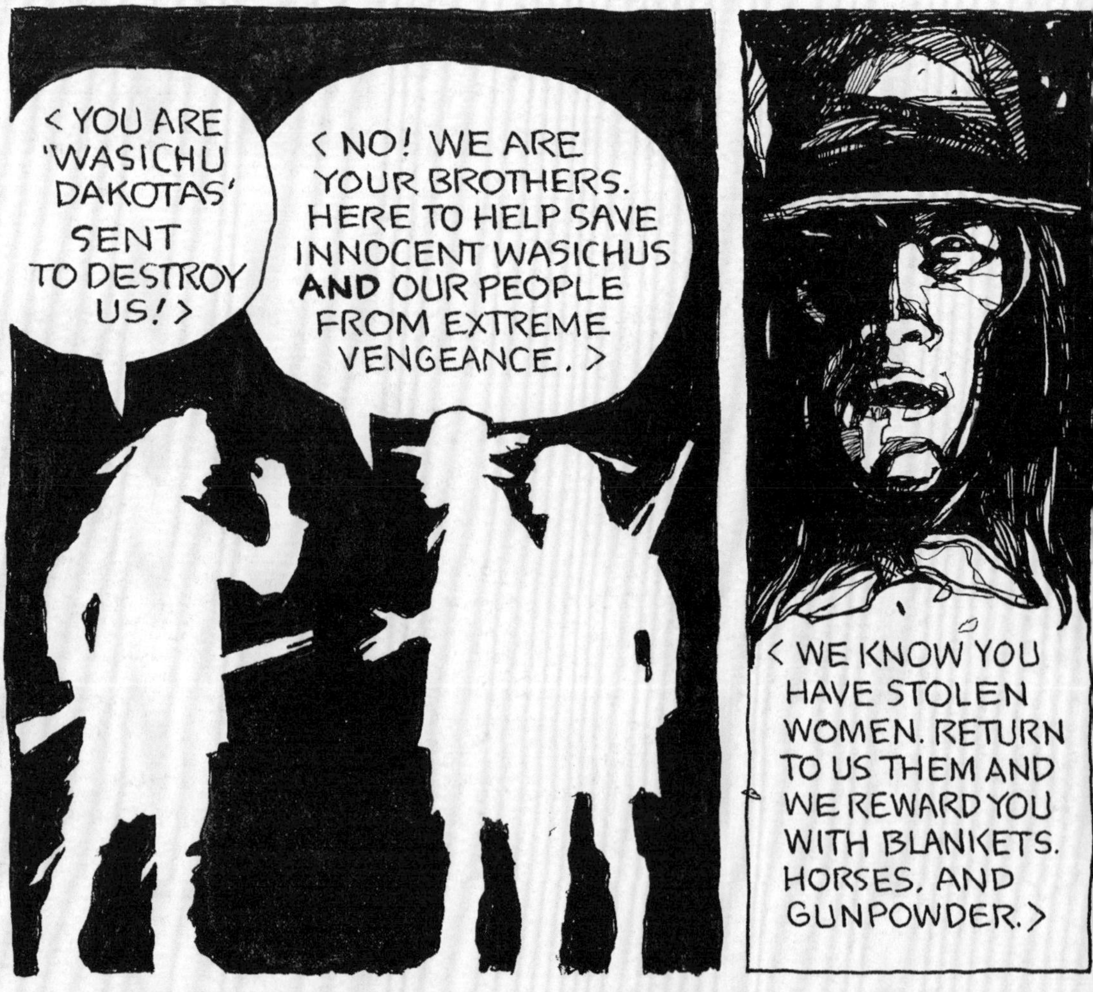
<YOU ARE 'WASICHU DAKOTAS' SENT TO DESTROY US!>
<NO! WE ARE YOUR BROTHERS. HERE TO HELP SAVE INNOCENT WASICHUS AND OUR PEOPLE FROM EXTREME VENGEANCE.>
<WE KNOW YOU HAVE STOLEN WOMEN. RETURN TO US THEM AND WE REWARD YOU WITH BLANKETS. HORSES, AND GUNPOWDER.>

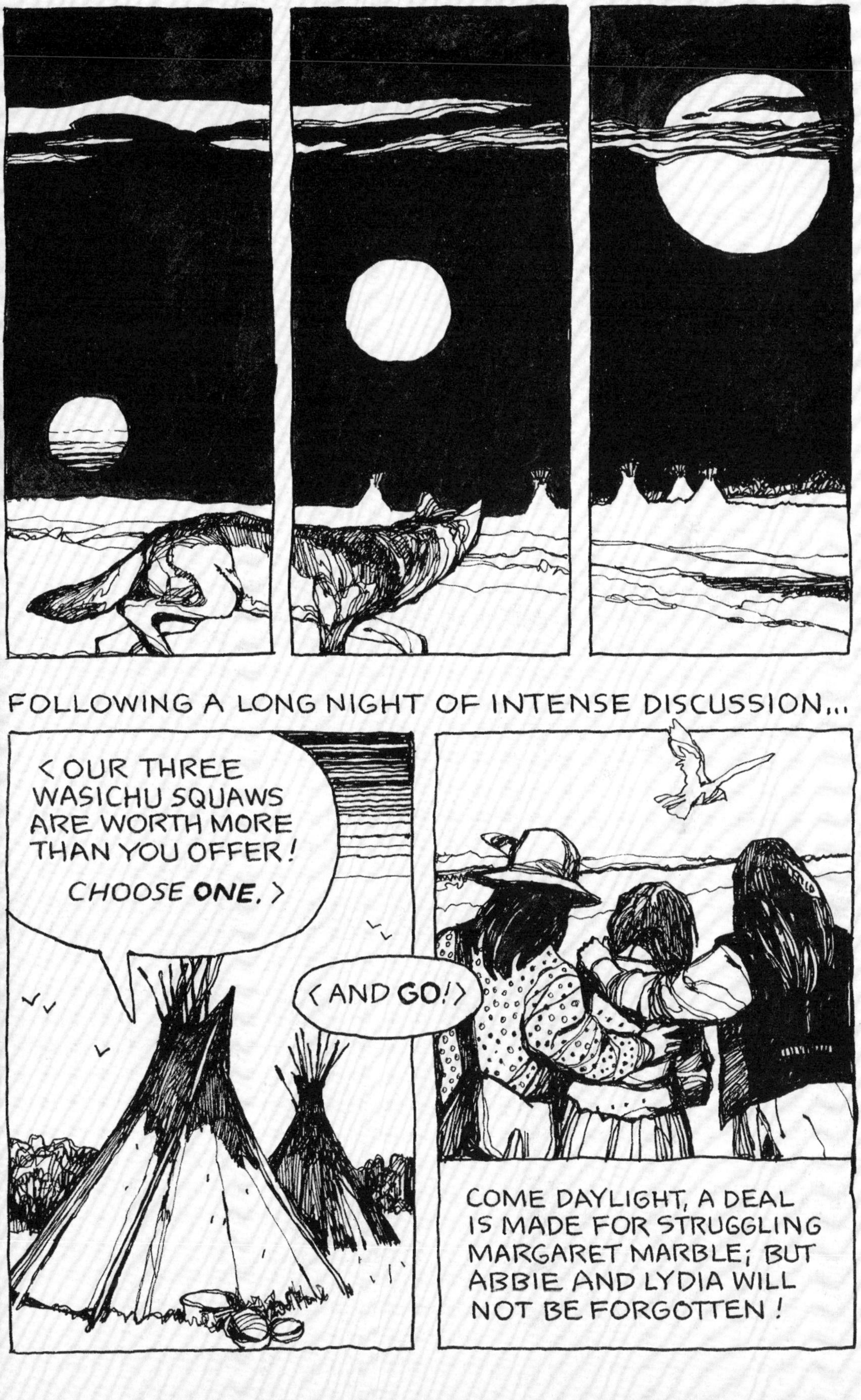
FOLLOWING A LONG NIGHT OF INTENSE DISCUSSION...
< OUR THREE WASICHU SQUAWS ARE WORTH MORE THAN YOU OFFER! CHOOSE ONE. >
< AND GO! >
COME DAYLIGHT, A DEAL IS MADE FOR STRUGGLING MARGARET MARBLE; BUT ABBIE AND LYDIA WILL NOT BE FORGOTTEN!

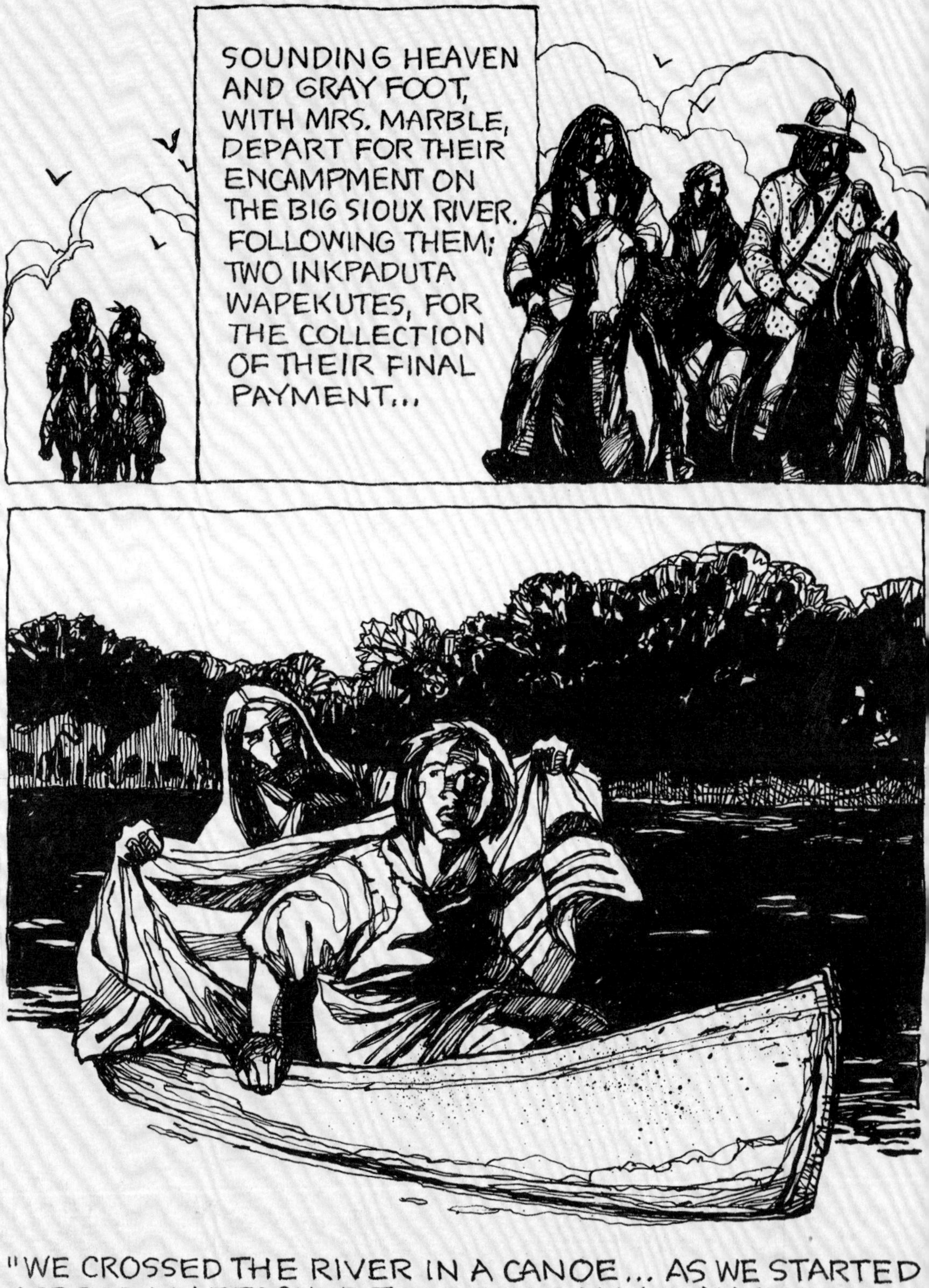
SOUNDING HEAVEN AND GRAY FOOT, WITH MRS. MARBLE, DEPART FOR THEIR ENCAMPMENT ON THE BIG SIOUX RIVER. FOLLOWING THEM; TWO INKPADUTA WAPEKUTES, FOR THE COLLECTION OF THEIR FINAL PAYMENT...

"WE CROSSED THE RIVER IN A CANOE... AS WE STARTED ACROSS, MY RESCUER THREW BACK MY BLANKET FROM MY SHOULDERS, SO AS THE INDIANS COULD ALL SEE, THEY HAD PURCHASED AND RESCUED A WHITE WOMAN ...IT WAS EVIDENT THEY WERE PROUD OF THEIR NEW POSSESSION. I FOUND THAT FORTUNE HAD VASTLY CHANGED FOR ME!" — MARGARET MARBLE

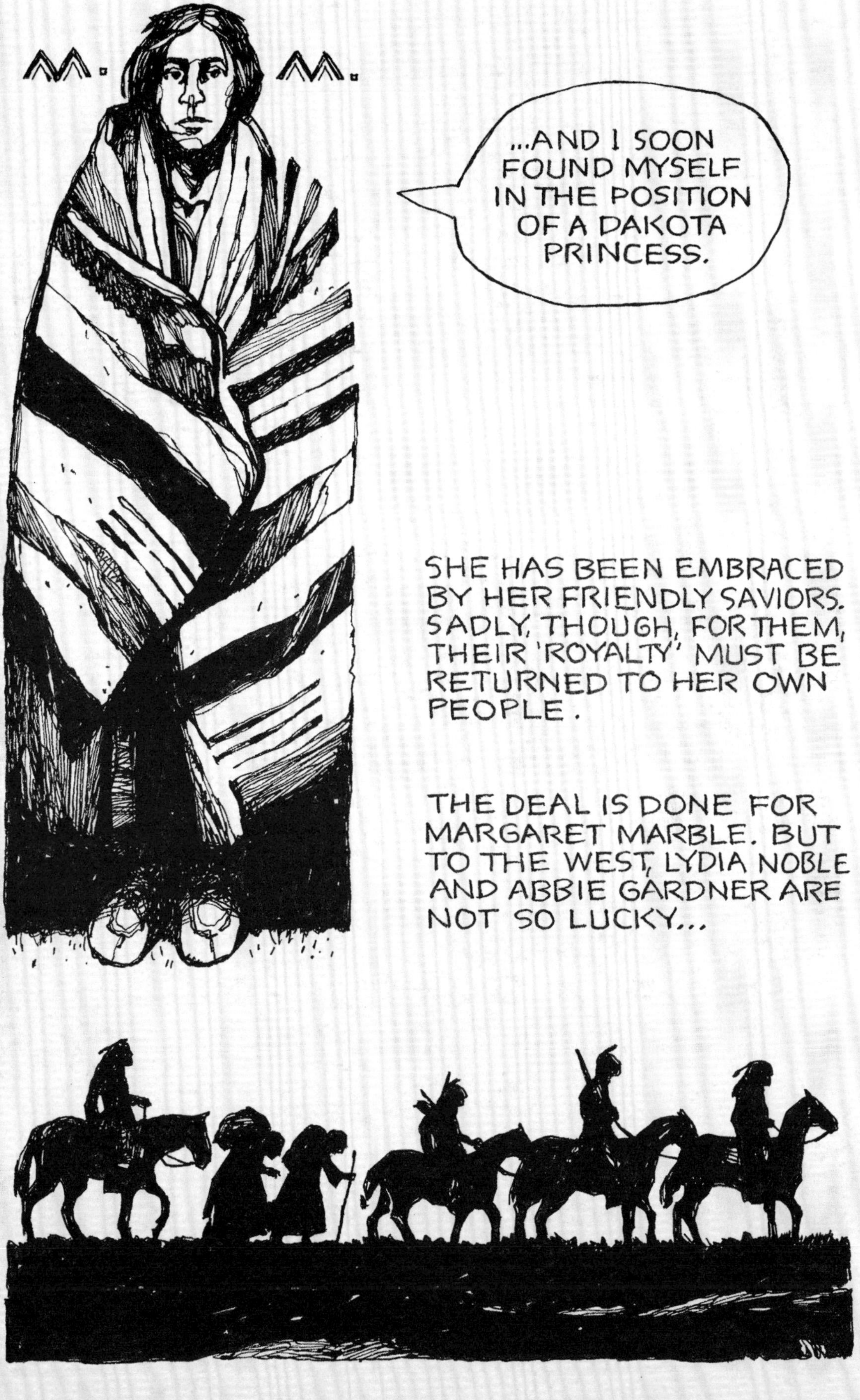
M. M.
...AND I SOON FOUND MYSELF IN THE POSITION OF A DAKOTA PRINCESS.
SHE HAS BEEN EMBRACED BY HER FRIENDLY SAVIORS. SADLY, THOUGH, FOR THEM, THEIR 'ROYALTY' MUST BE RETURNED TO HER OWN PEOPLE.
THE DEAL IS DONE FOR MARGARET MARBLE. BUT TO THE WEST, LYDIA NOBLE AND ABBIE GARDNER ARE NOT SO LUCKY...

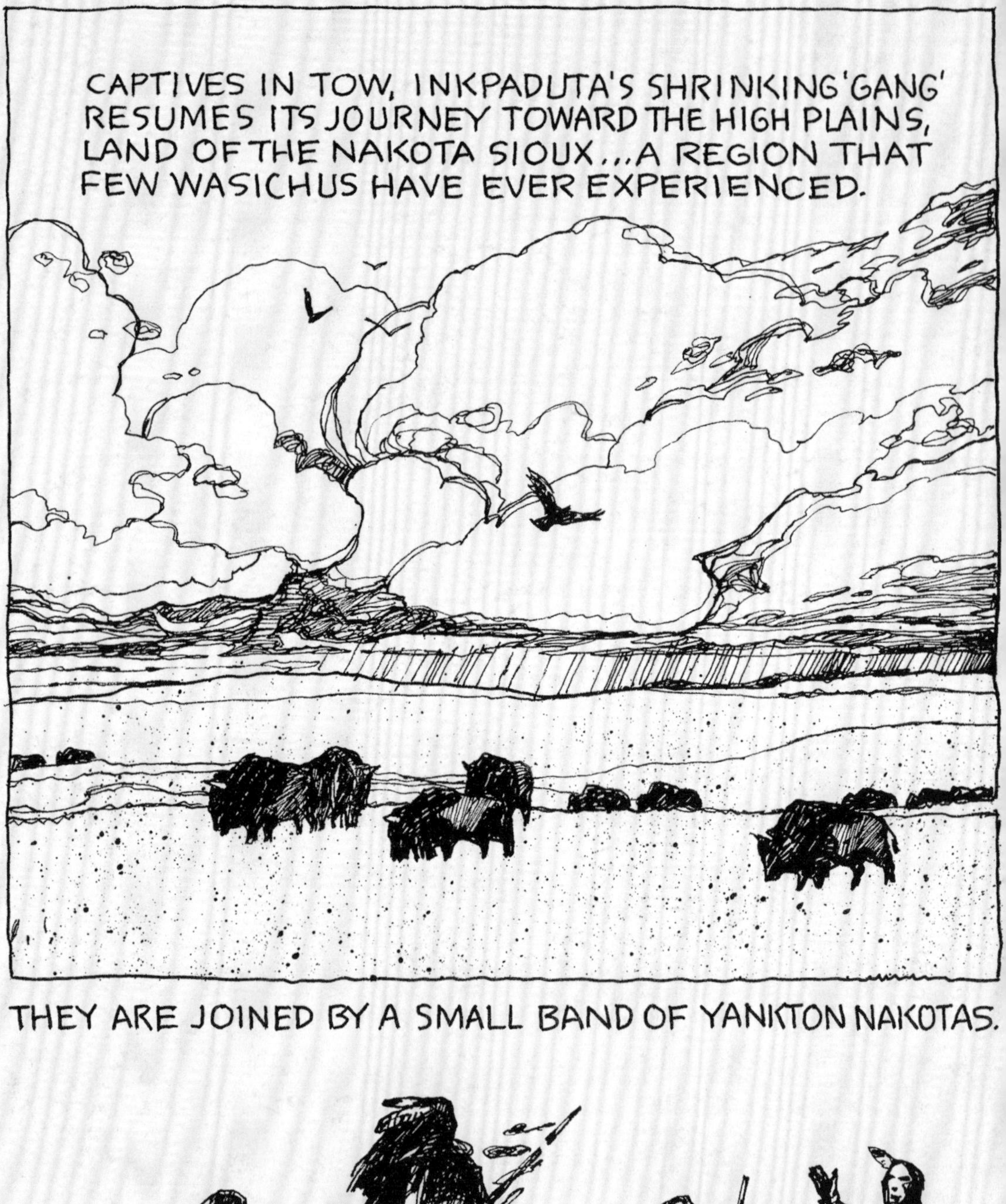
CAPTIVES IN TOW, INKPADUTA'S SHRINKING 'GANG' RESUMES ITS JOURNEY TOWARD THE HIGH PLAINS, LAND OF THE NAKOTA SIOUX...A REGION THAT FEW WASICHUS HAVE EVER EXPERIENCED.

THEY ARE JOINED BY A SMALL BAND OF YANKTON NAKOTAS.

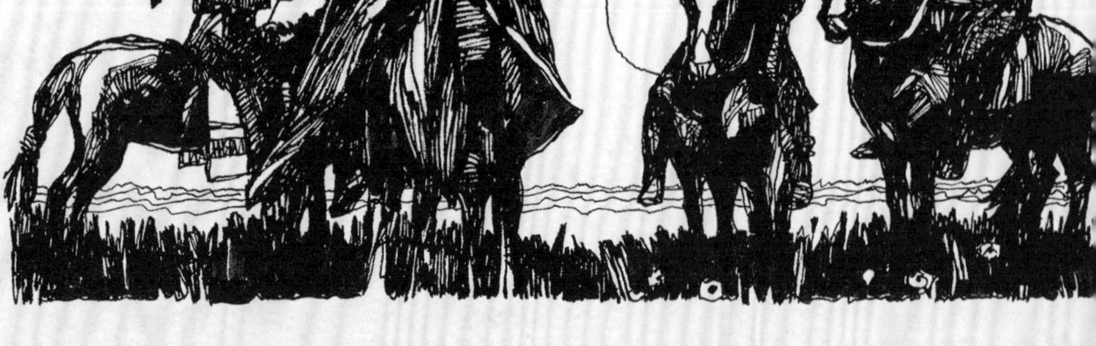

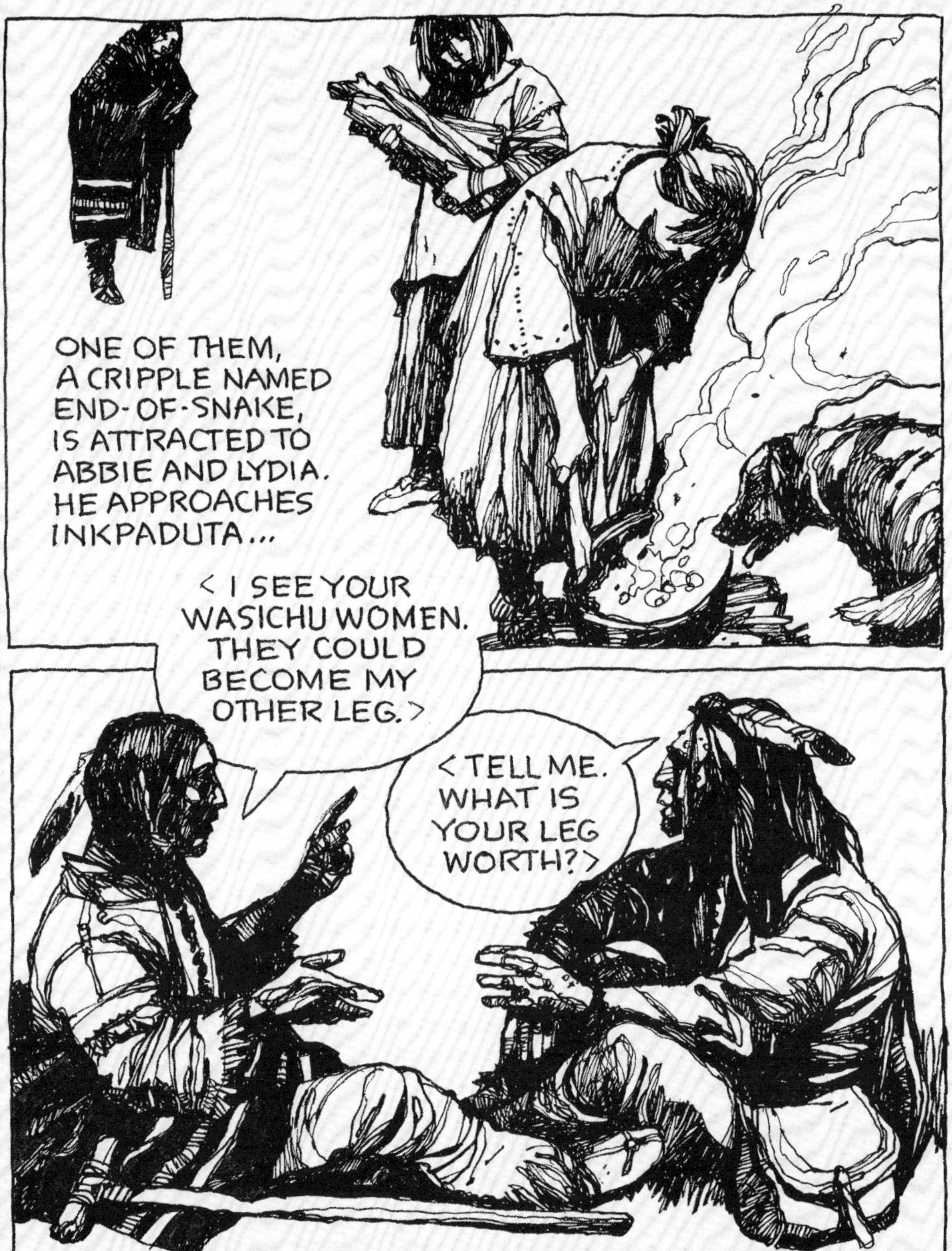
ONE OF THEM, A CRIPPLE NAMED END-OF-SNAKE, IS ATTRACTED TO ABBIE AND LYDIA. HE APPROACHES INKPADUTA...
< I SEE YOUR WASICHU WOMEN. THEY COULD BECOME MY OTHER LEG. >
< TELL ME. WHAT IS YOUR LEG WORTH? >
THE CONVERSATION EVOLVES INTO A TRADE DEAL. ABBIE GARDNER AND LYDIA NOBLE NOW BELONG TO A ONE-LEGGED YANKTON. HIS INTENTION; TO SOMEDAY PROFIT FROM 'SELLING' THEM TO A WHITE MAN. AN INDIAN AGENT.
...A GLIMMER OF HOPE FOR THE CAPTIVES?

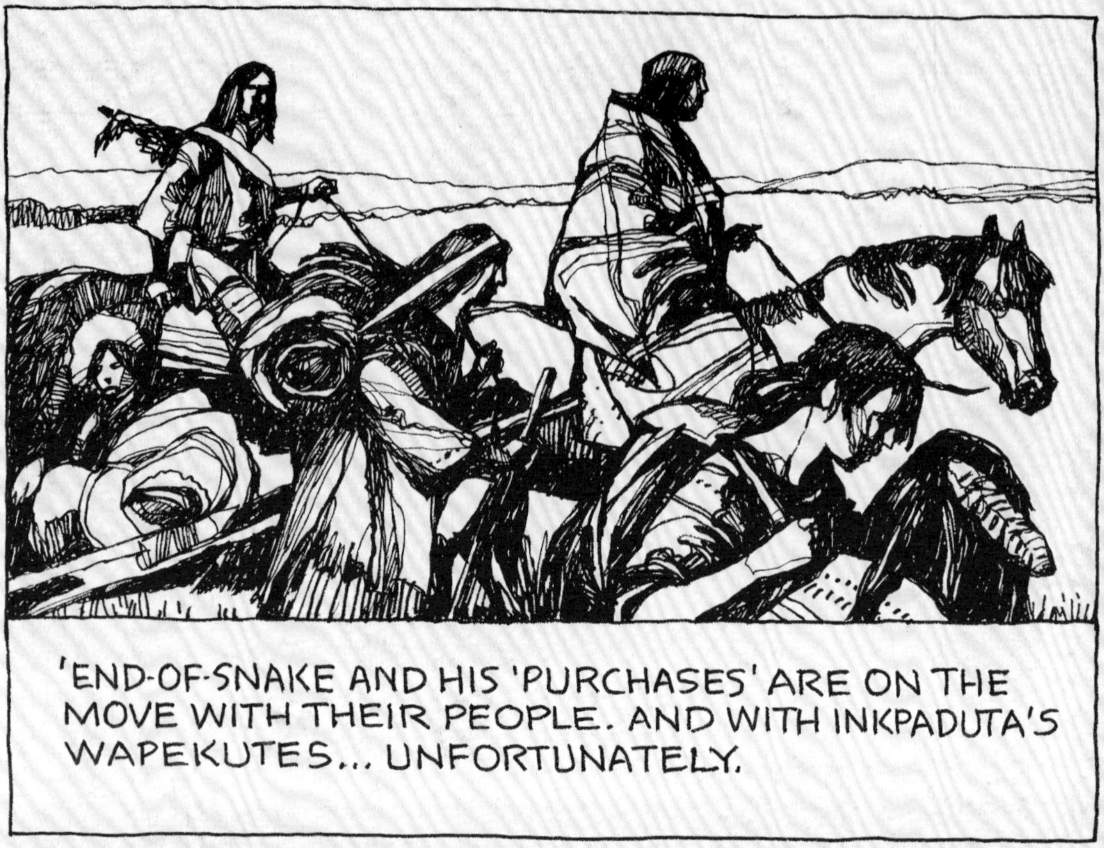
'END-OF-SNAKE AND HIS 'PURCHASES' ARE ON THE MOVE WITH THEIR PEOPLE. AND WITH INKPADUTA'S WAPEKUTES... UNFORTUNATELY.

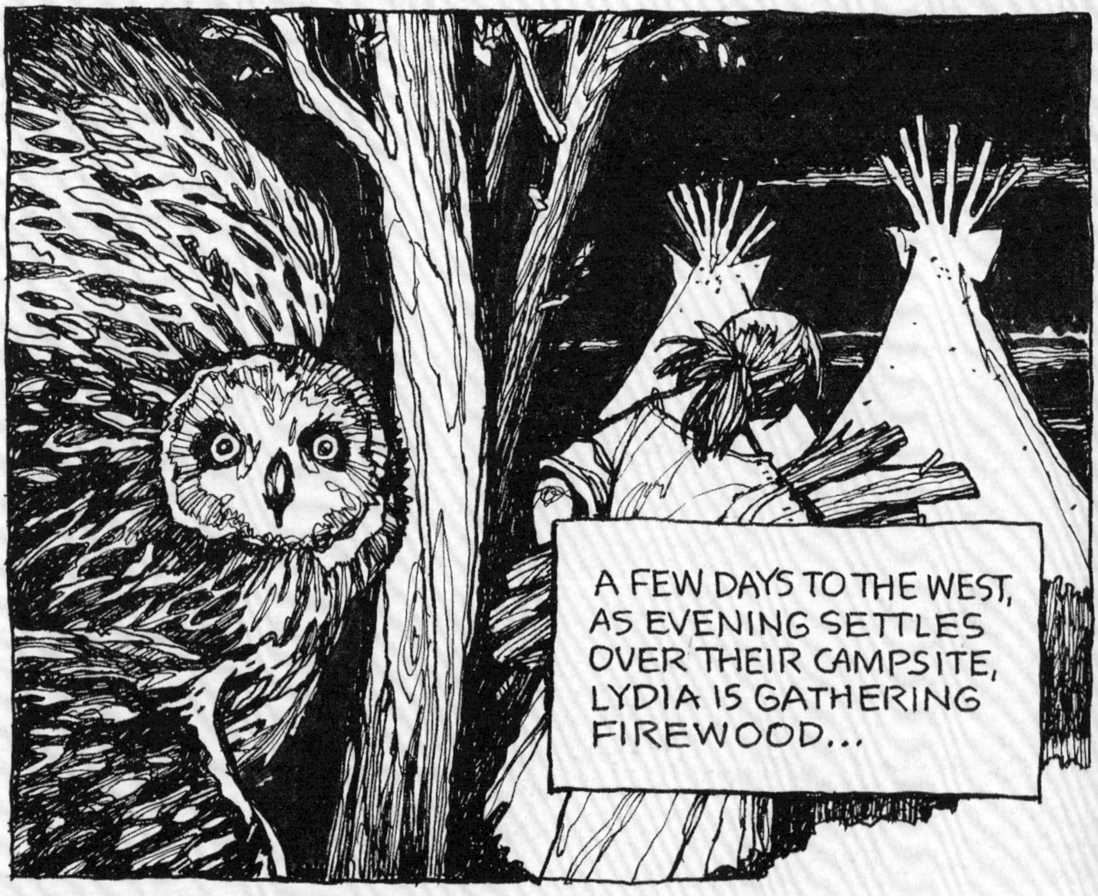
A FEW DAYS TO THE WEST, AS EVENING SETTLES OVER THEIR CAMPSITE, LYDIA IS GATHERING FIREWOOD...

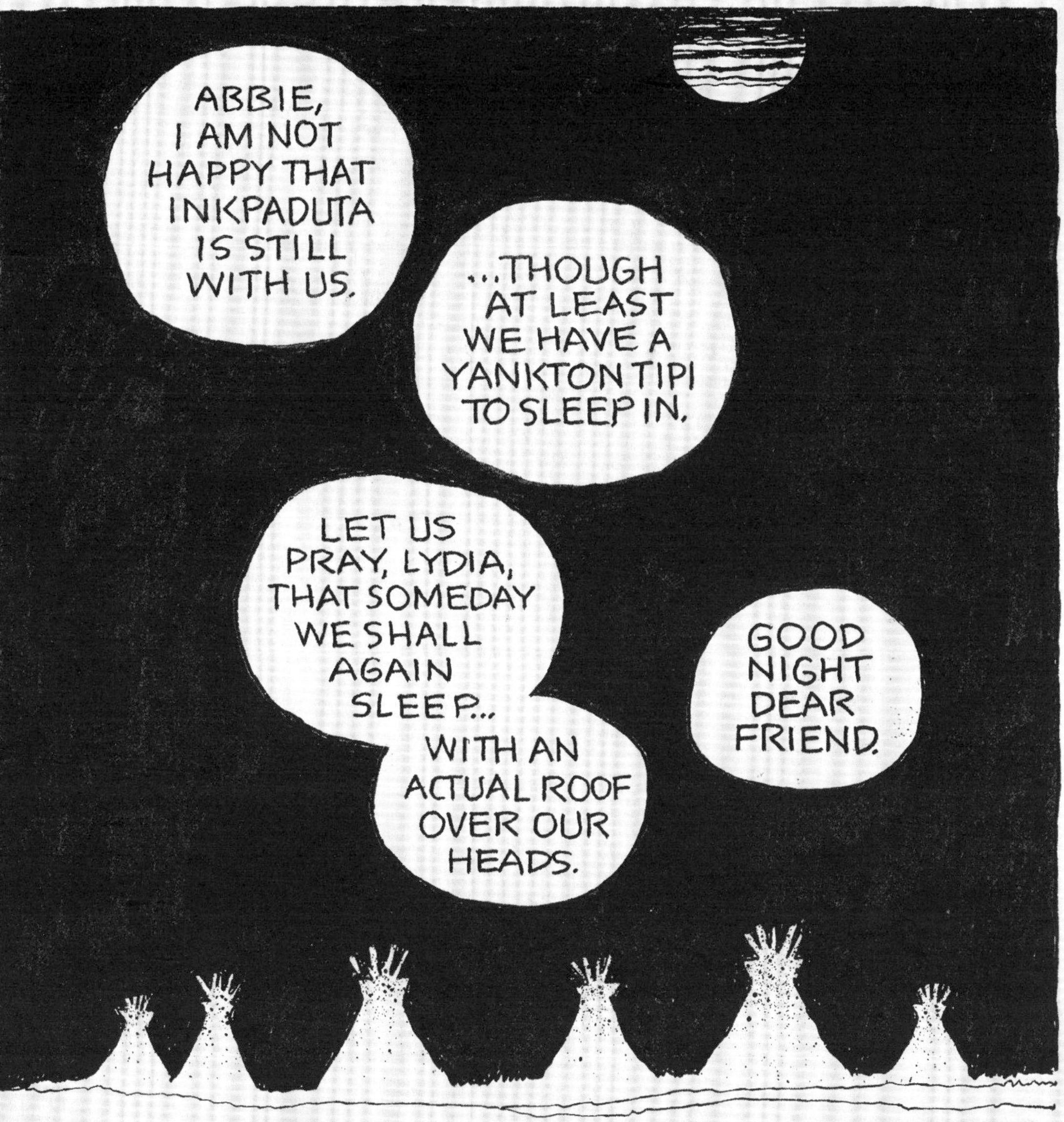
ABBIE, I AM NOT HAPPY THAT INKPADUTA IS STILL WITH US.
...THOUGH AT LEAST WE HAVE A YANKTON TIPI TO SLEEP IN.
LET US PRAY, LYDIA, THAT SOMEDAY WE SHALL AGAIN SLEEP...
WITH AN ACTUAL ROOF OVER OUR HEADS.
GOOD NIGHT DEAR FRIEND.

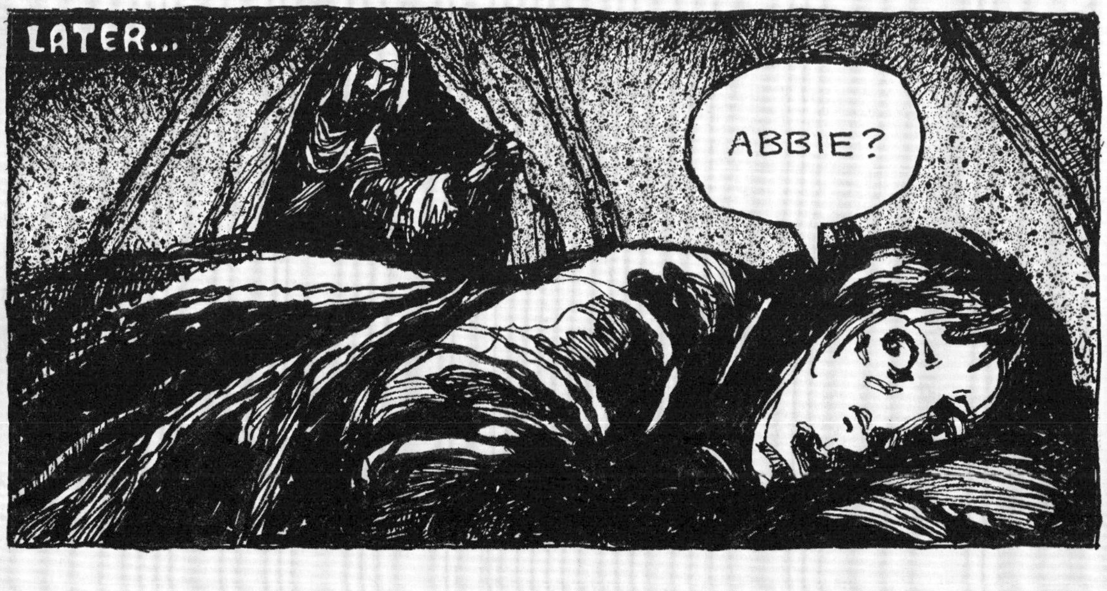
LATER...
ABBIE?

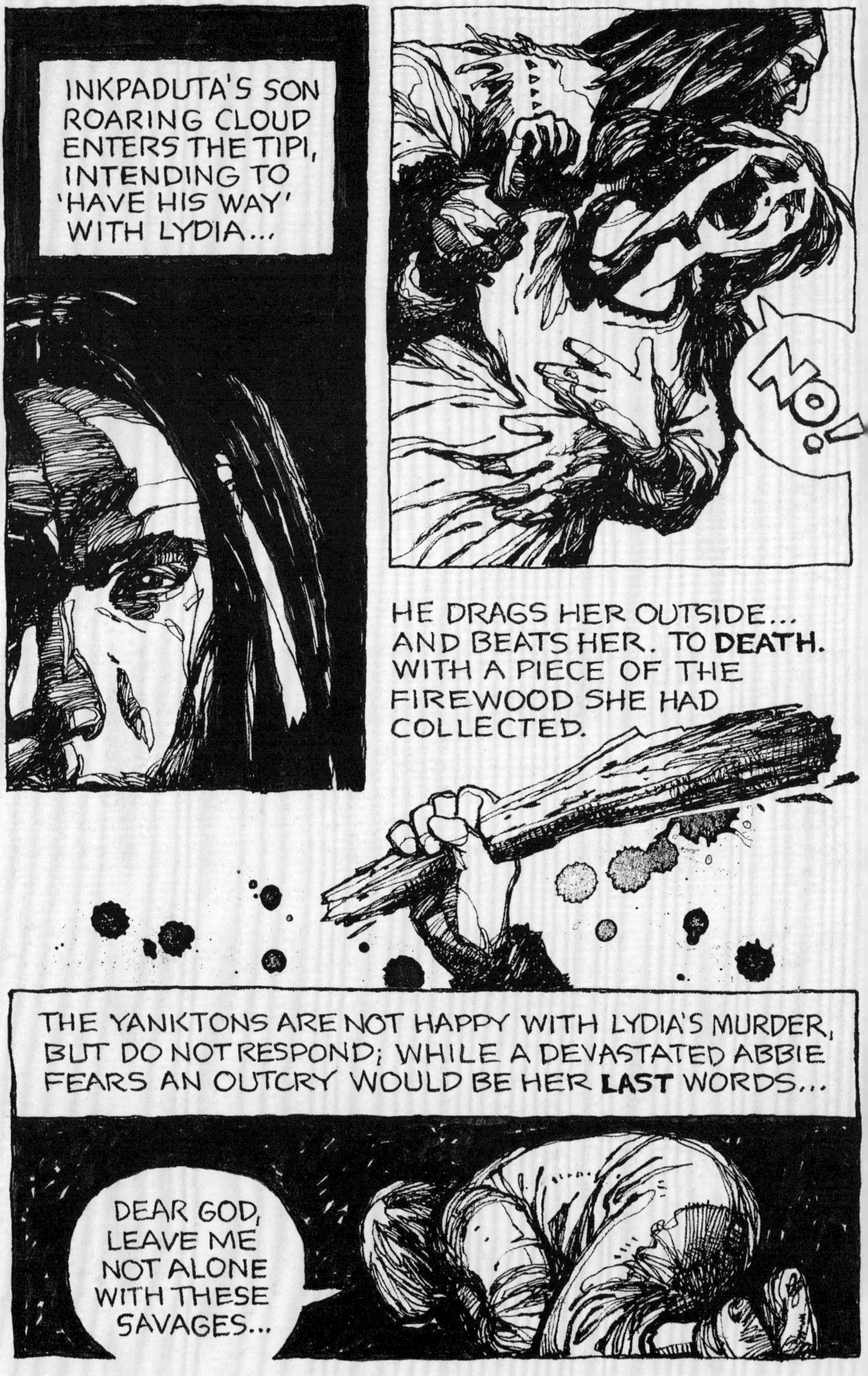
INKPADUTA'S SON ROARING CLOUD ENTERS THE TIPI, INTENDING TO 'HAVE HIS WAY' WITH LYDIA...
NO!
HE DRAGS HER OUTSIDE... AND BEATS HER. TO DEATH. WITH A PIECE OF THE FIREWOOD SHE HAD COLLECTED.
THE YANKTONS ARE NOT HAPPY WITH LYDIA'S MURDER, BUT DO NOT RESPOND; WHILE A DEVASTATED ABBIE FEARS AN OUTCRY WOULD BE HER LAST WORDS...
DEAR GOD, LEAVE ME NOT ALONE WITH THESE SAVAGES...

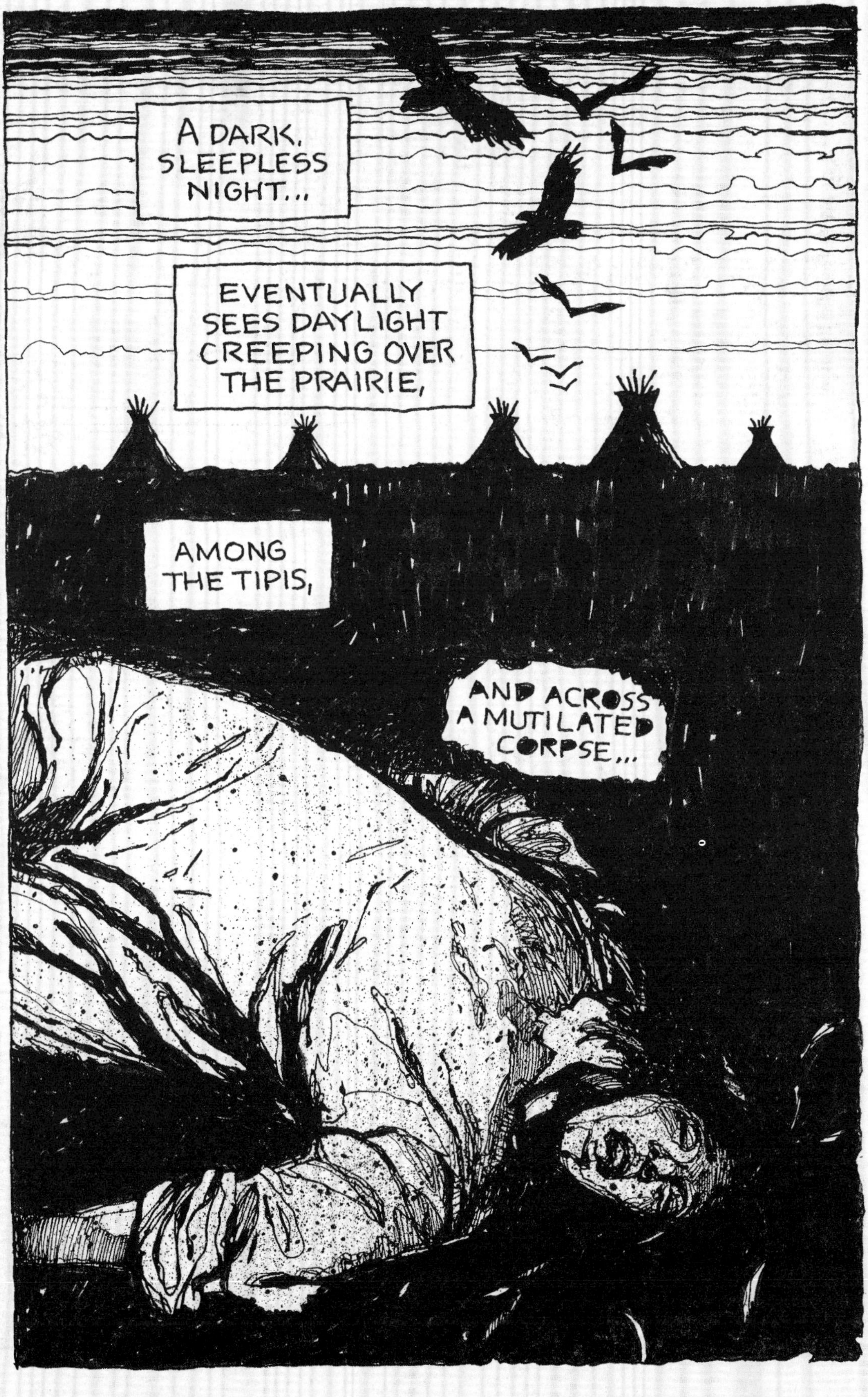
A DARK, SLEEPLESS NIGHT...
EVENTUALLY SEES DAYLIGHT CREEPING OVER THE PRAIRIE,
AMONG THE TIPIS,
AND ACROSS A MUTILATED CORPSE...

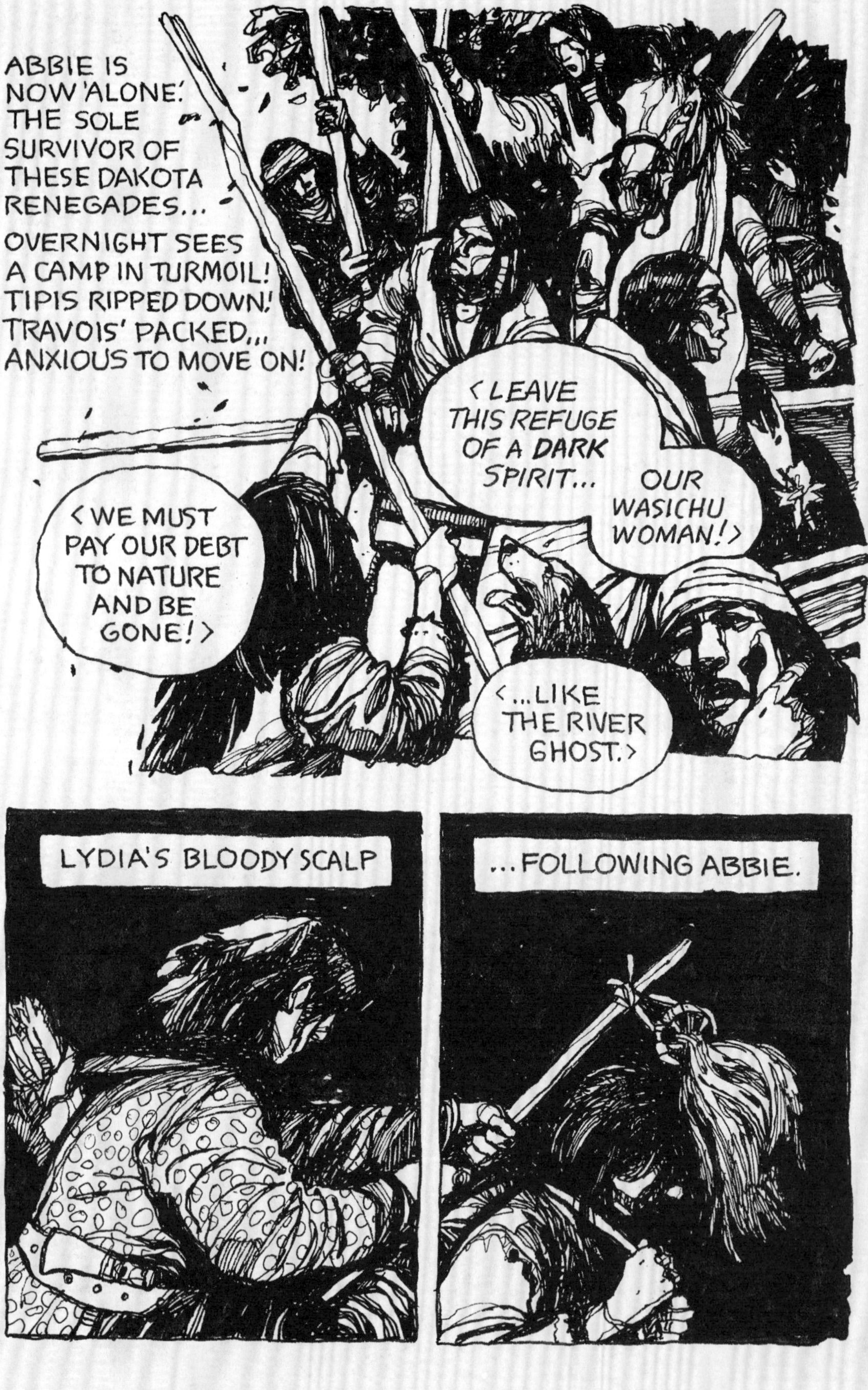
ABBIE IS NOW 'ALONE.' THE SOLE SURVIVOR OF THESE DAKOTA RENEGADES...
OVERNIGHT SEES A CAMP IN TURMOIL! TIPIS RIPPED DOWN! TRAVOIS' PACKED... ANXIOUS TO MOVE ON!
<LEAVE THIS REFUGE OF A DARK SPIRIT... OUR WASICHU WOMAN!>
<WE MUST PAY OUR DEBT TO NATURE AND BE GONE!>
<...LIKE THE RIVER GHOST.>
LYDIA'S BLOODY SCALP
...FOLLOWING ABBIE.

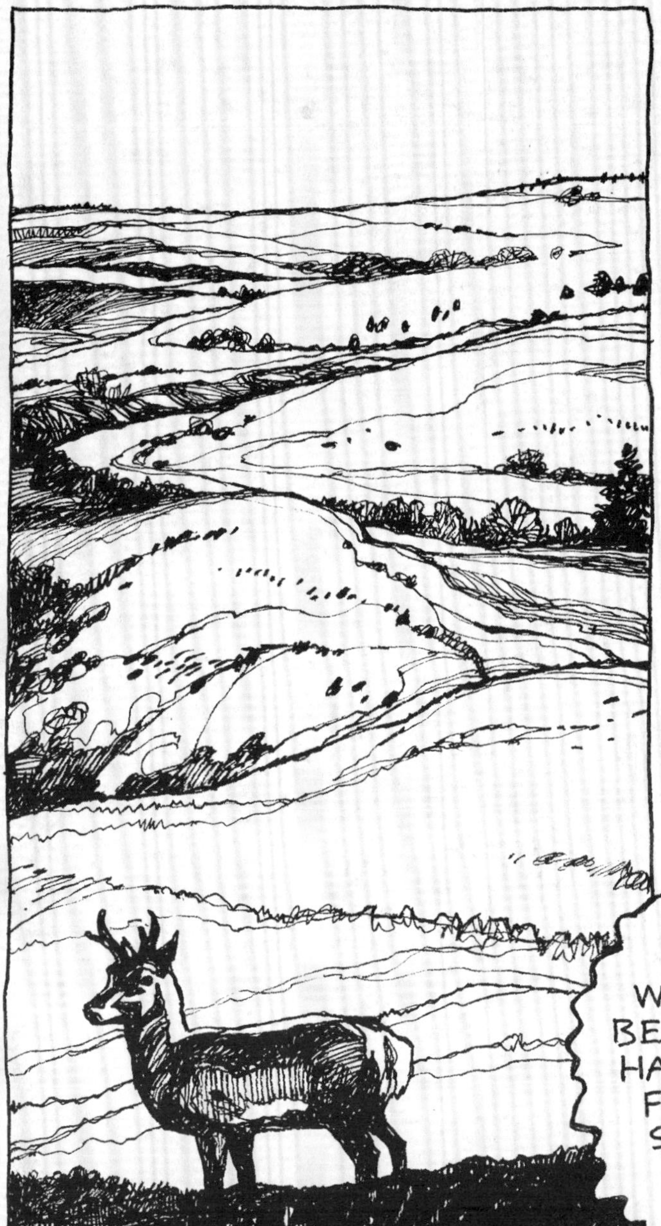

DESPITE THE GLOOM.

DESPITE THE DOOM.

THE VAST AND OPEN PRAIRIES ARE IN BLOOM; LATE MAY ON THE RIM OF THE GREAT PLAINS.

INKPADUTA'S PEOPLE, WITH THEIR YANKTON COMPANIONS, ARE THRIVING ON BISON. ON WILDFOWL. AND, OCCASIONALLY, THE ELUSIVE ANTELOPE.

THEY'VE BEEN ON THE MOVE NOW, FROM THE IOWA GREAT LAKES, SINCE EARLY MARCH.

UNFORTUNATELY... FOR ABBIE, IN THE WRONG DIRECTION.

BEYOND 'CIVILIZATION.'

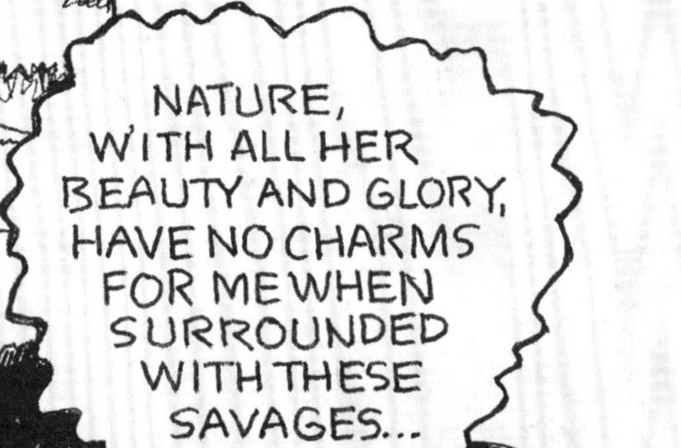
NATURE, WITH ALL HER BEAUTY AND GLORY, HAVE NO CHARMS FOR ME WHEN SURROUNDED WITH THESE SAVAGES...

...BUT FOR ABBIE'S CAPTORS, A DESTINATION FOR THE BETTER. THE HOMELANDS OF THEIR REBEL KINSMEN... NAKOTAS. LAKOTAS. AND THEIR ULTIMATE NECESSITY; HERDS OF BISON, WANDERING ENDLESS GRASSLANDS.

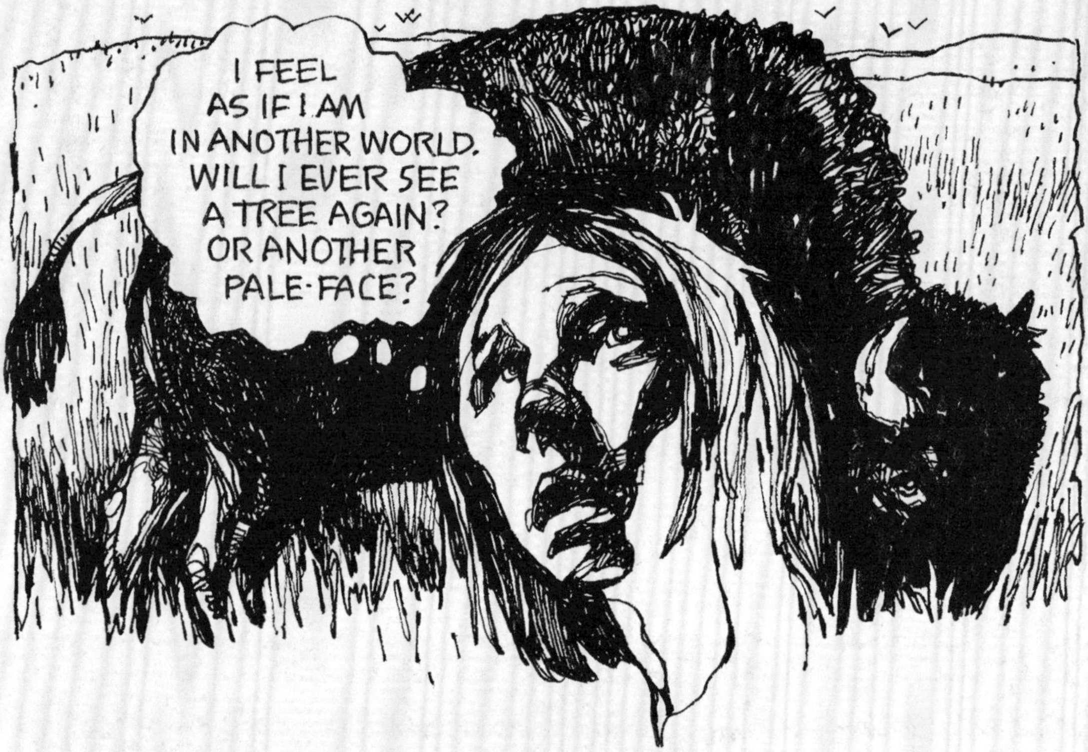
I FEEL AS IF I AM IN ANOTHER WORLD. WILL I EVER SEE A TREE AGAIN? OR ANOTHER PALE-FACE?

WITH HOPE, STILL, AGENT FLANDRAU CANNOT DISMISS THE MASSACRE AT THE IOWA LAKES.

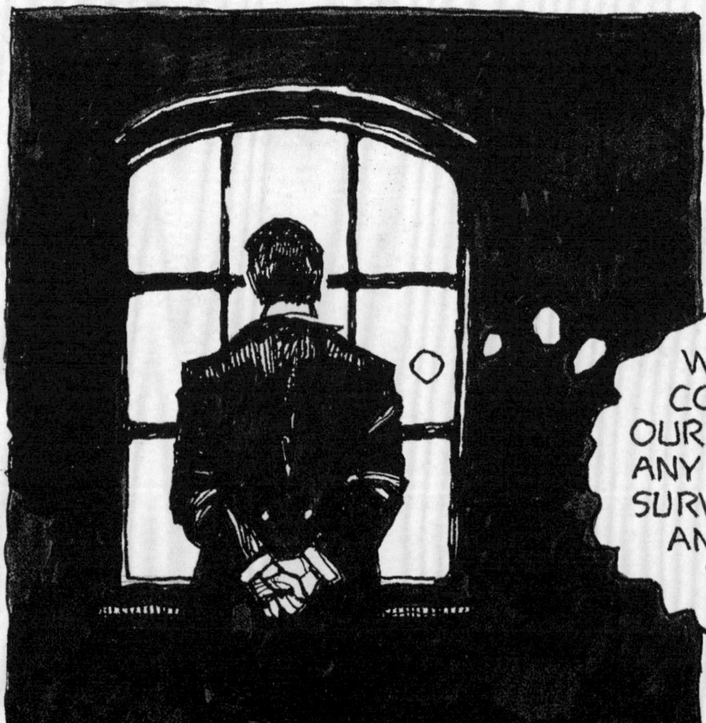
WE MUST CONTINUE OUR SEARCH FOR ANY REMAINING SURVIVORS STILL AMONG THE SIOUX.

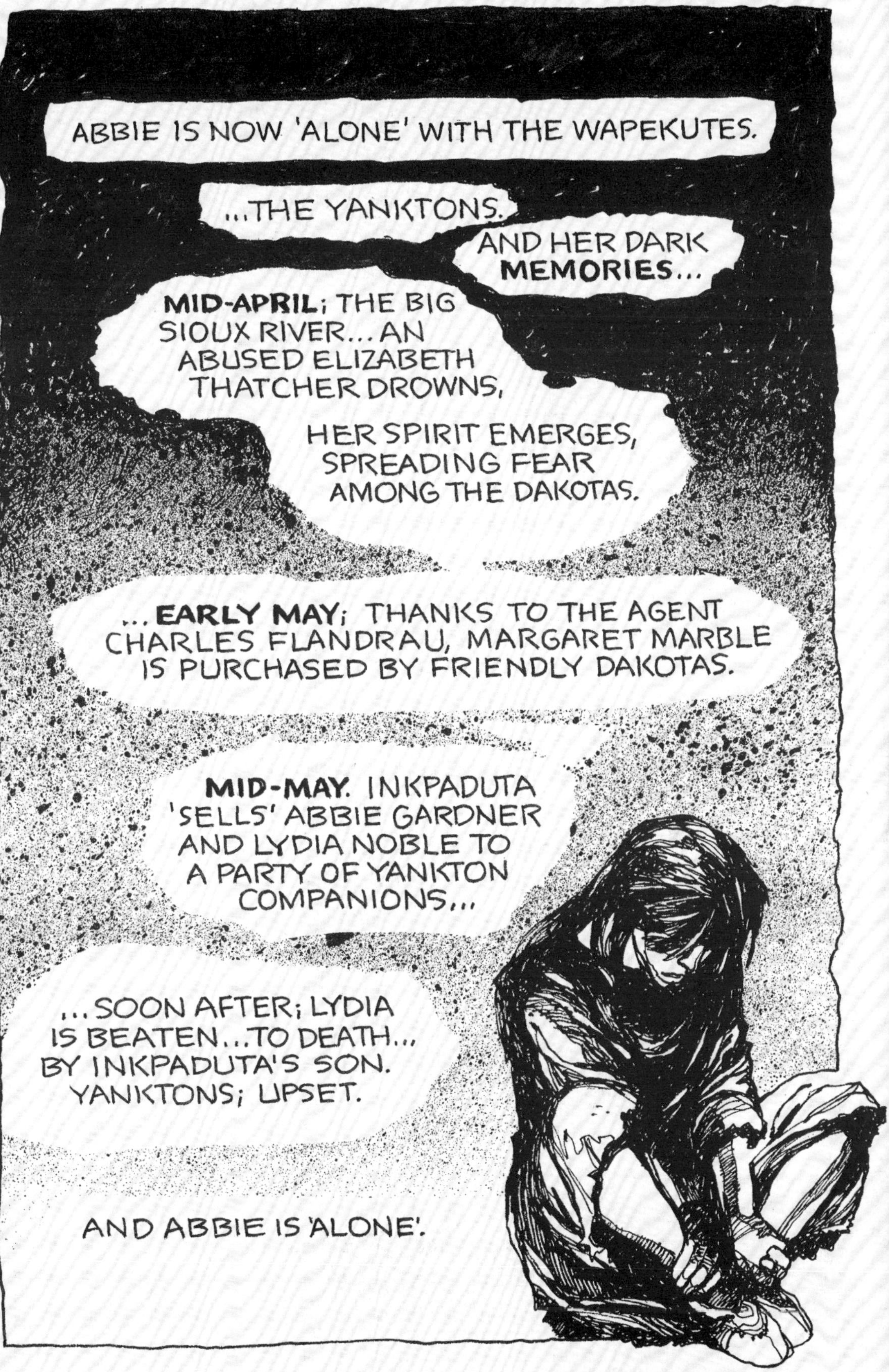
ABBIE IS NOW 'ALONE' WITH THE WAPEKUTES.
...THE YANKTONS.
AND HER DARK **MEMORIES**...
MID-APRIL; THE BIG SIOUX RIVER... AN ABUSED ELIZABETH THATCHER DROWNS,
HER SPIRIT EMERGES, SPREADING FEAR AMONG THE DAKOTAS.
...**EARLY MAY**; THANKS TO THE AGENT CHARLES FLANDRAU, MARGARET MARBLE IS PURCHASED BY FRIENDLY DAKOTAS.
MID-MAY. INKPADUTA 'SELLS' ABBIE GARDNER AND LYDIA NOBLE TO A PARTY OF YANKTON COMPANIONS...
...SOON AFTER; LYDIA IS BEATEN...TO DEATH... BY INKPADUTA'S SON. YANKTONS; UPSET.
AND ABBIE IS 'ALONE'.

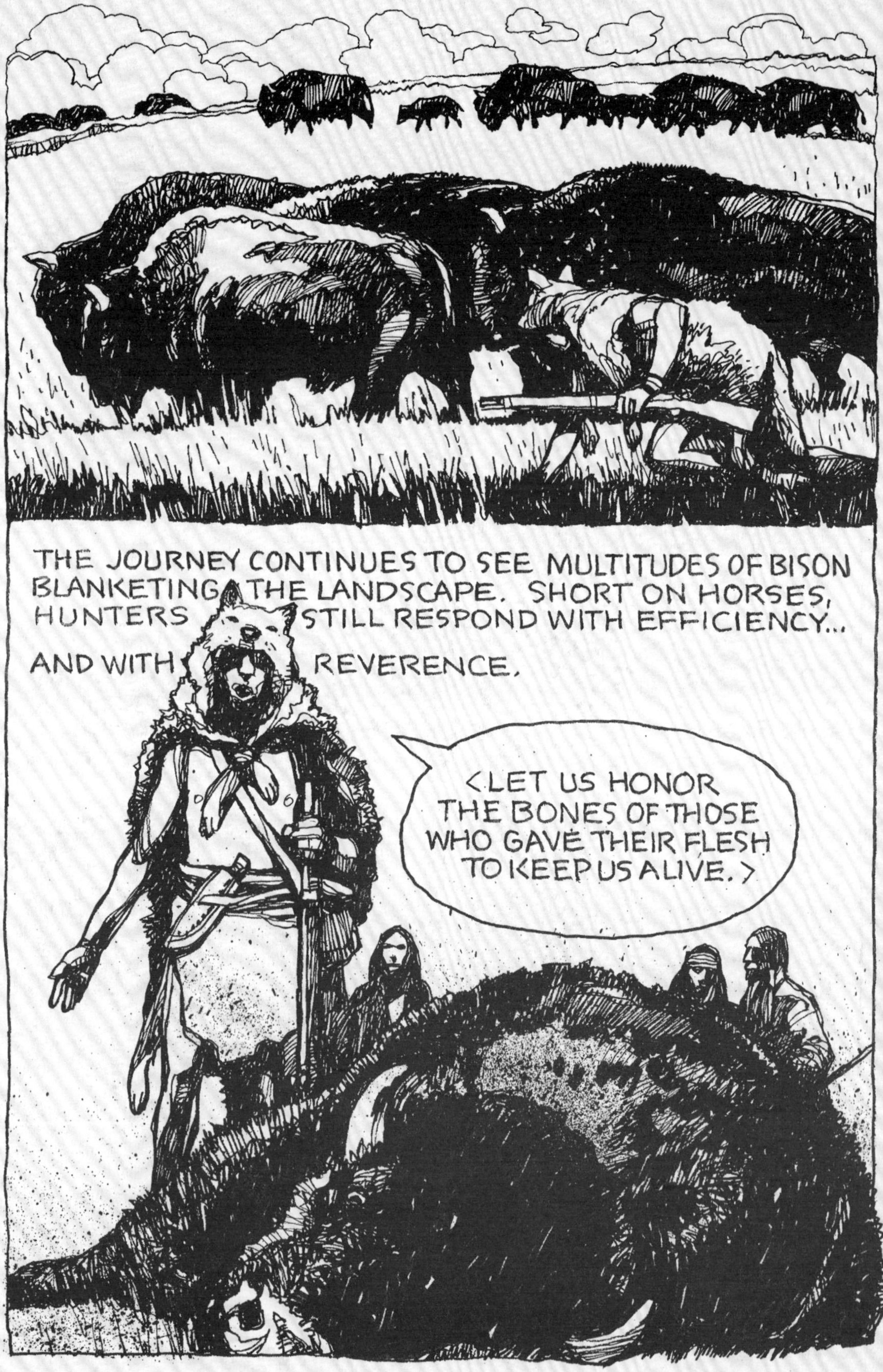
THE JOURNEY CONTINUES TO SEE MULTITUDES OF BISON BLANKETING THE LANDSCAPE. SHORT ON HORSES, HUNTERS STILL RESPOND WITH EFFICIENCY...
AND WITH REVERENCE.
<LET US HONOR THE BONES OF THOSE WHO GAVE THEIR FLESH TO KEEP US ALIVE.>

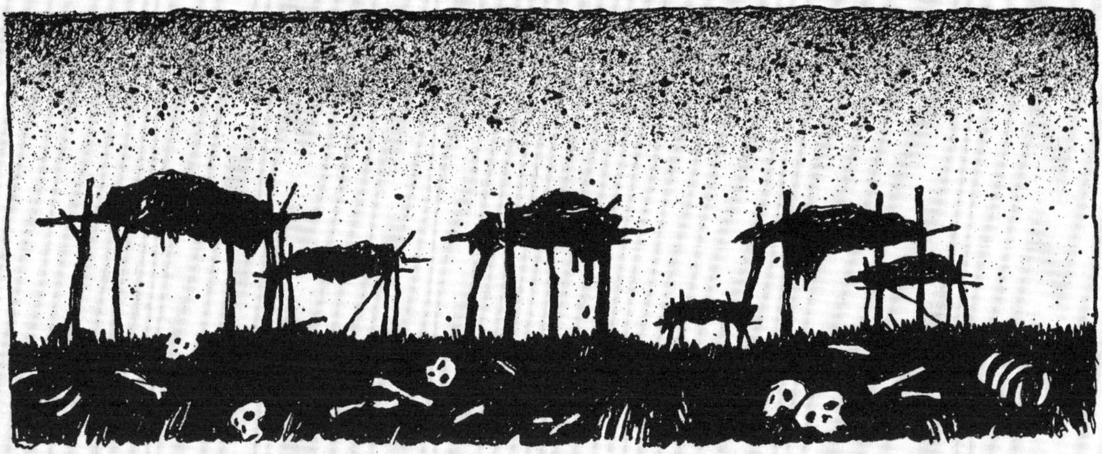

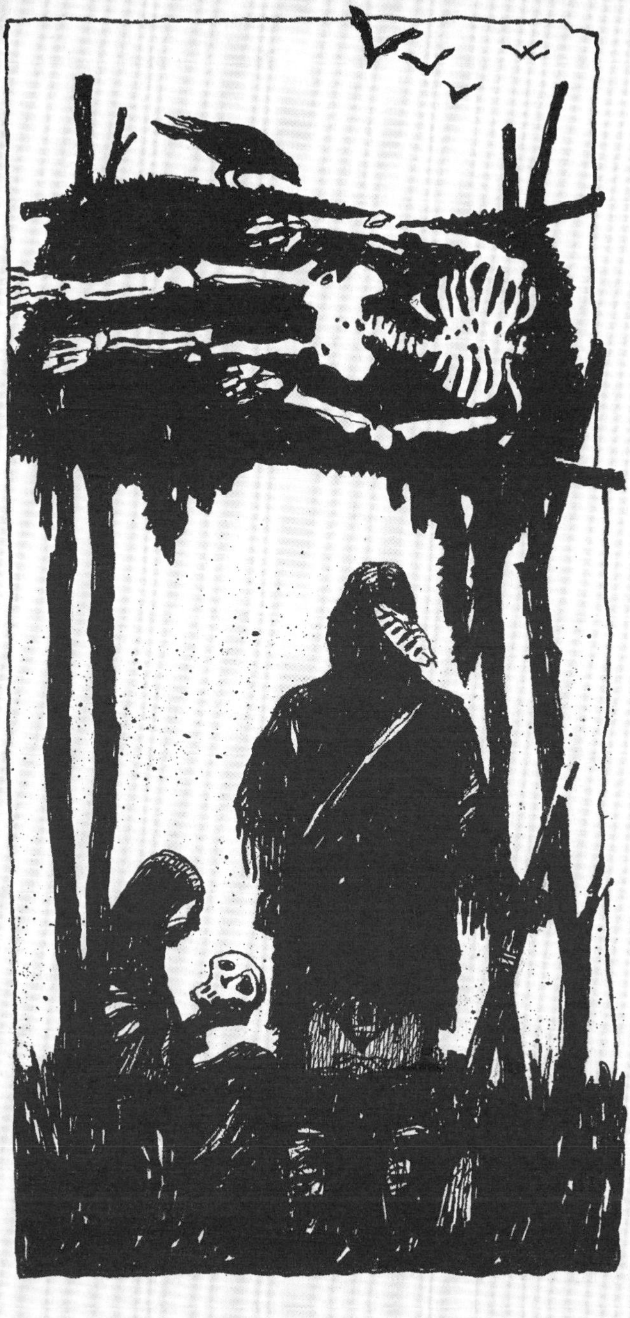

A FEW DAYS BEYOND THEIR BUFFALO HUNT, AND ITS SCATTERED REMAINS, INKPADUTA'S PEOPLE COME ACROSS ANOTHER SCATTERING, OF HUMAN REMAINS. A BURIAL SITE, LIKELY THE RESULT OF A LONG-AGO TRIBAL CONFLICT. BONES AND MEMORIES ON THEIR SCAFFOLDS... 'ASLEEP'.....IN THEIR HAPPY HUNTING GROUND.

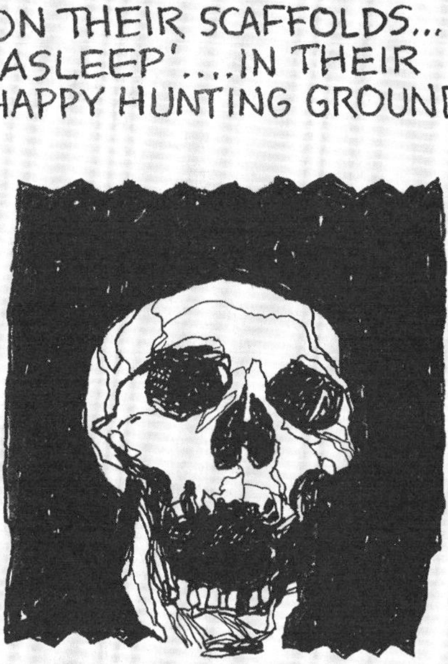

MORBIDLY CURIOUS, BUT WITH RESPECT, THE WAPEKUTES FIND THESE HUMAN SKULLS MOST FASCINATING...

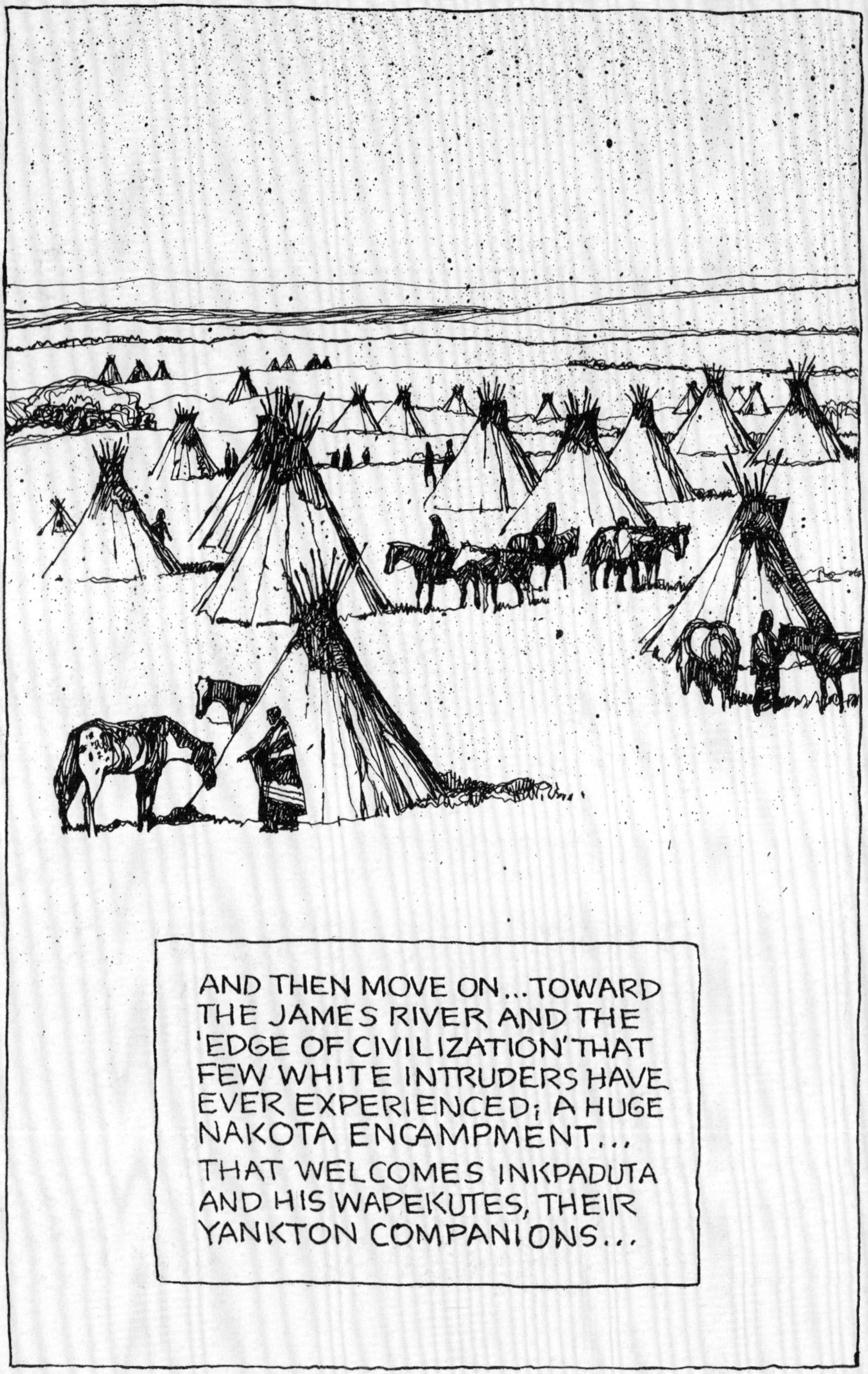
AND THEN MOVE ON...TOWARD THE JAMES RIVER AND THE 'EDGE OF CIVILIZATION' THAT FEW WHITE INTRUDERS HAVE EVER EXPERIENCED; A HUGE NAKOTA ENCAMPMENT...
THAT WELCOMES INKPADUTA AND HIS WAPEKUTES, THEIR YANKTON COMPANIONS...

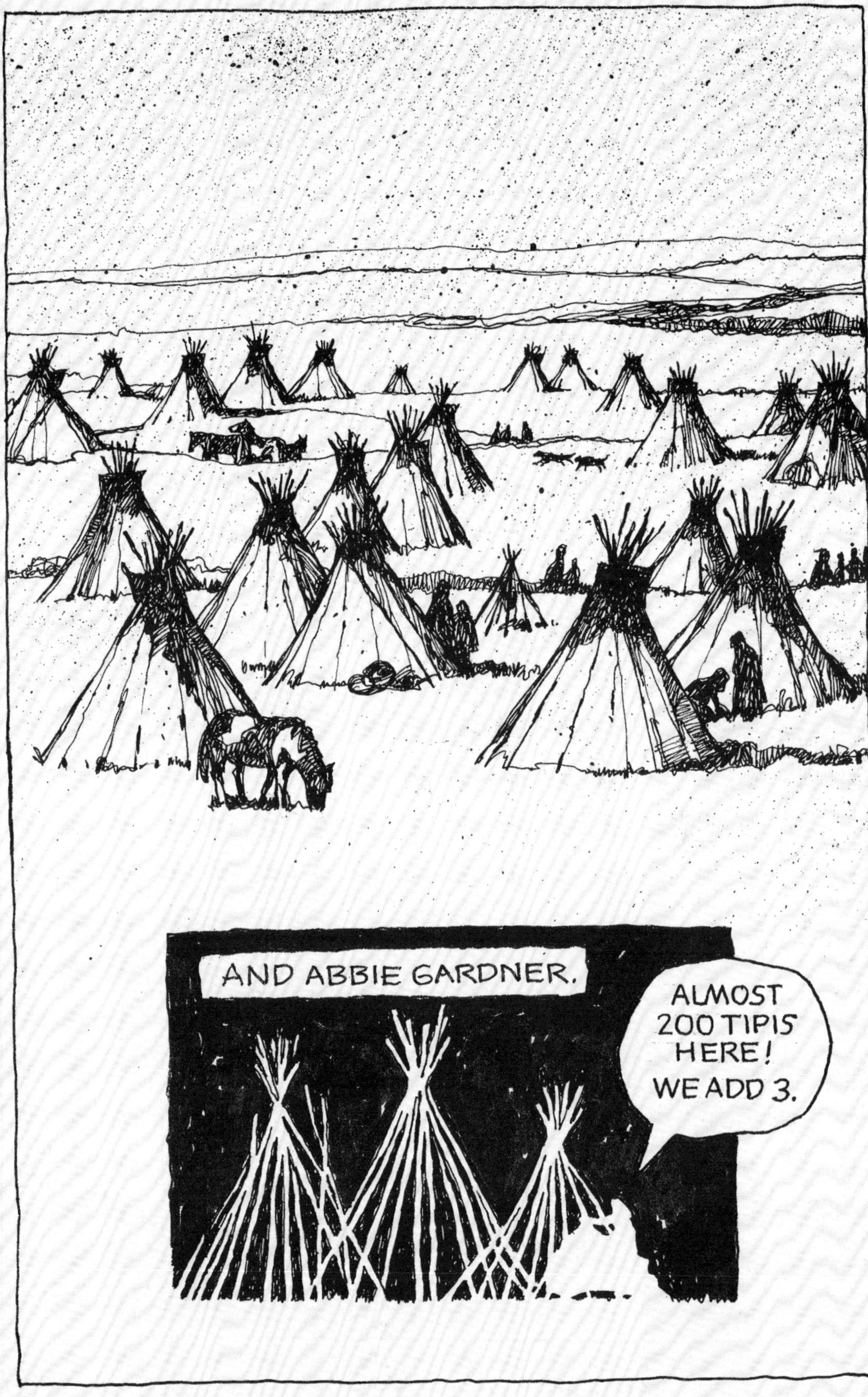
AND ABBIE GARDNER.
ALMOST 200 TIPIS HERE! WE ADD 3.

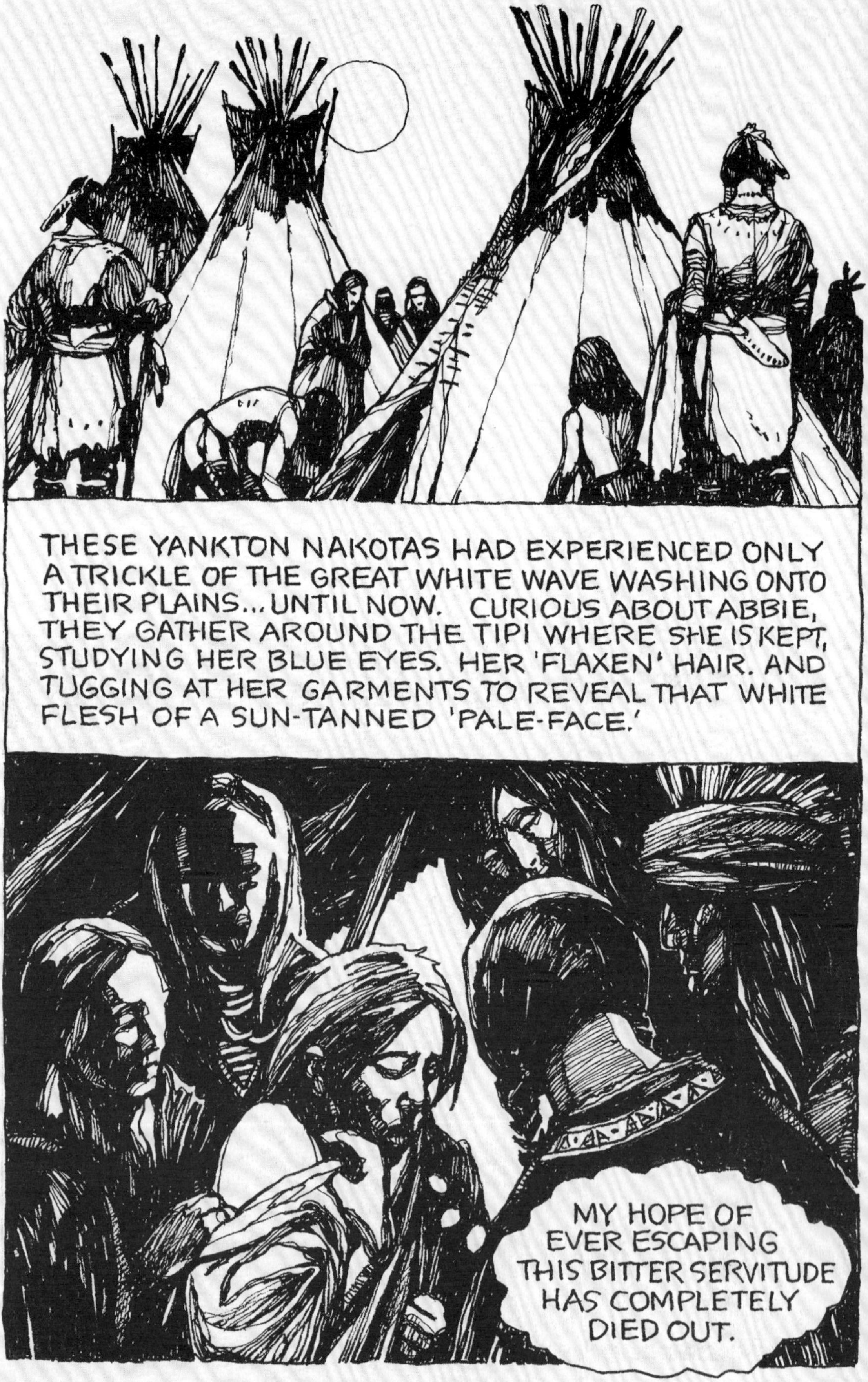
THESE YANKTON NAKOTAS HAD EXPERIENCED ONLY A TRICKLE OF THE GREAT WHITE WAVE WASHING ONTO THEIR PLAINS... UNTIL NOW. CURIOUS ABOUT ABBIE, THEY GATHER AROUND THE TIPI WHERE SHE IS KEPT, STUDYING HER BLUE EYES. HER 'FLAXEN' HAIR. AND TUGGING AT HER GARMENTS TO REVEAL THAT WHITE FLESH OF A SUN-TANNED 'PALE-FACE.'
MY HOPE OF EVER ESCAPING THIS BITTER SERVITUDE HAS COMPLETELY DIED OUT.

"THE MORNING OF MAY 30TH DAWNED AS FAIR; LOVELY; AS ANY MORTAL EYE HAS EVER SEEN, BUT ALL BEAUTY AND BRIGHTNESS OF NATURE COULD NOT SYMBOLIZE THE BRIGHTNESS OF THAT DAY TO ME." ABBIE GARDNER

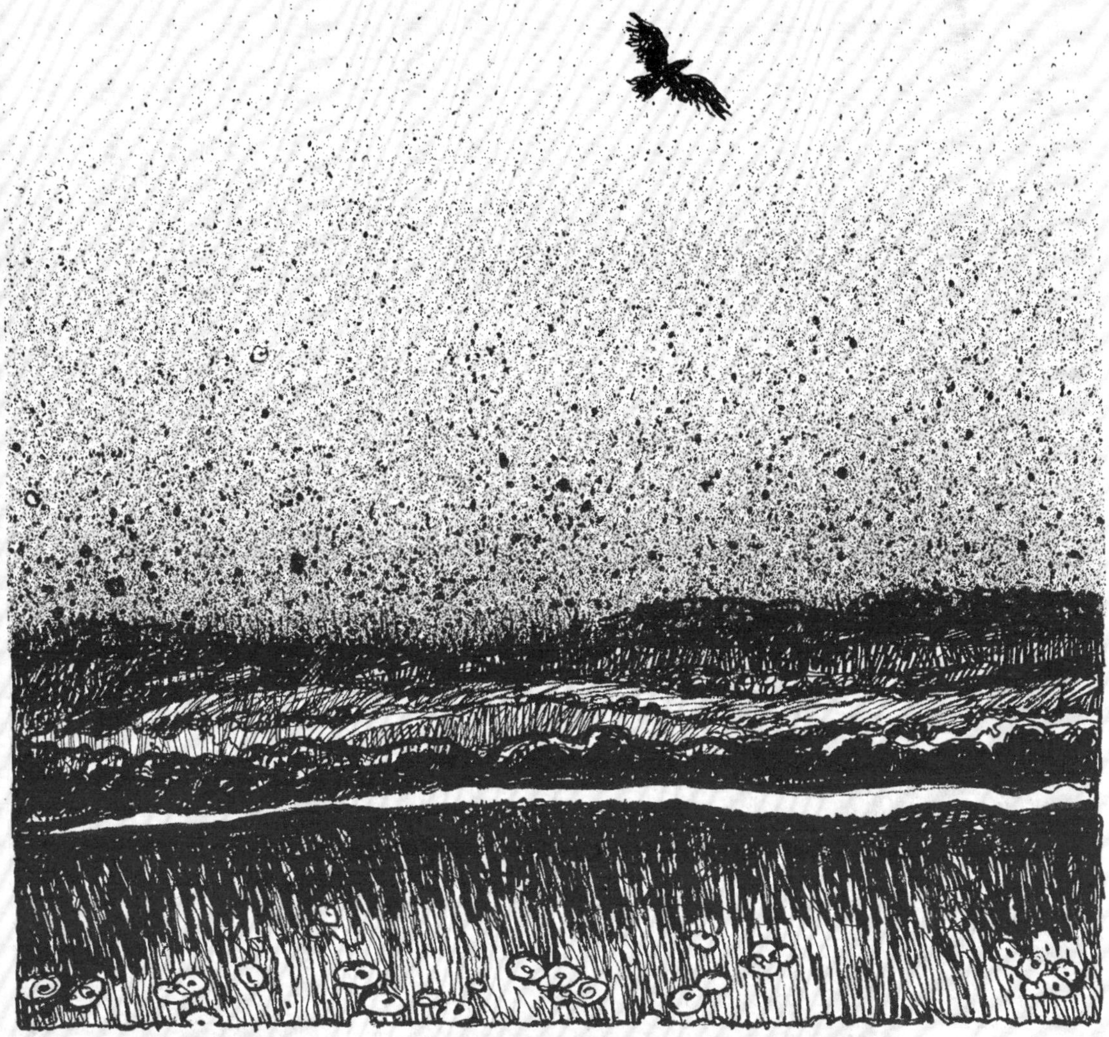

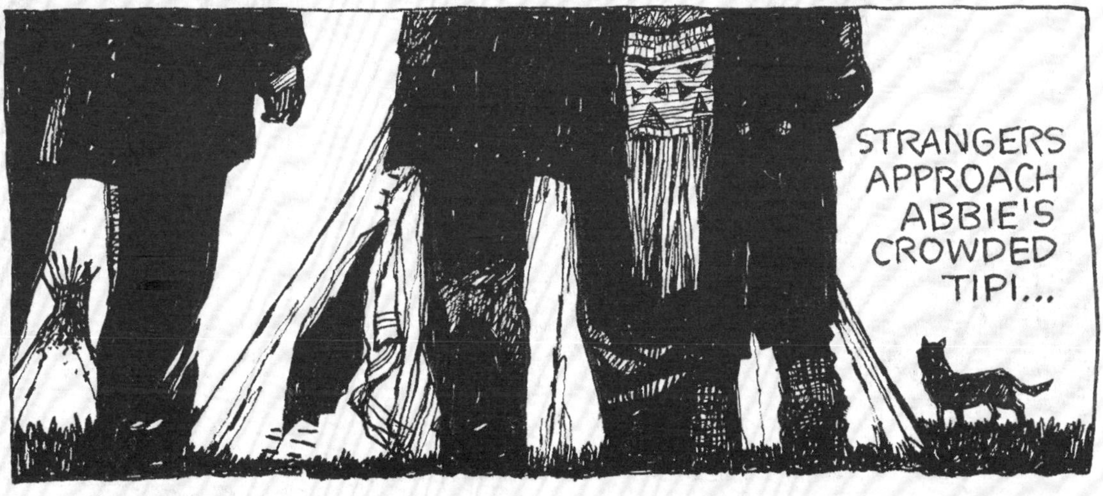
STRANGERS APPROACH ABBIE'S CROWDED TIPI...

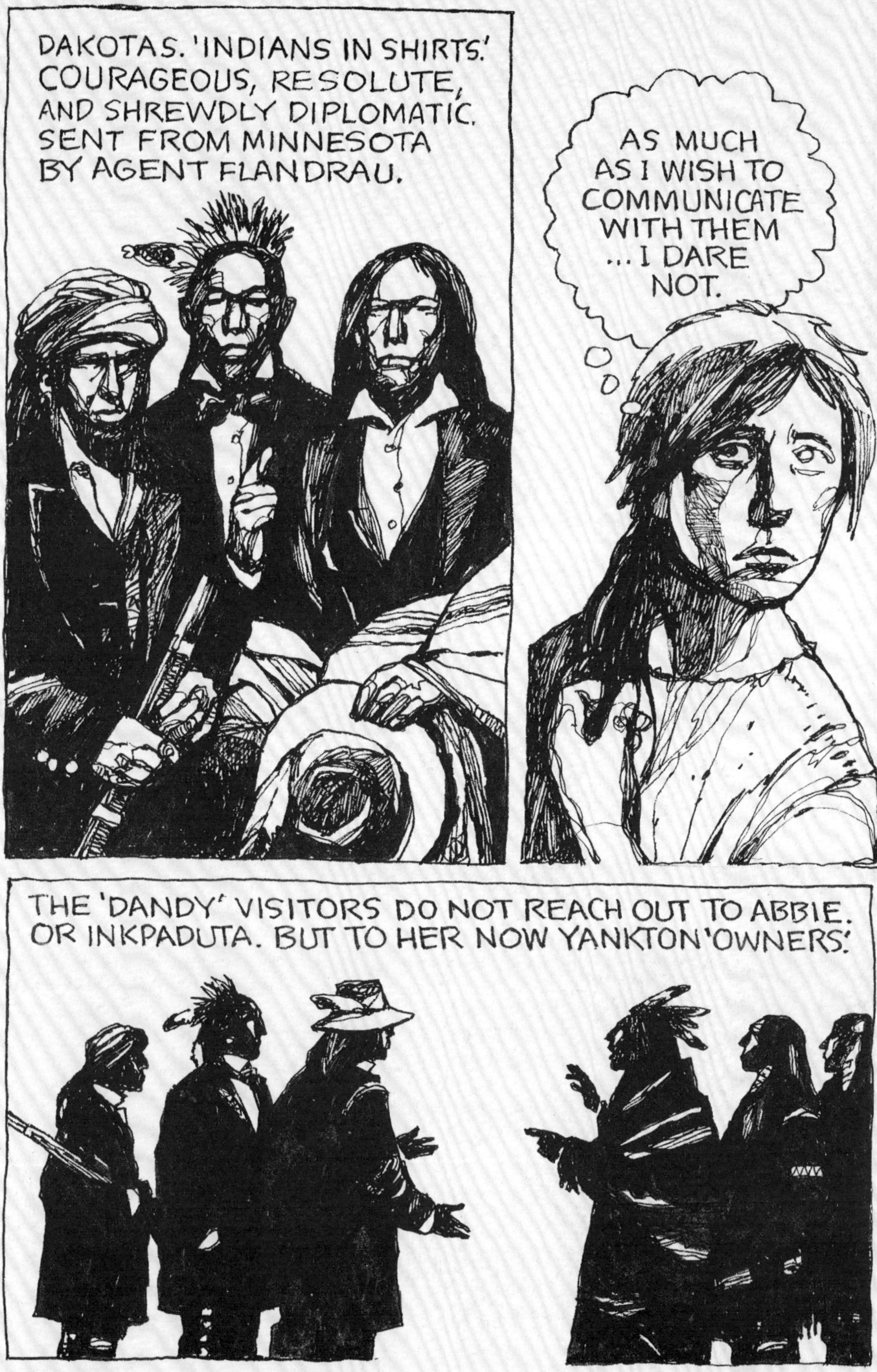

DAKOTAS. 'INDIANS IN SHIRTS.' COURAGEOUS, RESOLUTE, AND SHREWDLY DIPLOMATIC. SENT FROM MINNESOTA BY AGENT FLANDRAU.
AS MUCH AS I WISH TO COMMUNICATE WITH THEM ...I DARE NOT.
THE 'DANDY' VISITORS DO NOT REACH OUT TO ABBIE. OR INKPADUTA. BUT TO HER NOW YANKTON 'OWNERS.'

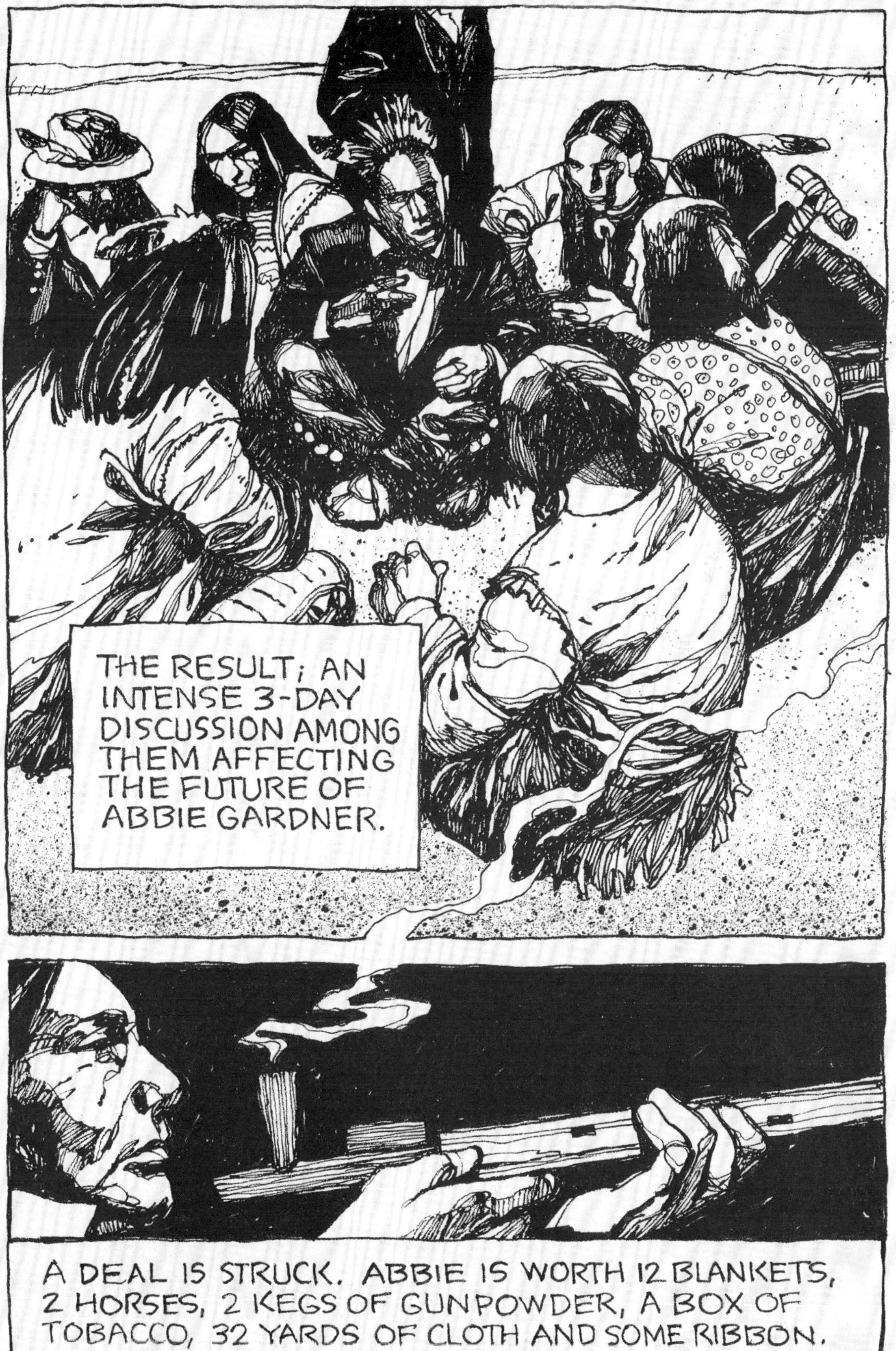
THE RESULT; AN INTENSE 3-DAY DISCUSSION AMONG THEM AFFECTING THE FUTURE OF ABBIE GARDNER.
A DEAL IS STRUCK. ABBIE IS WORTH 12 BLANKETS, 2 HORSES, 2 KEGS OF GUNPOWDER, A BOX OF TOBACCO, 32 YARDS OF CLOTH AND SOME RIBBON.

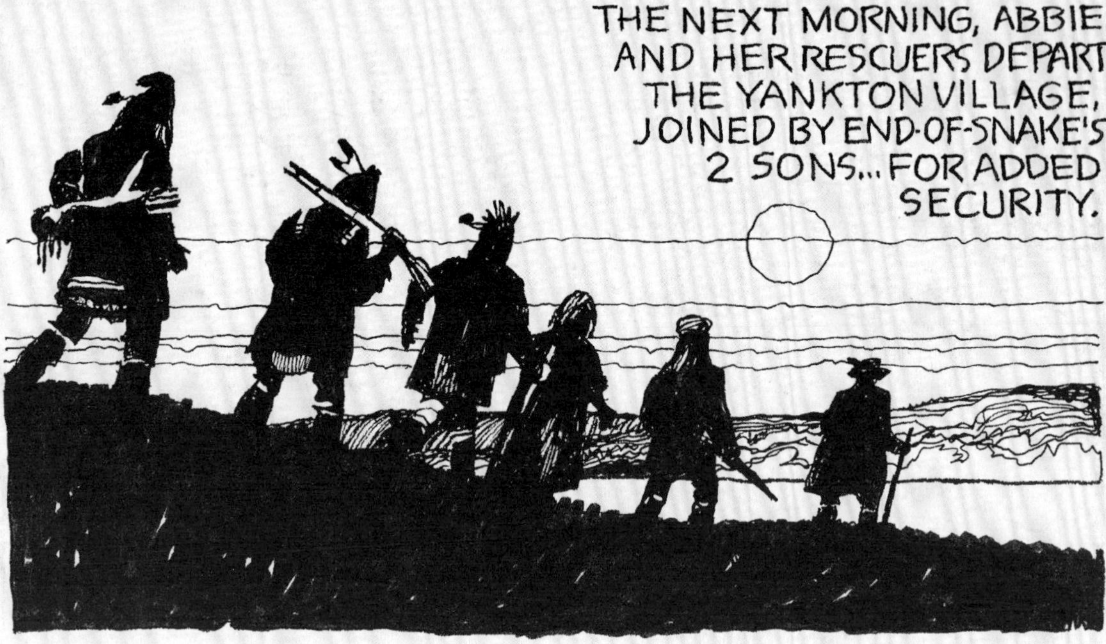
THE NEXT MORNING, ABBIE AND HER RESCUERS DEPART THE YANKTON VILLAGE, JOINED BY END-OF-SNAKE'S 2 SONS... FOR ADDED SECURITY.

THE GROUP HEADS EAST TO THE BANK OF THE NEARBY JAMES RIVER. THERE THEY UNCOVER A TINY HIDDEN BUFFALO-HIDE BOAT; SENDING ABBIE OUT ONTO THE WATER IN IT, ALONE. WITH HER DARK MEMORIES OF THE BIG SIOUX RIVER... AND ELIZABETH THATCHER.

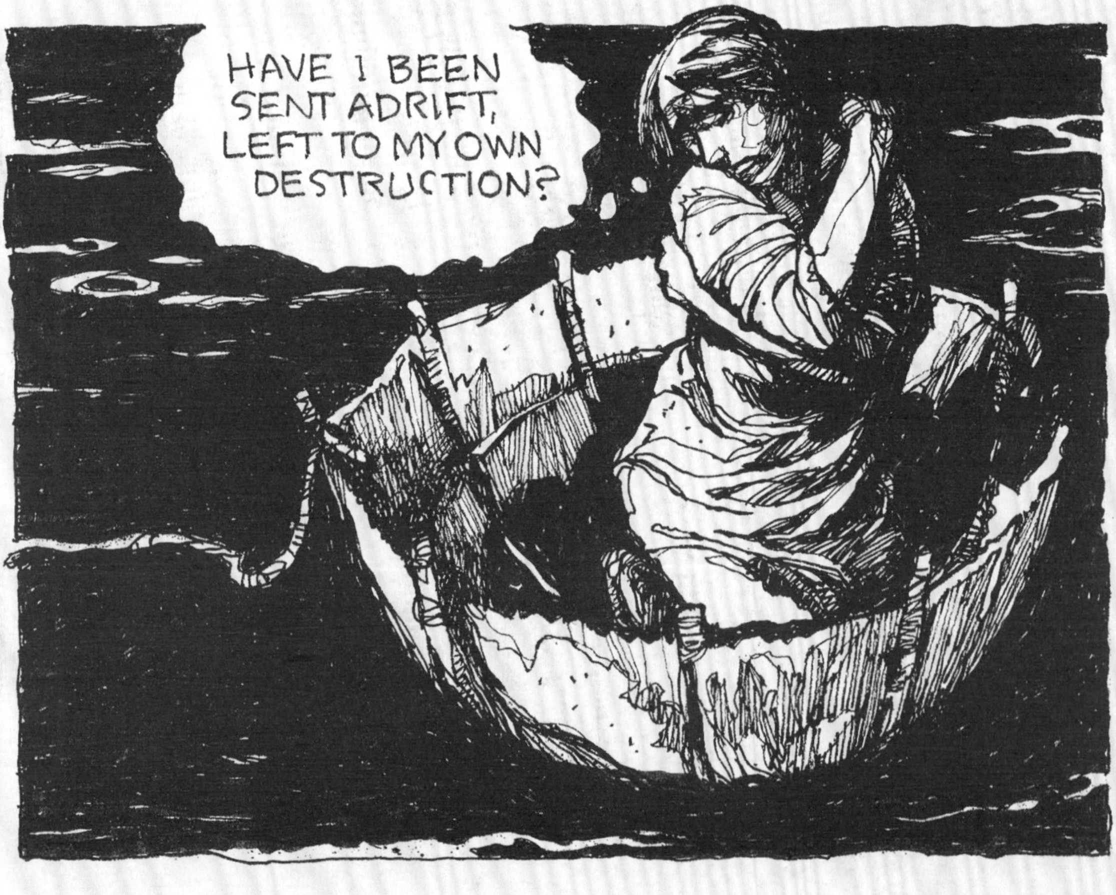
HAVE I BEEN SENT ADRIFT, LEFT TO MY OWN DESTRUCTION?

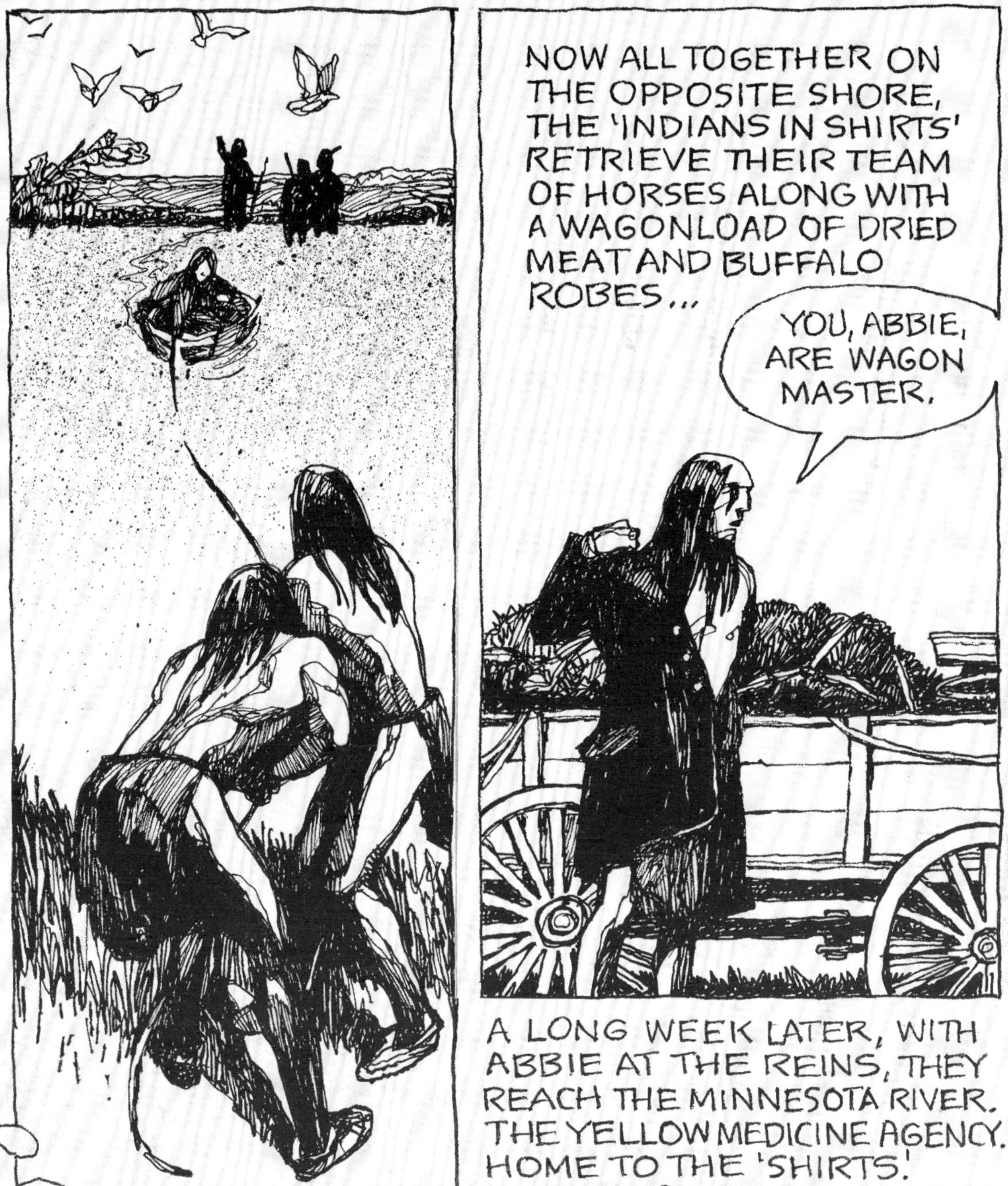
No.
A PAIR OF FLANDRAU DAKOTAS SWIM THE RIVER WITH A TOW ROPE . . . THEN PULL ABBIE'S BOAT AFTER THEM.
'CLOSER TO HOME.'
NOW ALL TOGETHER ON THE OPPOSITE SHORE, THE 'INDIANS IN SHIRTS' RETRIEVE THEIR TEAM OF HORSES ALONG WITH A WAGONLOAD OF DRIED MEAT AND BUFFALO ROBES...
YOU, ABBIE, ARE WAGON MASTER.
A LONG WEEK LATER, WITH ABBIE AT THE REINS, THEY REACH THE MINNESOTA RIVER. THE YELLOW MEDICINE AGENCY. HOME TO THE 'SHIRTS.'

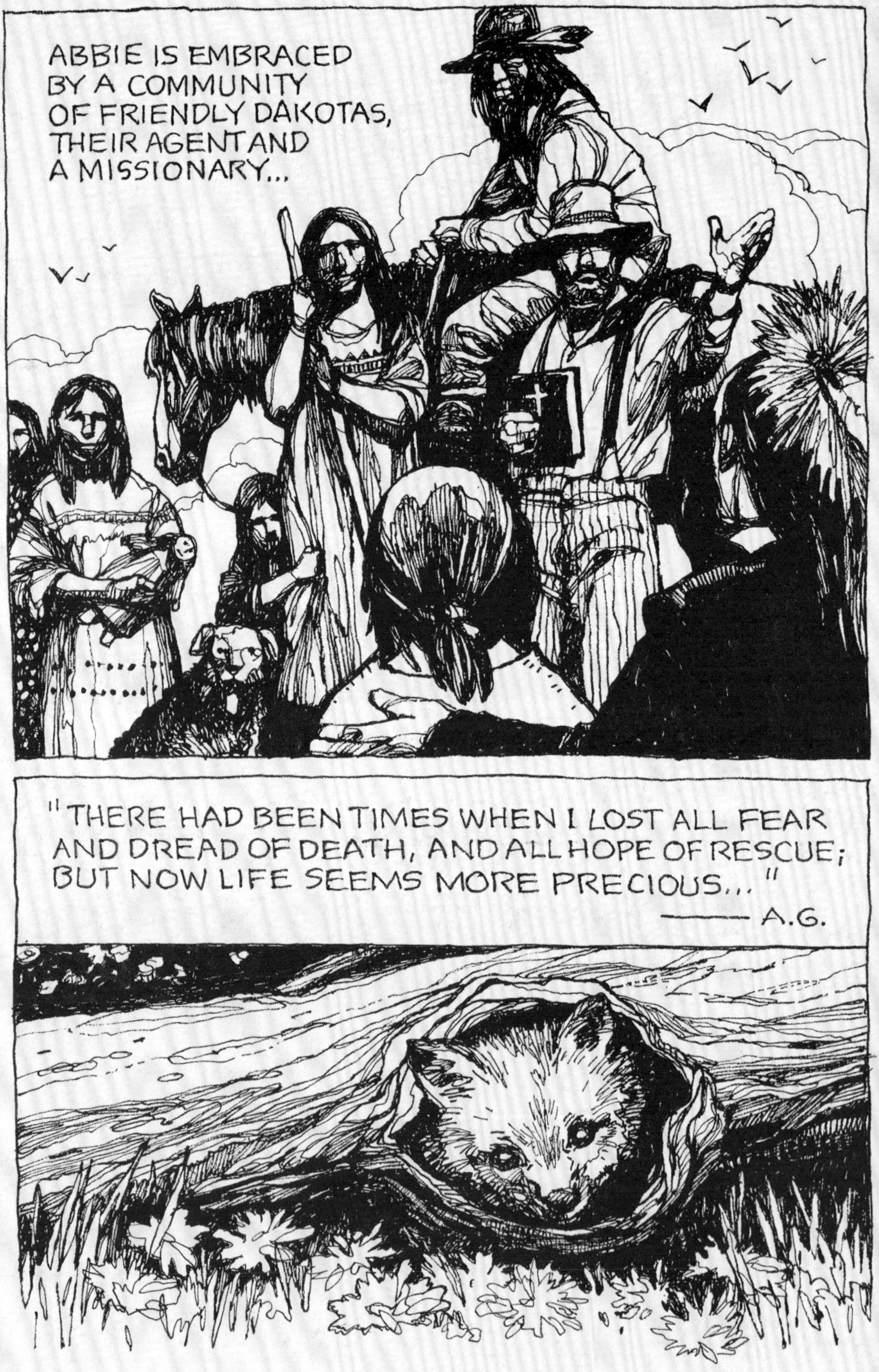
ABBIE IS EMBRACED BY A COMMUNITY OF FRIENDLY DAKOTAS, THEIR AGENT AND A MISSIONARY...
"THERE HAD BEEN TIMES WHEN I LOST ALL FEAR AND DREAD OF DEATH, AND ALL HOPE OF RESCUE; BUT NOW LIFE SEEMS MORE PRECIOUS..."
—— A.G.

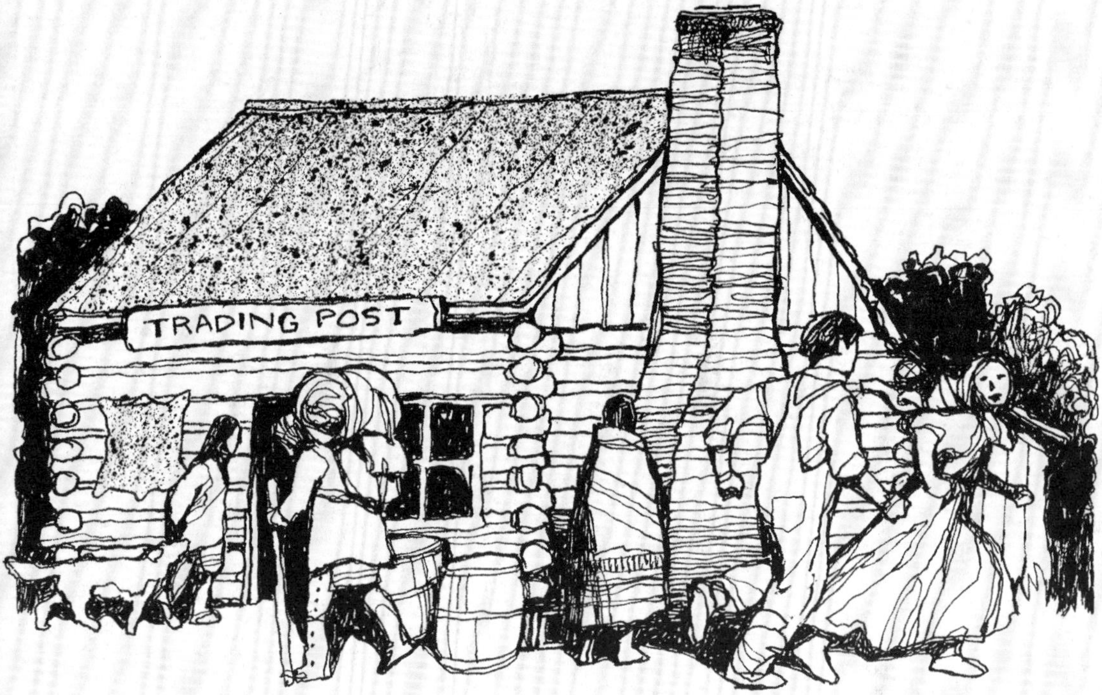
TRADING POST

THE TRADING POST INHABITED BY A BLENDED FAMILY OFFERS ABBIE THE FIRST ACTUAL ROOF OVER HER HEAD IN 3 MONTHS... AND SOME HOPEFUL WORDS.

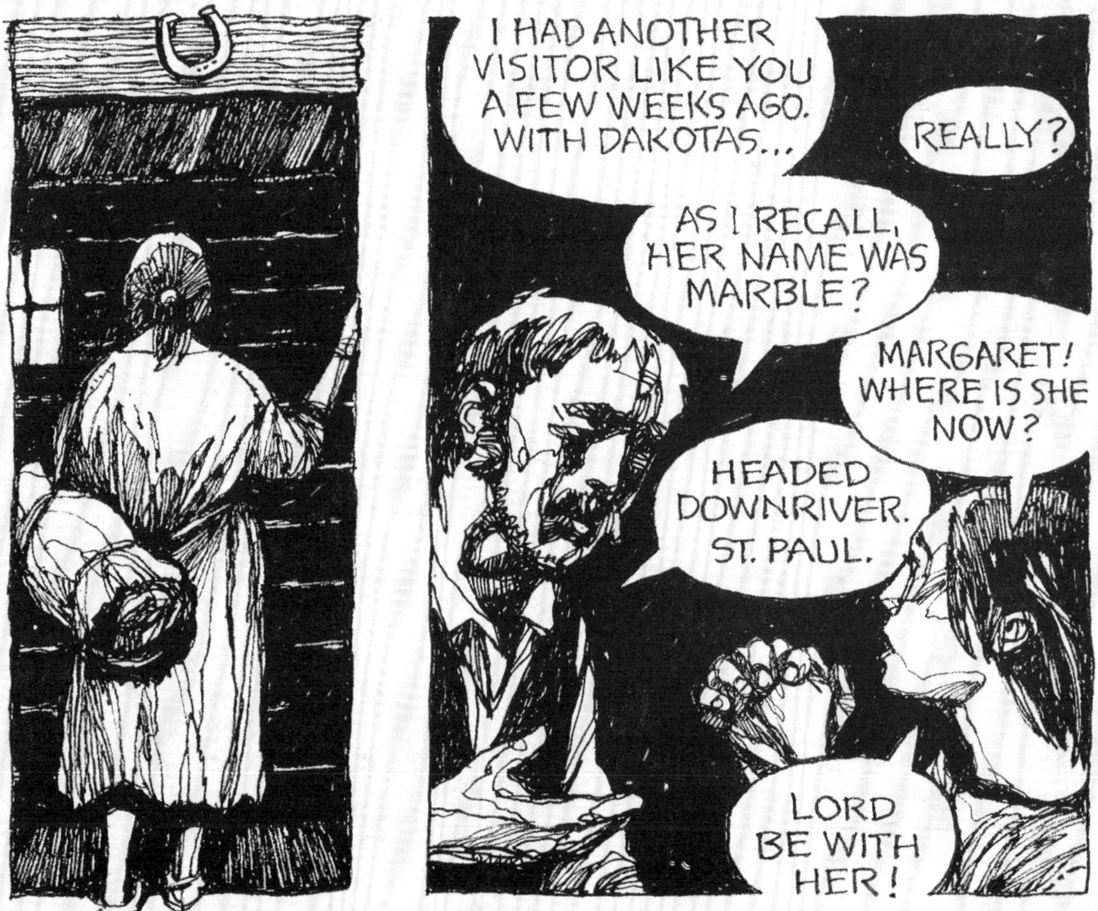
I HAD ANOTHER VISITOR LIKE YOU A FEW WEEKS AGO. WITH DAKOTAS...
REALLY?
AS I RECALL, HER NAME WAS MARBLE?
MARGARET! WHERE IS SHE NOW?
HEADED DOWNRIVER. ST. PAUL.
LORD BE WITH HER!

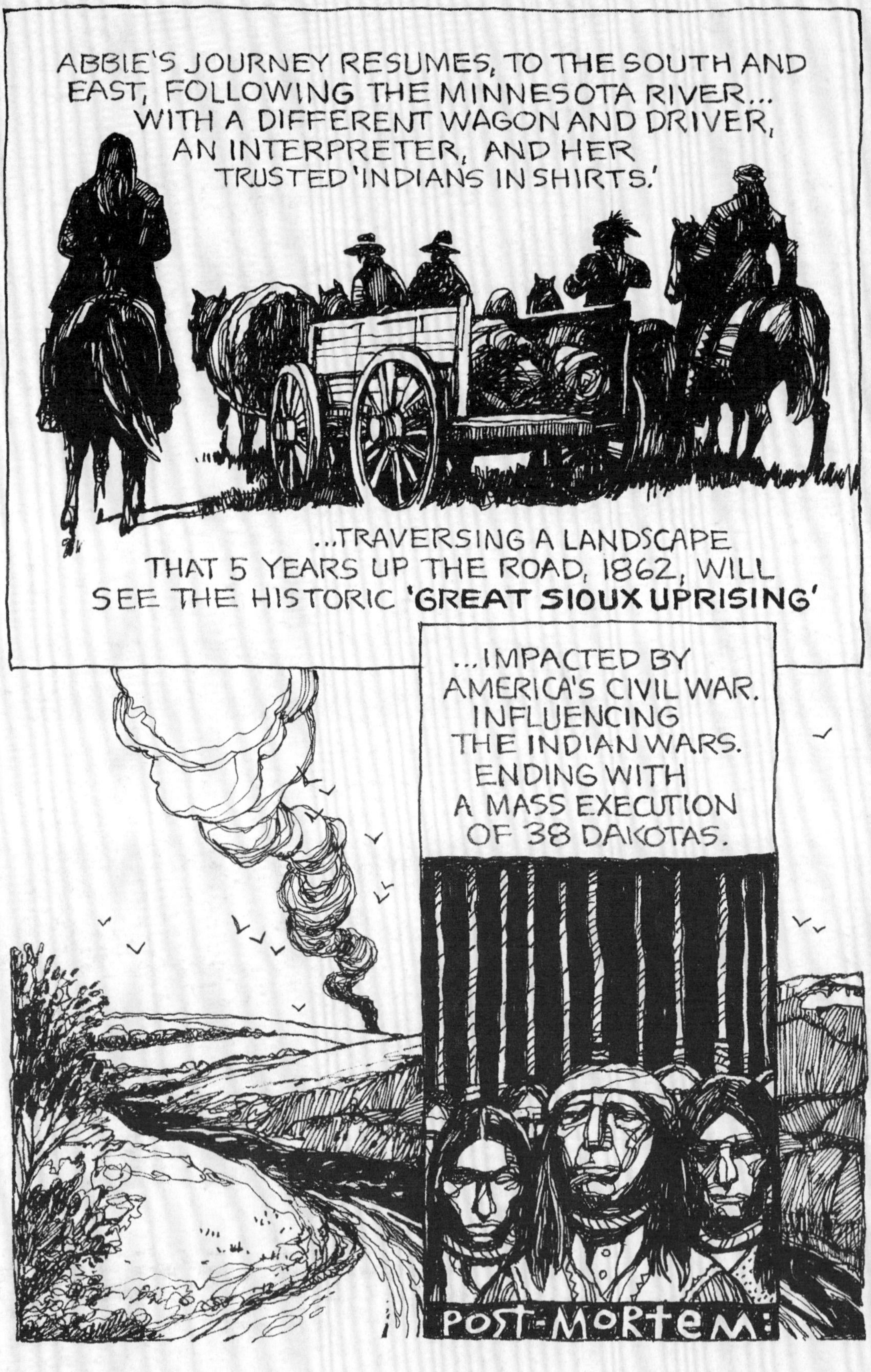
ABBIE'S JOURNEY RESUMES, TO THE SOUTH AND EAST, FOLLOWING THE MINNESOTA RIVER... WITH A DIFFERENT WAGON AND DRIVER, AN INTERPRETER, AND HER TRUSTED 'INDIANS IN SHIRTS.'
...TRAVERSING A LANDSCAPE THAT 5 YEARS UP THE ROAD, 1862, WILL SEE THE HISTORIC **'GREAT SIOUX UPRISING'**
...IMPACTED BY AMERICA'S CIVIL WAR. INFLUENCING THE INDIAN WARS. ENDING WITH A MASS EXECUTION OF 38 DAKOTAS.
POST-MORTEM:

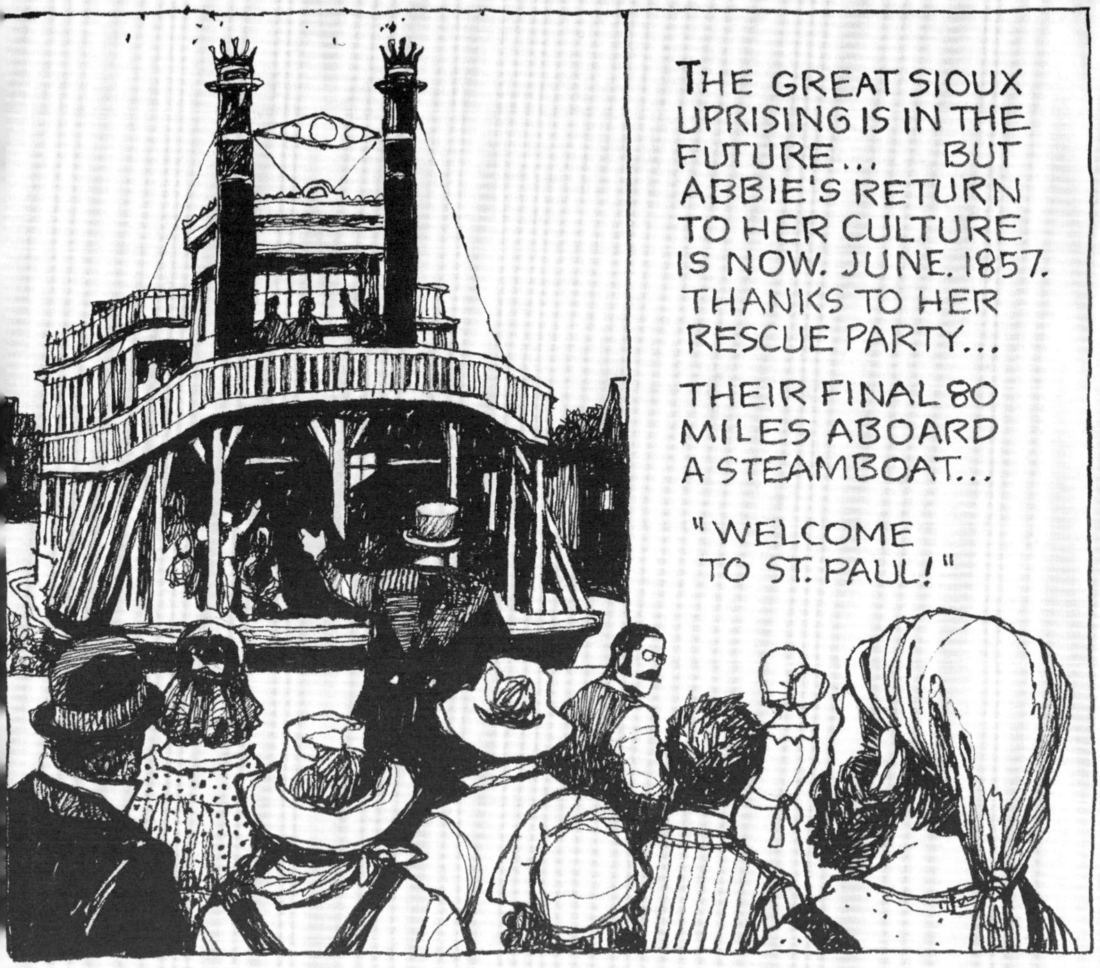
THE GREAT SIOUX UPRISING IS IN THE FUTURE... BUT ABBIE'S RETURN TO HER CULTURE IS NOW. JUNE. 1857. THANKS TO HER RESCUE PARTY...
THEIR FINAL 80 MILES ABOARD A STEAMBOAT...
"WELCOME TO ST. PAUL!"

THAT EVENING, MINNESOTA GOVERNOR MEDARY HOSTS A SPECIAL RECEPTION FOR ABBIE AND HER HEROES.

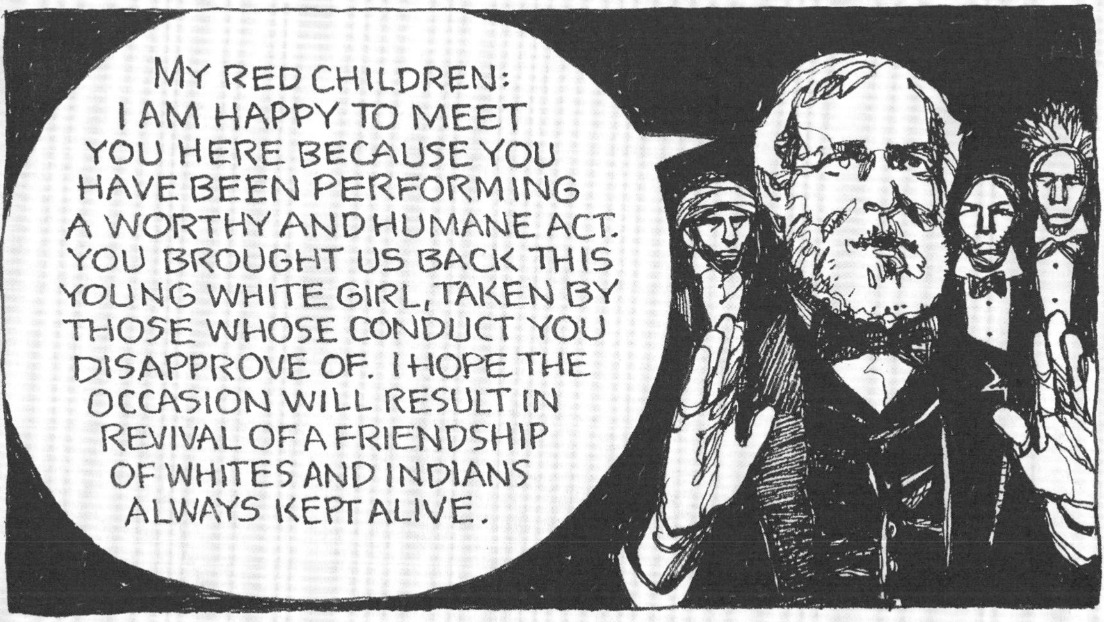
MY RED CHILDREN: I AM HAPPY TO MEET YOU HERE BECAUSE YOU HAVE BEEN PERFORMING A WORTHY AND HUMANE ACT. YOU BROUGHT US BACK THIS YOUNG WHITE GIRL, TAKEN BY THOSE WHOSE CONDUCT YOU DISAPPROVE OF. I HOPE THE OCCASION WILL RESULT IN REVIVAL OF A FRIENDSHIP OF WHITES AND INDIANS ALWAYS KEPT ALIVE.

WHILE IN ST. PAUL, ABBIE IS BLESSED WITH SOME GOOD NEWS; SISTER ELIZA, LIVING WITH DOCTOR STRONG'S FAMILY IN SPRINGFIELD, MINNESOTA, SURVIVED THE INKPADUTA RAID ON THEIR TOWN... AND SINCE, RETURNED TO IOWA, NOW MARRIED TO A YOUNG HOMESTEADER IN HAMPTON.

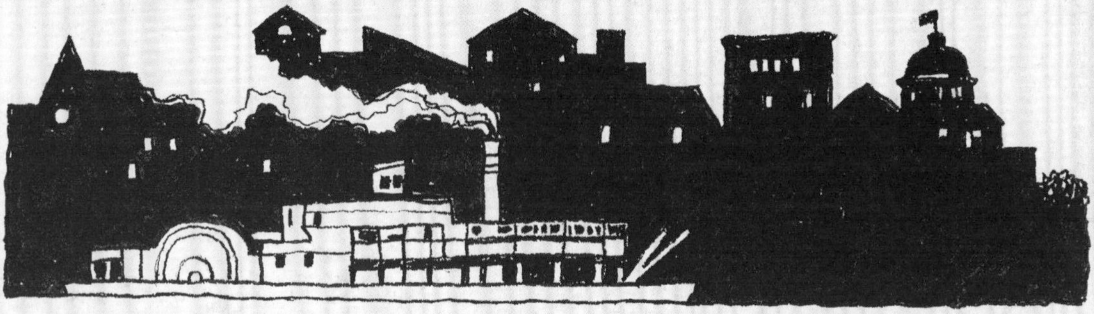

ABBIE DEPARTS ST. PAUL, TRAVELING SOUTHWARD BY RIVERBOAT, THEN STAGECOACH...

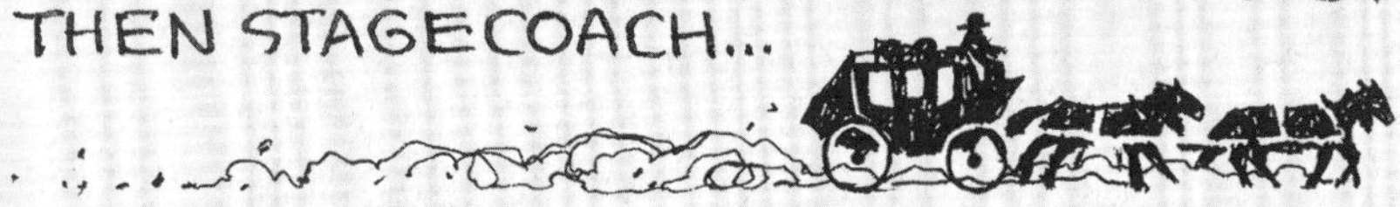

TO RECONNECT WITH HER SIBLING...

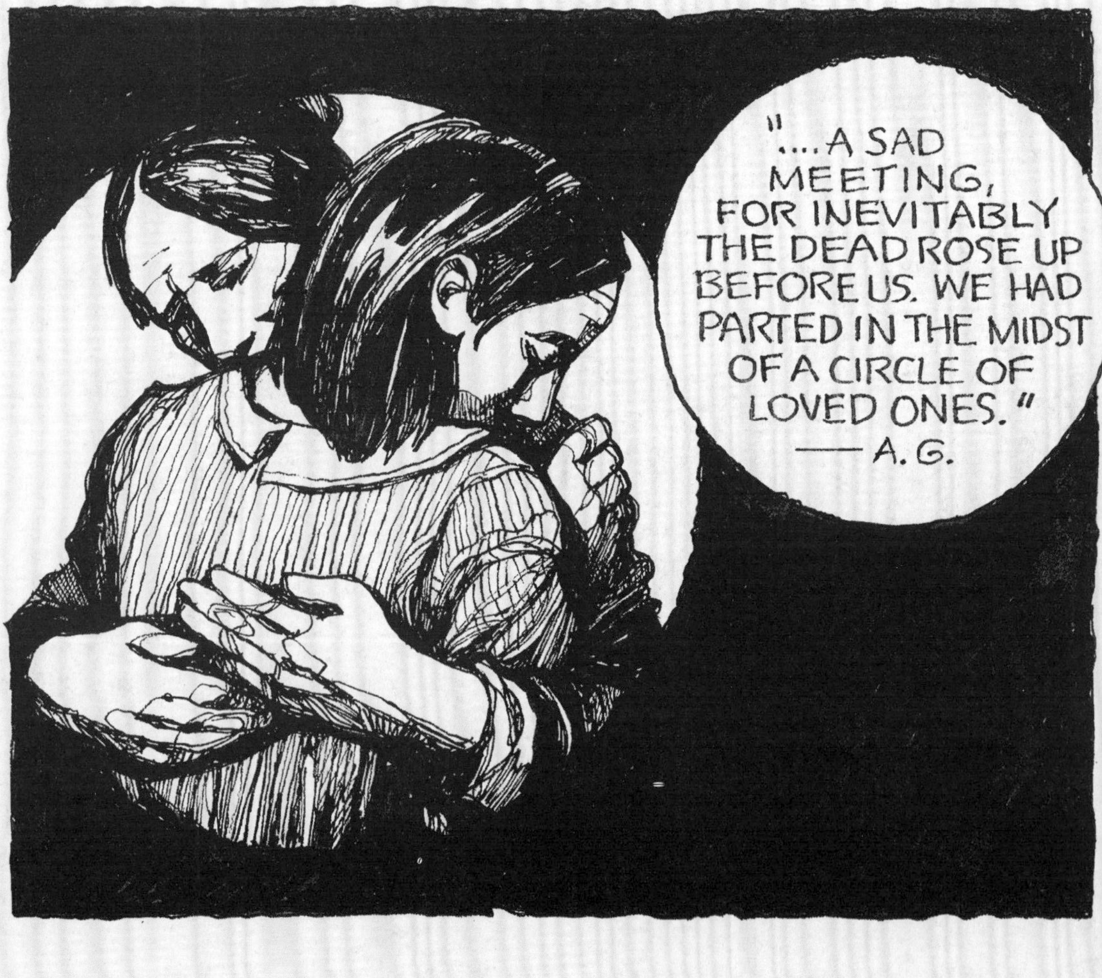
"....A SAD MEETING, FOR INEVITABLY THE DEAD ROSE UP BEFORE US. WE HAD PARTED IN THE MIDST OF A CIRCLE OF LOVED ONES."
— A. G.

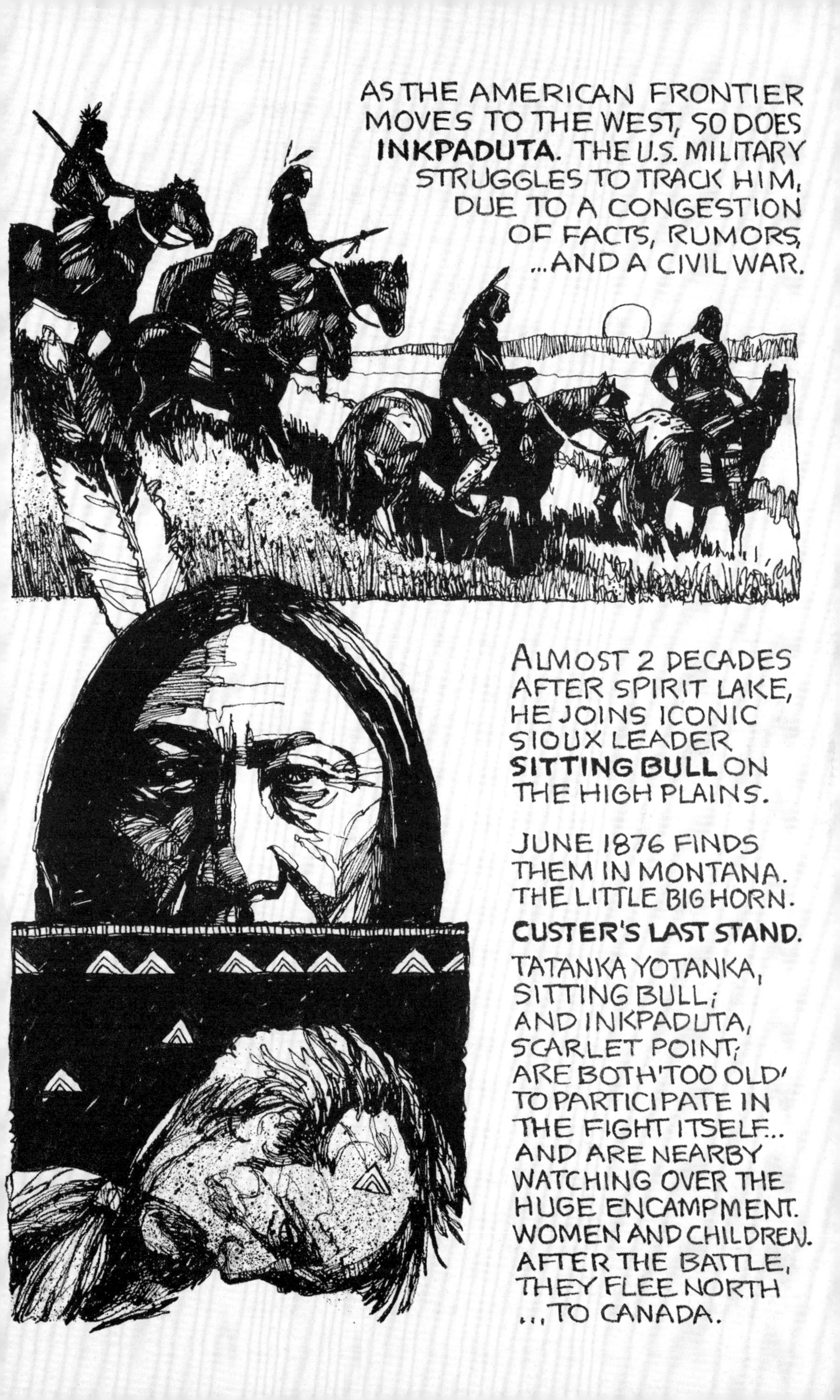
AS THE AMERICAN FRONTIER MOVES TO THE WEST, SO DOES **INKPADUTA**. THE U.S. MILITARY STRUGGLES TO TRACK HIM, DUE TO A CONGESTION OF FACTS, RUMORS, ...AND A CIVIL WAR.
ALMOST 2 DECADES AFTER SPIRIT LAKE, HE JOINS ICONIC SIOUX LEADER **SITTING BULL** ON THE HIGH PLAINS.
JUNE 1876 FINDS THEM IN MONTANA. THE LITTLE BIG HORN.
CUSTER'S LAST STAND.
TATANKA YOTANKA, SITTING BULL; AND INKPADUTA, SCARLET POINT; ARE BOTH 'TOO OLD' TO PARTICIPATE IN THE FIGHT ITSELF... AND ARE NEARBY WATCHING OVER THE HUGE ENCAMPMENT. WOMEN AND CHILDREN. AFTER THE BATTLE, THEY FLEE NORTH ...TO CANADA.

WHEN SITTING BULL RETURNS FROM CANADA, HE IS A HERO AMONG HIS PEOPLE AND EVENTUALLY JOINS BUFFALO BILL'S WORLD-FAMOUS WILD WEST SHOW.

TIMES CHANGE. IN 1890, NEAR WOUNDED KNEE, SOUTH DAKOTA, HE'S MURDERED BY INDIAN POLICE.

INKPADUTA HAS FADED... INTO HISTORY...

A VAGUE, FOREVER DARK IMAGE.

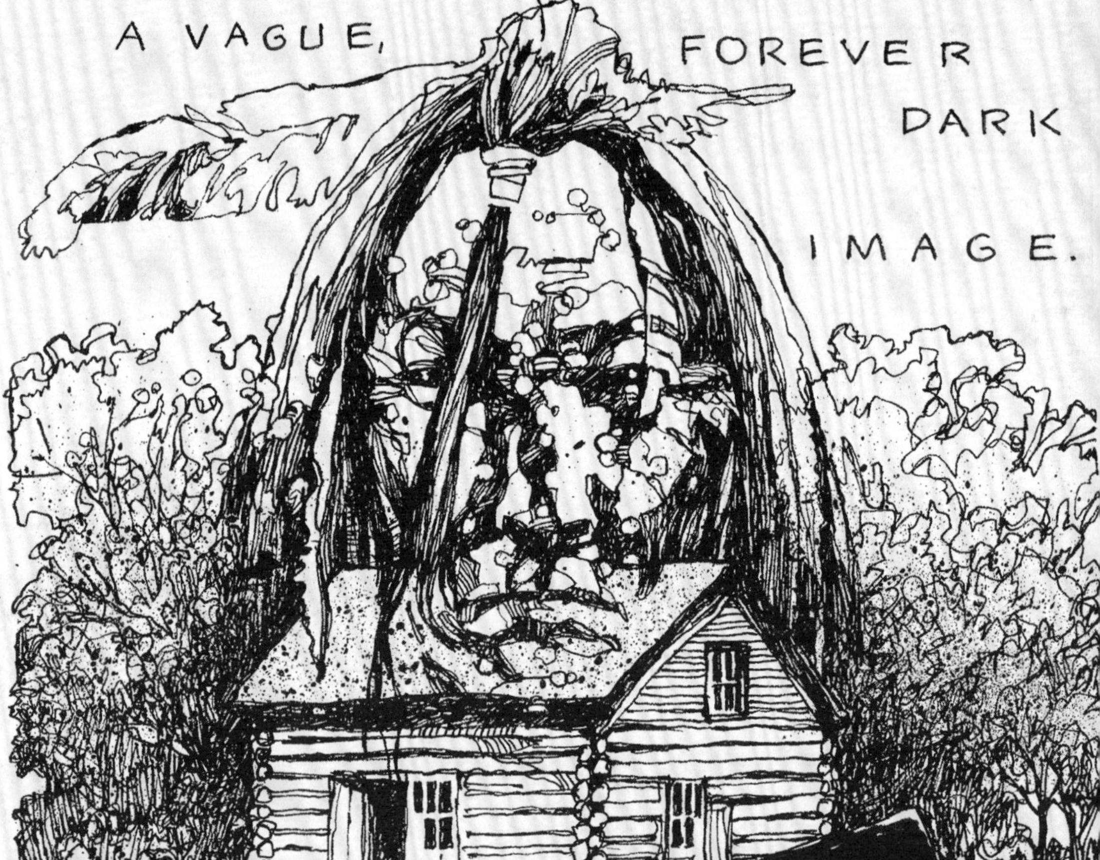

1891 AFTER SPENDING TIME IN MISSOURI AND KANSAS, **ABBIE GARDNER** RETURNS HOME TO IOWA. TO HER FAMILY CABIN ON WEST LAKE OKOBOJI, NEAR A YOUNG ARNOLDS PARK AND ITS NEW WOODEN ROLLERCOASTER.

SHE PASSES AWAY IN EARLY 1921... THE LAST REMAINING SURVIVOR OF THE 1857 SPIRIT LAKE MASSACRE.

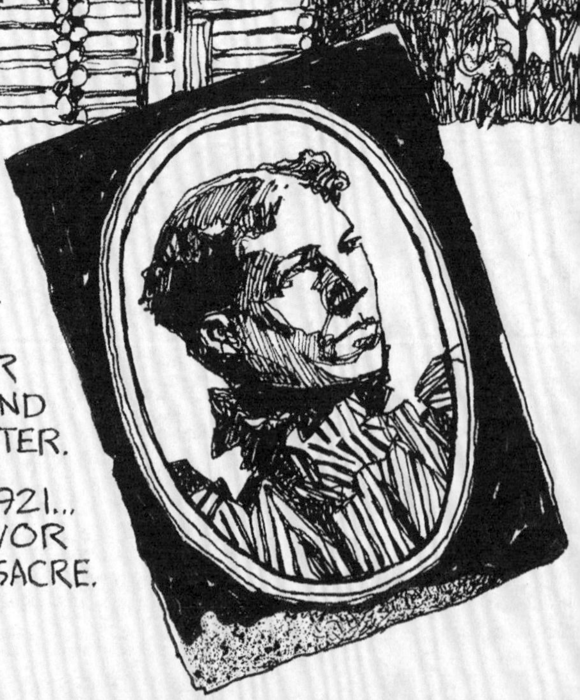

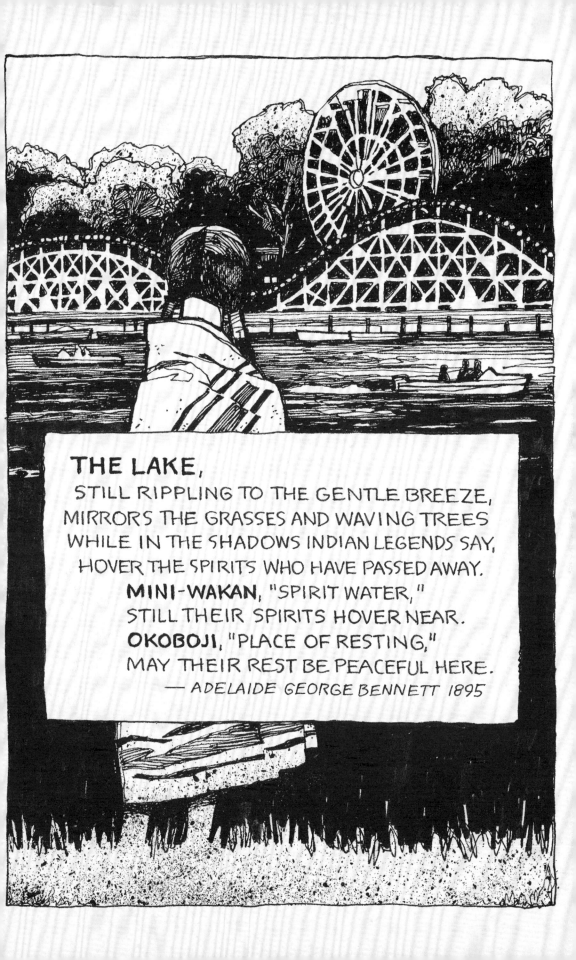

THE LAKE,
STILL RIPPLING TO THE GENTLE BREEZE,
MIRRORS THE GRASSES AND WAVING TREES
WHILE IN THE SHADOWS INDIAN LEGENDS SAY,
HOVER THE SPIRITS WHO HAVE PASSED AWAY.
MINI-WAKAN, "SPIRIT WATER,"
STILL THEIR SPIRITS HOVER NEAR.
OKOBOJI, "PLACE OF RESTING,"
MAY THEIR REST BE PEACEFUL HERE.
— ADELAIDE GEORGE BENNETT 1895

POST MORTEM:

Minnewakan—Spirit Lake—has long cast a spell over its indigenous visitors. The very first seeds of Indian corn, maize, were conjured up from the depths of Minnewakan by the Wapiya Wicasta. The Dakota medicine people. In the long ago they traveled a familiar trail from the center of the world in Minnesota to this supernatural place. About the time Christopher Columbus, the medicine people designated one of their own to stand watch over Minnewakan and her sister lakes. Since then that sentry, embodied in a cedar tree, has watched faithfully the days, the months, and the years come and go. He has watched the Dakota come and go. And he has watched the Wasichu, the white man, come and stay. He was watching when they arrived from France to explore the upper Mississippi. He was watching when Lewis and Clark passed nearby on their journey to the Pacific. And he was watching on a late winter night in 1857 as Wasichu cabins burned on the opposite shore. The Spirit Lake Massacre.

Today, after five centuries the Medicine Tree watches a world of power boats and luxury homes while across the water where cabins burned, an amusement park lights up the night.

AN ANCIENT CEDAR TREE IS STILL
WATCHING OVER WEST LAKE OKOBOJI
AND ITS DISTANT WOODED SHORELINE
WITH ABBIE GARDNER'S 1857 CABIN...
— G. KELLEY sketchbook 2018

SOURCES

NORTHERN BORDER BRIGADE
published early 1900's
no other information available.

HISTORY OF THE SPIRIT LAKE MASSACRE
Abigail Gardner Sharp
Wallace-Homestead Book Co. Des Moines, IA

SPIRIT LAKE MASSACRE
Thomas Teakle
State Historical Society of Iowa, 1918

SPIRIT LAKE
Mackinlay Kantor
The World Publishing Co., 1962

INKPADUTA-DAKOTA LEADER
Paul N. Beck
University of Oklahoma Press, 2008

WOMEN AND INDIANS ON THE FRONTIER
Glenda Riley
University of New Mexico Press, 1984

BLACK ELK SPEAKS
John G. Neihardt (Flaming Rainbow)
University of Nebraska Press, 1961

THE SOUL OF THE INDIAN
Charles A. Eastman (Oniyesa)
University of Nebraska Press, 1980

THE LAND OF THE DAKOTA
Gwen Westerman & Bruce White
Minnesota Historical Society Press, 2012

INDIAN SPIRIT—REVISED AND ENLARGED
Edited by Oren Fitzgerald &
Judith Fitzgerald
World Wisdom, Inc., 2006

TRIBES OF THE SIOUX NATION
Michael Johnson
Osprey Publishing, 2000

THE DAKOTA WAR OF 1862
Kenneth Carley
Minnesota Historical Society Press, 1976

A HISTORY OF THE PIPESTONE
NATIONAL MONUMENT—MINNESOTA
Robert A. Murray
Pipestone Indian Shrine Association, 1965

IOWA—PORTRAIT OF THE LAND
Iowa Department of Natural Resources, 2000

Plus conversations with Mike Koppert,
curator at the Gardner Cabin Historical
Site in Arnold's Park, Iowa.

The Ice Cube Press began publishing in 1991 to focus on how to live with the natural world and to better understand how people can best live together in the communities they share and inhabit. Using the literary arts to explore life and experiences in the heartland of the United States we have been recognized by a number of well-known writers including: Bill Bradley, Gary Snyder, Gene Logsdon, Wes Jackson, Patricia Hampl, Greg Brown, Jim Harrison, Annie Dillard, Ken Burns, Roz Chast, Jane Hamilton, Daniel Menaker, Kathleen Norris, Janisse Ray, Craig Lesley, Alison Deming, Harriet Lerner, Richard Lynn Stegner, Richard Rhodes, Michael Pollan, David Abram, David Orr, and Barry Lopez. We've published a number of well-known authors including: Mary Swander, Jim Heynen, Mary Pipher, Bill Holm, Connie Mutel, John T. Price, Carol Bly, Marvin Bell, Debra Marquart, Ted Kooser, Stephanie Mills, Bill McKibben, Craig Lesley, Elizabeth McCracken, Derrick Jensen, Dean Bakopoulos, Rick Bass, Linda Hogan, Pam Houston, and Paul Gruchow. Check out Ice Cube Press books on our web site, join our email list, Facebook group, or follow us on Twitter. Visit booksellers, museum shops, or any place you can find good books and support our truly honest to goodness independent publishing projects and discover why we continue striving to "hear the other side."

Ice Cube Press, LLC (Est. 1991)
North Liberty, Iowa, Midwest, USA
Resting above the Silurian and Jordan aquifers
steve@icecubepress.com
Check us out on twitter and facebook
www.icecubepress.com

To Fenna Marie, the all-time "GK"! The corona-cation
will be with you forever, and, has somehow
increased your greatness! I pray you are protected
by magical medicine just like Spirit Lake.